Theme & Improvisation: Kandinsky & the American Avant-Garde, 1912-1950

A Bulfinch Press Book   Little, Brown and Company   Boston • Toronto • London

Theme & Improvisation:
KANDINSKY
& the American Avant-Garde   1912-1950

Gail Levin and Marianne Lorenz

An Exhibition Organized by the Dayton Art Institute   Marianne Lorenz, Curator

"Kandinsky and Regional America" and "Kandinsky and American Abstraction: New York and Europe in the 1930s and 1940s" copyright © 1992 Dayton Art Institute

"Kandinsky's Debut in America"; "Kandinsky and the First American Avant-Garde"; "Marsden Hartley, Albert Bloch, and Kandinsky in Europe"; and "Kandinsky and Abstract Expressionism" copyright © 1976, 1992 Gail Levin

Theme & Improvisation: Kandinsky and the American Avant-Garde, 1912–1950, was made possible by a generous grant from *Dayton Daily News* and funding from the National Endowment for the Arts. Additional support was made possible by the Mead Corporation.

Exhibition Schedule

The Phillips Collection, Washington, D.C., September 19–November 29, 1992

Dayton Art Institute, Dayton, Ohio, December 12, 1992–January 31, 1993

Terra Museum of American Art, Chicago, Illinois, February 13–April 25, 1993

Amon Carter Museum, Fort Worth, Texas, May 14–August 1, 1993

First Edition

Library of Congress Cataloging-in-Publication Data
Lorenz, Marianne.
    Theme & improvisation : Kandinsky and the American avant-garde, 1912–1950 / Dayton Art Institute; essays by Marianne Lorenz and Gail Levin. —
1st ed.
        p.   cm.
    "A Bulfinch Press book."
    Includes bibliographical references and index.
    ISBN 0-8212-1921-9 (hc)
    ISBN 0-8212-1927-8 (pb)
    1. Painting, American — Exhibitions.   2. Painting, Modern — 20th century — United States — Exhibitions.   3. Avant-garde (Aesthetics) — United States — History — 20th century — Exhibitions.   4. Kandinsky, Wassily, 1866–1944 — Influence — Exhibitions.   I. Levin, Gail, 1948–   .   II. Dayton Art Institute. III. Title.   IV. Title: Theme and improvisation.
ND212.L66   1992
759.13'09'0407473 — dc20   92-7777

Designed by William Wondriska, Wondriska Associates Inc.
Type set in Garamond by Eastern Typesetting, Inc.
Printed on Mead Signature® Dull 100 lb. Text and Cover by Eastern Press, Inc.
Bound by Acme Bookbinding

Bulfinch Press is an imprint and trademark of Little, Brown and Company (Inc.)
Published simultaneously in Canada by Little, Brown & Company (Canada) Limited

Contents

Acknowledgments

An exhibition such as this is not accomplished without the cooperation and collaboration of a great many people and institutions whose goodwill and expertise are vital to its success and completion. To the many lenders to the exhibition, who have consented to part with their works for the duration of the tour, I express sincere appreciation. Thanks go also to the directors and curators of the museums participating in the tour of the exhibition. At The Phillips Collection in Washington, D.C., we express gratitude to Laughlin Phillips, Director, and Eliza Rathbone, Curator; at the Terra Museum of American Art in Chicago, to Harold P. O'Connell, Jr., Director, and D. Scott Atkinson, Curator; and at the Amon Carter Museum in Fort Worth, Texas, to Jan Keene Muhlert, Director, and Doreen Bolger, Curator of Paintings and Sculpture.

Many people have been involved in helping us to locate important works of art for inclusion in the exhibition. Martin and Harriet Diamond were instrumental in this regard, and I would like to acknowledge and thank them for their enthusiasm, knowledge, and support. Special thanks are also extended to Michael Rosenfeld, Michael Rosenfeld Gallery; James Yohe, Andre Emmerich Gallery; N. P. Naud, Hirschl & Adler Galleries; Virginia Zabriskie, Zabriskie Gallery; Steve Turner, Steve Turner Gallery; Toby Moss, Toby Moss Gallery; Steven Lowy of Portico; and John Cram, Blue Spiral 1 Gallery.

We have been most fortunate in having the support of a number of scholars and artists who have generously given their time, expertise, and resources to this project. Co-author and curatorial consultant Gail Levin's contributions to the exhibition and publication have been invaluable. I discovered Ms. Levin's doctoral dissertation, "Kandinsky and the American Avant-Garde, 1912–1950," shortly after I had conceived of the project and had begun research. Research on the Transcendental Painting Group was greatly facilitated by Tiska Blankenship at the Jonson Gallery; former TPG artists Bill Lumpkins, Ed Garman, and Florence Pierce; Walt Wiggins; David Witt at the Harwood Foundation; Dennis Reid of the Art Gallery of Ontario; Elizabeth Cunningham at the Anschutz Collection; and Margaret Stainer. Andrew Martinez, Archivist at the Art Institute of Chicago and Douglas Dreishpoon of Hirschl & Adler Galleries made available valuable information on the Chicago art scene in the 1930s and William S. Schwartz. To Elfriede Fischinger and William Moritz I extend my thanks for opening the Fischinger Archives and for their insights on Fischinger's art and films. The discussion of Will Henry Stevens was significantly enhanced by the assistance of the artist's daughter Janet McDowell and Bernard Lemann. Ward Jackson, Archivist at the Guggenheim Museum, greatly facilitated my research there. Harriet Tannin graciously opened her files and research on Rolph Scarlett to me. Rae Ferren was also most helpful in providing information on John Ferren. Barbara Haskell is also to be thanked for her help with the Burgoyne Diller material.

Gail Levin has asked that I thank on her behalf Matthew Baigell, Vivian Endicott Barnett, Anna Francis Bloch, Suzaan Boettger, Aileen Cramer, William Dove, Norman Fainstein, Natalie Henderson, Rose-Carol Washton Long, W. Ann Reynolds, Martica Sawin, Peg Weiss, Amy Winter, Judith K. Zilczer, and especially John Van Sickle.

A large part of the credit for this exhibition goes to the staff of the Dayton Art Institute. Their expertise and commitment to the project have made its success possible. Bruce Evans, former Director of the Dayton Art Institute, was an ardent supporter of this project from its inception. My thanks go out to Lois Mann, Director of Development, who was instrumental in securing funding for the exhibition and whose constant support and belief in the project were a source of inspiration. I am indebted to Dominique H. Vasseur, Registrar, and Patti Huls, Assistant Registrar and Curatorial Secretary, for their efficient handling of the many details of shipping, insurance, photographs, and conservation. Eileen Carr and Robin Crum of the Education Department are to be recognized for organizing superb programs to accompany the exhibition. In Marketing and Public Relations I thank Pat Koepnick for her efforts on behalf of this project. Jane Dunwoodie, Julie Bengala, and Suzanne Gourlie of the DAI library must also be recognized for their help in my research for the exhibition and catalogue. Curatorial interns Raina Bajpai, Alexandra Fink, and Molly Miller were also instrumental in researching the exhibition.

To the Board of Trustees of the Dayton Art Institute I am most appreciative for providing ongoing support to the DAI's exhibition program. The Chair of the Collections and Programs Committee, Bob Shiffler, is gratefully recognized here, not only for his help with the project but for his belief in and support for the DAI staff charged with carrying it out. Ted Lienesch of Thompson, Hine and Flory helped see the project through a variety of contracts and legal issues. For his encouragement and generous donation of services and expertise I am extremely thankful.

This exhibition would not have been possible without the generous support of the *Dayton Daily News*. I would also like to thank Drew Oliver at the National Endowment for the Arts. Kathryn Strawn, Manager, Corporate Contributions at the Mead Corporation, must be thanked for facilitating Mead's donation of paper for this publication.

In completing this book, we have been fortunate to have the support of our editor, Brian Hotchkiss of Bulfinch Press. His skillful guidance of us through the editing and publication process is gratefully acknowledged.

Marianne Lorenz
Director, Collections and Programs Division
Dayton Art Institute

Introduction

Within the diverse and complex field of American art from 1912 to 1950 the legacy of Kandinsky is clearly discernible across a wide geographic and generational span. In order for us to demonstrate this thesis, careful documentation and selection of particular works by specific artists was necessary. Those works that would best illustrate Kandinsky's impact but that were not available for loan to the exhibition are discussed and reproduced in this catalogue.

In our task, we have been aided by a number of pioneering studies that precede this publication. Thomas M. Messer's 1966 "Kandinsky in America," published in *XXᵉ Siècle*, was the first essay to discuss Kandinsky's impact in America. This was followed ten years later by Gail Levin's doctoral dissertation, "Wassily Kandinsky and the American Avant-Garde, 1912–1950," which gave thorough consideration to Kandinsky's importance to the first American avant-garde and members of the Abstract Expressionist group. Since that time our access to and knowledge of American modernism, particularly the art of the 1930s and early 1940s, has expanded considerably, enabling us to present a much more complete survey of the continued influence of Kandinsky on the development of American art to 1950. Of particular importance in this regard are John Lane and Susan Larsen's *Abstract Painting and Sculpture in America, 1927–1944*, Virginia Mecklenburg's *The Patricia and Phillip Frost Collection: American Abstraction 1930–1945*, and Susan Ehrlich's *Turning the Tide: Early Los Angeles Modernists, 1920–1956*. These provided us the ground upon which we could undertake a more specialized study, and their importance is manifest in the number of references to them made in chapters 4 and 5 of this book.

The work and ideas of Kandinsky provide the unifying theme for the exhibition and catalogue, but it is the Americans who hold center stage and whose story we wish to tell. The picture that most accurately reveals the story of American art also distorts at times the one we may have of Kandinsky. Often the Americans read Kandinsky's ideas in inadequate translations, as we have learned from Kenneth Lindsay (in his 1951 Ph.D. dissertation, "An Examination of the Fundamental Theories of Wassily Kandinsky," University of Wisconsin) and Peg Weiss (*Kandinsky in Munich*, 1985), who have demonstrated the shortcomings of English translations of Kandinsky's *Über das Geistige in der Kunst*, including Michael Sadler's 1914 *The Art of Spiritual Harmony*. This was the version most often read by American artists between 1914 and 1946, when the Museum of Non-Objective Painting published Hilla Rebay's translation, entitled *On the Spiritual in Art*, which itself proved problematic. These early translations, as well as interpretations of Kandinsky's work and ideas by influential figures such as Rebay, Katherine Dreier, and Galka Scheyer, inadvertently misrepresented to some degree Kandinsky's ideas and intentions. These misconceptions have, by necessity, been reported here as part and parcel of the story of Kandinsky and America.

Nowhere are the perils of mistranslation and distortion more evident than in the use of the words *spiritual, mysticism,* and *the occult,* which not only defy exact translation from the German but which also held distinct meanings for almost every artist under discussion here. Weiss, for example, has noted that the word *spiritual* in English embodies our concept of the soul and the supernatural, which ally it to the religious, whereas the German word *Geist* as intended by Kandinsky connotes the ineffable realm of the intellect that is capable of being expressed only by the artist. Even the most cursory review of the literature reveals that each artist who read Kandinsky's treatise chose to read the term in such a way that it would support his or her individual objectives, and that strict adherence to what Kandinsky *actually* said or meant was neither desired nor achieved. By its very ambiguity, the term *spiritual* proffered access to realms at once personal, universal, and (for some) dogmatic—subject only to the artist's intent. Our approach, therefore, has been to discover for each artist what such terms signified and to trace the extent to which the quality and magnitude of their presence in the artist's work and thought were attributable to Kandinsky's influence.

Kandinsky's importance for American artists during the formative years of American abstraction, while extensive, is by no means exclusive. To deny the profound impact of cubism, the art of Matisse, Miró, Mondrian, Léger, and the surrealists (to name only a few) on the art of the period and to set Kandinsky up as the primogenitor of American modernism has not been our aim. Indeed, much of the power of the story is found in the recombinant, eclectic manner in which artists exploited Kandinsky's art and ideas in conjunction with a diversity of other sources. What does reveal itself, however, is the legacy of Kandinsky in this country and the myriad ways in which American artists found him useful in shaping their work and furthering their own aesthetic goals.

Gail Levin and Marianne Lorenz

Kandinsky's Debut in America

Gail Levin

Kandinsky first astounded a broad public in America during the notorious Armory Show of 1913.[1] The previous year, his art and theories already had begun to attract attention among the cognoscenti. In July 1912, Alfred Stieglitz published translated extracts from Kandinsky's *Über das Geistige in der Kunst* in *Camera Work,* the magazine that Stieglitz had been using to promote avant-garde photography, painting, and aesthetics since 1903. Stieglitz, whose German was fluent, probably made the translation himself. The appeal of Kandinsky's writing for Stieglitz rested in the painter's embrace of the new art and their common background amid late nineteenth-century symbolists. Stieglitz chose a passage that reflected his own interest in Cézanne, Matisse, Picasso, and symbolism. It begins: "These are the seekers of the inner spirit in outer things . . ."[2]

At this time Stieglitz was already well established as America's pioneer promoter of modern art. His center of activity was his Photo-Secession Gallery at 291 Fifth Avenue, where he held exhibitions of European and American avant-garde art and published *Camera Work.* From 1883, when he abandoned his studies in engineering in Berlin to take up photography, Stieglitz, who was a philosophical anarchist, demonstrated his independent spirit. This spirit was behind his organizing a group of photographers in 1902 to form the Photo-Secession in opposition to the academic salon, and, later, his openness to all new forms of expression.

Publishing Kandinsky's text in *Camera Work* epitomized Stieglitz's visionary tastes and dedication to the promotion of modernism. His interests extended beyond photography and the artworks he exhibited to the writings of Kandinsky, Gertrude Stein, and others in touch with the avant-garde. Stieglitz's excerpt from Kandinsky's *Über das Geistige in der Kunst* appeared two years before the first complete English translation was published in 1914 under the title *The Art of Spiritual Harmony.*[3] When Stieglitz published Kandinsky in 1912, he brought the Russian to the attention of the magazine's readership, which included many young American artists, among them Marsden Hartley, Oscar Bluemner, Max Weber, Arthur Dove, Arthur B. Carles, Konrad Cramer, and Abraham Walkowitz.

Less than a year later, during the winter of 1912–13, Kandinsky's art was first exhibited in America. His work had caught the eye of Martin Birnbaum, the manager of the New York branch of the Berlin Photographic Company, a German publisher. Birnbaum traveled to Germany in search of contemporary graphic art to exhibit at the gallery in the New York office of his firm. Along with Kandinsky, Birnbaum chose examples by some eighty other artists for his December 1912 exhibition. To represent Kandinsky, Birnbaum chose *Composition No. 4,* a woodcut based on an abstract painting of the same title from 1911.[4]

Kandinsky's print caught the eye of W. H. de B. Nelson, who reviewed the show for *International Studio,* where he was editor. He noted that "it is a long cry from Kandinsky, with 'Composition No. 4,' to the work of Slevogt," comparing the latter's German impressionist style to Kandinsky's more radical abstract work.[5] But, he cautioned presciently, "Let us not jeer. They are in earnest and theirs may be the art of tomorrow. The movement is hydraheaded. Guillaume Apollinaire shouts its doctrines from the Paris rooftops. Kill Cubists and you have Conceptionalists; decimate these, Orphists and Instinctivists arise. Que faire?"[6]

In his introductory essay in the show's catalogue, Birnbaum himself admitted: "Kandinsky we frankly fail as yet to understand, but we hesitate to sneer, for a survey of these anarchistic works only impresses us with the freedom of art in our day."[7] In calling Kandinsky's work "anarchistic," Birnbaum, a Hungarian immigrant, employed a metaphor that would have carried diverse political and cultural implications for different readers. Some may have associated Kandinsky's Russian background with that of prominent Russian anarchists like Kropotkin, Bakunin, and Tolstoy. For others, the association was more immediate, linking the artist to one of the most visible ideological cultural movements in 1912 New York. At that time, the major gathering place for anarchists was the Ferrer Center, where Robert Henri and George Bellows taught art in night classes for adults.[8] At the center, which was frequented by modernists like Max Weber and Man Ray, freedom in artistic expression was coupled with libertarian thinking.

Linking Kandinsky's art to anarchism, Birnbaum foreshadowed the history of Kandinsky's impact in America, where his radical abstract style would again and again be associated with cultural innovation. Birnbaum may have read *Über das Geistige in der Kunst,* where Kandinsky had spoken of the "spiritual turning-point" making itself felt in literature, music, and art and criticized "the materialistic 'credo'" of those whose "fear, distaste, and hatred . . . are today directed at the term anarchy, about which they know nothing save the terrifying name."[9] He might also have read *Der Blaue Reiter,* the almanac edited by Kandinsky and Franz Marc, where in his essay "On the Question of Form" Kandinsky described contemporary art created without external limits as "truly anarchistic," reflecting "the spiritual standpoint already conquered but also . . . the spirit as a materializing force, ripe for revelation."[10] If so, Birnbaum would have known Thomas Von Hartmann's essay "On Anarchy in Music," which claims that "the principle of anarchy in art should be welcomed. . . . Art should rather lead to an even greater, more conscious freedom."[11]

Birnbaum explained: "Germany is, after all, artistically a youthful country, full of vitality and promise, without centuries of cultivated tradition behind her, like France; and now that the doctrines of Severini and other Italian futurists are being accepted . . . no one can say whither the movement may lead."[12] His understanding of reactionary American critics and the conservative public was such that he warned: "Merely to hurl shafts of cheap ridicule at new work is easy enough, but to prove conclusively that it is silly, or even grotesque, is not so simple."[13] In 1913, Birnbaum's exhibition traveled around the country to several museums, among them the Albright Art Gallery at the Buffalo Fine Art Academy, the City Art Museum in St. Louis, and the Carnegie Institute in Pittsburgh. The single Kandinsky woodcut, *Composition No. 4,* was thus able to challenge viewers in several American communities.

At the same time, a review of Kandinsky's first one-man show at Galerie Der Sturm in Berlin appeared in *American Art News.* Although he was referred to as "Wassilli Kaudansky," at least some New Yorkers may have made the connection with the artist then showing at the Berlin Photographic Company. The brief review described Kandinsky as "the Russian artist, who has caused a sensation in art circles."[14]

The first Kandinsky painting to be shown in America, *Improvisation No. 27* (fig. 1.1), was purchased out of the Armory Show by Stieglitz on March 8, 1913, less than three weeks after the controversial show opened. He paid $500 for this work, the only example of the artist included in the exhibition.[15] Stieglitz reportedly bought the Kandinsky for two reasons: "He felt it should stay in America for young workers to see and because he anticipated that

people would be saying that [Marsden] Hartley, who had gone to Germany, was imitating Kandinsky and he wished to provide a check against such statements."[16] Stieglitz's willingness to pay $500 for the Kandinsky indicates how strongly he must have felt about this purchase; his other seven acquisitions at the Armory Show together totaled only $267.50.[17] In a letter to Israel White, a reporter for the *Newark Evening News,* Stieglitz defended his major purchase, responding to that paper's characterization of Kandinsky as one of "the revolutionists":[18]

> It is true that Kandinsky's picture was bought for the little place at "291." You know very well that we have very little money and certainly none to waste. You must know me well enough to realize that there must be some very definite reason why I should have decided to procure the Kandinsky for ourselves. From a certain point of view—that is considering the future development of a certain phase of painting— the Kandinsky was possibly the most important feature in the whole show.[19]

Less than a year later, visitors to 291 could study *Improvisation No. 27,* a first-rate example of Kandinsky's art, as well as Stieglitz's collection of other key works of the modern movement. Stieglitz's acquisition of Kandinsky's painting was motivated in part by indignation, as he explained in a letter to the artist:

> I really had no moral right, nor even the money to buy your picture. I was so insenced [sic] at the stupidity of the people who visited the Exhibition, and also more than incen [sic] at the stupidity of most of those in charge of the Exhibition, in not realizing the importance of your picture that I decided to buy it. Thus I knew I might influence the people to look at the picture, which I thought of importance to themselves.[20]

In referring to "the stupidity of the people who visited the Exhibition," Stieglitz could have had in mind an anonymous review in the *New York Herald* entitled "Art Extremists in Broadsides of Lurid Color Invade New York and Capture Armory" that ridiculed *Improvisation No. 27* less than three weeks before Stieglitz purchased it.[21]

The lengthy treatment that Kandinsky received in the press is all the more remarkable because, unlike the other artists who were found to be especially provocative, such as Marcel

Duchamp, Francis Picabia, and Henri Matisse, who were represented by multiple works, Kandinsky had only one painting in the show. Still, this painting was one of fifty-seven works of art chosen for reproduction as a postcard for sale at the show. The picture caught the attention of Royal Cortissoz, the critic for the *New York Tribune*, who is said to have been "normally courteous"; yet he, too, was baffled by *Improvisation No. 27*, which he referred to as "fragments of refuse thrown out of a butcher's shop upon a bit of canvas."[22]

That *Improvisation No. 27* was as provocative as it was should not surprise us. To the American public in 1913, *Improvisation No. 27*, subtitled *Garden of Love*, pushed beyond the anti-naturalistic color schemes of fauvist paintings and the cubist dissolution of recognizable objects. Moving toward a totally abstract style, or what has since been called "non-objective" art, Kandinsky's painting challenged spectators to sanction his expression of his inner feelings through form and color. For those who had already had access to his writing, his explanations of his goals offered assistance. Still, the boldly chosen colors and abstract forms of *Improvisation No. 27* exasperated many first-time viewers. On confronting Kandinsky's painting, visitors to the Armory Show could not ignore the dynamic, emotional composition.

Kandinsky's correspondence with Stieglitz was originally prompted by their mutual friendship with Marsden Hartley, who encouraged Kandinsky to write to Stieglitz to settle certain practical questions with regard to the purchase of his painting from the Armory Show.[23] Kandinsky evidently hoped to circumvent the various dealers' commissions in Munich and New York and wanted to ensure that he would be represented when the Armory Show traveled to Chicago and Boston; Kandinsky also requested that Stieglitz photograph *Improvisation No. 27* for him for inclusion in an upcoming book. Responding to Stieglitz's reply (May 26, 1913) to his queries, Kandinsky wrote that he was pleased with Stieglitz's explanation of his decision to purchase *Improvisation No. 27*. In that same letter, Stieglitz, promising only an introduction "in the proper spirit and with understanding," had mentioned the possibility of a Kandinsky exhibition at "291." Kandinsky replied that a small exhibition at "291" would be agreeable and suggested showing watercolors with some small oil paintings.[24] Before the logistics of a New York exhibition could be settled, the outbreak of the First World War interrupted their plans. Stieglitz was never to organize a one-man exhibition of Kandinsky's work; in fact, Kandinsky's first one-man show in New York did not take place until ten years later.

When the heart of the Armory Show traveled to Chicago and then to Boston, *Improvisation No. 27* was included. The exhibition made quite a splash in Chicago, where it was shown at the Art Institute and promoted by lectures given by several supporters of modern art, including Arthur Jerome Eddy. Eddy, an adventurous art collector who already owned works by Manet and Whistler, saw the Armory Show in New York, rather than wait for the exhibition's Chicago showing.

The *Chicago Record-Herald* reported with unconcealed skepticism that "cubist art, whether it be sane or insane, freakish or really 'higher art,' is getting Chicago's money anyway. While critics criticised and laymen laughed, several patrons of art stepped forward yesterday and exchanged real dollars for what are termed the 'wooziest of the woozy' pictures at the cubist exhibition."[25] This article also labeled Eddy "chief purchaser" of the new art, but the rumored purchase of Kandinsky's painting by an anonymous Chicagoan provoked a special headline, "PAYS $8,000 FOR ONE," followed by "Another Chicagoan, a patron of music and aviation, is reported to have paid $8,000 for Wassily Kandinsky's 'Improvisation.' This is admitted by all lay visitors to be a wonderful smear of many colors, the meaning of which is a secret."[26]

This rumor was, of course, a great exaggeration of the $500 that Stieglitz, a New Yorker, had actually paid for the painting.

Eddy, known for his audacious tastes and enamored of anything new and unusual, "reputed to have been the first to ride a bicycle in Chicago and the first to own an automobile,"[27] must have regretted that he had missed the opportunity to acquire such a bold and controversial painting as *Improvisation No. 27*. He later made up for this by acquiring a number of important Kandinsky paintings.[28]

Eddy gave his first lecture in defense of modern art during the Armory Show's stay in Chicago. About a thousand people attended the talk, and Eddy repeated it because of the interest demonstrated. This popular response probably prompted him to write *Cubists and Post-Impressionism,* which was published in March 1914, exactly a year after the Armory Show.[29] The book pays a great deal of attention to Kandinsky, whom Eddy refers to as "the most extreme man not only of Munich but of the entire modern art movement."[30] In his lecture in defense of the new art, Eddy asserted: "To me these pictures are like an explosion of fireworks. And as I like fireworks, I bought a Roman candle or two. I'm going to have a great deal of pleasure exploding them before friends."[31]

Eddy soon felt that Kandinsky's art had the greatest impact of all and began to study Kandinsky's writings and correspond with the artist. His research was facilitated when *The Art of Spiritual Harmony* appeared in 1914. Eddy wrote to the artist:

> Last night I read your book and it throws a great deal of light upon your art. There is much fine thinking in the book. I like your attitude toward art and your attitude toward life. It is the attitude of a fine mind. I hope painters, generally, will read your book for, even if they are not prepared to accept all your theories, they certainly will be inspired by your ideals.[32]

Not long after the opening of the Armory Show, Eddy had acquired his first paintings by Kandinsky. In his book, Eddy recalled the single Kandinsky painting in the Armory Show and the public's reaction to it:

> Visitors who paused to look at it dismissed it as meaningless splotches of paint, and passed on. There is this to be said for the public, that with no word of explanation one of Kandinsky's Improvisations does seem—at first glance—the last word in extravagance; on fourth or fifth glance it appears to have a charm of color that is fascinating; on study it begins to sound like color music.[33]

Eddy included in *Cubists and Post-Impressionism* excerpts of art critic Roger Fry's laudatory comments on Kandinsky's work, which appeared in his review for *The Nation* of the July 1913 exhibition of the Allied Artists at Albert Hall, London:

> By far the best pictures there seemed to me to be the three works by Kandinsky. They are of peculiar interest, because one is a landscape in which the disposition of the forms is clearly prompted by a thing seen, while the other two are improvisations. In these the forms and colors have no possible justification, except the rightness of their relations. This, of course, is really true of all art, but where representation of natural form comes in, the senses are apt to be tricked into acquiescence by the intelligence. In these improvisations, therefore, the form has to stand the test without any adventitious aids. It seemed to me that they did this, and established their right to be what they were. In fact, these seemed to me the most complete pictures in the exhibition, to be those which had the most definite and coherent expressive power. . . . The improvisations become more definite, more logical and more closely knit in

structure, more surprisingly beautiful in their color oppositions, more exact in their equilibrium. *They are pure visual music.*[34]

The important role Eddy's *Cubists and Post-Impressionism* played in introducing modern art to an American audience should not be underestimated. As late as 1931, Daniel Catton Rich wrote that the book "has done much to break down prejudice toward new art forms."[35] Rich contended: "The chapter on Kandinsky, with its valuable translations and excerpts from Kandinsky's letters, remains, perhaps, the outstanding contribution on his art, and certainly the only serious discussion of it in English."[36] Treating both Kandinsky's art and theories in depth, Eddy recognized *The Art of Spiritual Harmony* to be of major significance; so much so, that he claimed: "The keynote of the entire modern movement is found in the first sentence of his book, 'Every work of art is the child of its own times.' "[37] Eddy attempted to summarize and explain Kandinsky's theory of "inner necessity," as he understood it, and offered a detailed analysis and commentary on one of the Kandinsky paintings that he owned, *Improvisation No. 30,* complete with a color reproduction. Eddy was able to support his contention that this work, although an example of compositional painting, was not "absolutely pure" by publishing a letter from the artist answering his questions. Kandinsky had explained that

> the designation "Cannons," selected by me *for my own use,* is not to be conceived as indicating the "contents" of the picture.
>
> These contents are indeed what the spectator *lives,* or *feels* while under the effect of the *form and color combinations* of the picture. This picture is nearly in the shape of a cross. The centre—somewhat below the middle—is formed by a large, irregular blue plane. (The blue color in itself counteracts the impression caused by the cannons!). . . .
>
> The presence of the cannons in the picture could probably be explained by the constant war talk that had been going on throughout the year. But I did not intend to give a representation of war; to do so would have required different pictorial means; besides, such tasks do not interest me—at least not just now.
>
> This entire description is chiefly an analysis of the picture which I have painted rather subconsciously in a state of strong inner tension. So intensively did I feel the necessity of some of the forms . . .[38]

The timely publication of Eddy's book, just a year after the tumult of the Armory Show, resulted in excellent press coverage and no doubt a good deal of attention by a public seeking explanations for the baffling "new art." There was a three-quarter-page book review in the *New York Times* art section entitled "Cubists, Post-Impressionists, and Other Rebels against the Conventional Painting Analyzed in New Book—Interesting Pages on Cezanne, Van Gogh, and Many More Eccentric Artists."[39] In comparison to this, Willard Huntington Wright's *Modern Painting,* which appeared the following year, was given only a brief mention.[40] This was due in part to Wright's more historical approach, which began with the early nineteenth century, while Eddy began on page one with the Armory Show, which he referred to as "a Sensation." Eddy's enthusiasm for the new art seemed unbounded, fueled by his love of the scandalous and the shocking. The *New York Times* reviewer dutifully reported on the scope of Eddy's work and, like Eddy, gave particular attention to Kandinsky:

> Kandinsky is a logical and clear thinker, although by no means obvious to the easy going reader. He places his stress on spiritual expression, on the communication of the artist's inner feeling. The outer form must grow in art as in religion out of the inner spiritual necessity. A man must paint his most subtle emotions as a musician

other, and what gives life to one is the death of the other. The first is fluent and transitory while the latter is static and enduring. Music does not begin to exist until it has been liberated and its very being is a dying and when it is finished it is ended, while plastic art begins to exist only when it has become fixed in paints or clay and every stroke that contributes towards its completion gives it a more fixed and permanent character . . . [56]

Among the other critics to discuss this issue and others regarding Kandinsky were the contributors to *Camera Work,* where, after the excerpt from Kandinsky's treatise was published in July 1912, references to the Russian artist's ideas frequently appeared.

The American expatriate collector and writer Gertrude Stein rejected Kandinsky. So did her friend, the artist and future set designer Lee Simonson, who criticized the Russian painter's mystical theories and concluded that Kandinsky and other modern painters confused metaphysics with aesthetics. He asserted: "The revolutionary painter . . . has expressed again his own weariness, a desire to lose himself in a world his eye can no longer dominate or understand. The latest pamphlet calls this 'The Art of Spiritual Harmony.' "[57] Simonson's article, "Panic in Art," was published in November 1914, when Kandinsky's treatise was still much talked about in Paris after its appearance in mid-December 1911. Having actually visited Kandinsky's Paris studio in 1906 or 1907, where she reportedly looked at his tempera paintings and laughed, Stein remained unenthusiastic about his work, despite admiration for the artist among some of her friends. It must have annoyed her when an American critic, reviewing her 1914 book *Tender Buttons,* pointed out that Kandinsky had used word repetition in his treatise and that "Gertrude has beautifully followed this recipe."[58]

The 1914 English edition of *The Art of Spiritual Harmony* remained faithful to the basic form of the original German edition, reproducing the identical woodcuts and illustrative plates. Instead of including the foreword written by Kandinsky, Michael Sadler substituted a long foreword of his own, overstressing the idea that Kandinsky was painting music. Sadler also added explanatory footnotes of his own; he sometimes chose to disagree with or even to correct the author. Sadler later referred to his work on the English edition of the treatise as "a gallant effort which paid a sincere and prescient tribute to Kandinsky and his work. But aesthetic theory was then as much beyond my comprehension as it still is with the difference that now I am aware of the fact."[59]

In the light of Sadler's very personal interpretation of Kandinsky's theory, it is vital to consider what impression typical readers might have gained from Sadler's foreword, with which they would then approach the treatise itself. Calling Kandinsky "a visual musician," Sadler wrote that the artist's goal was "finding a common language of colour and line which shall stand alone as the language of sound and beat stands alone, without recourse to natural form or representation."[60] According to Sadler, who claimed that Kandinsky's aim was to create painting with the power of music, "The power of music to give expression without the help of representation is its noblest possession."[61] Sadler's overemphasis of Kandinsky's attempts at "colour-music" and on "the expression of the soul of nature and humanity," which the artist termed the "innerer Klang," perhaps accounts for the usual emphasis on these same matters by other critics and artists, often in rather narrow or otherwise distorted terms.[62]

Sadler's translation of *The Art of Spiritual Harmony* attracted the attention of the critic Sadakichi Hartmann. His various activities among the avant-garde in New York included associations with the anarchists at the Ferrer Center and writing for Stieglitz's *Camera Work.*

In May 1915, Hartmann wrote to Stieglitz, requesting "an order to write on the New Color Theory as brought out by color photography, upsetting Goethe's, Newton's and Chevreuil's theories, or a real critical review of Kandinsky's book."[63] Stieglitz's rejection of this proposal was certainly colored by his annoyance with Hartmann's criticism of the new journal, *291*, that Stieglitz had just begun to publish in March 1915, along with Francis Picabia, Paul Haviland, Marius de Zayas, and Agnes Meyer. Hartmann made the mistake of telling Stieglitz: "I just read '291' for the first and last time. . . . *Das ist ja kein blaue Reiter!*" (That sure is no Blaue Reiter!)[64] Since Hartmann unfavorably contrasted the new journal with the almanac edited by Kandinsky and Marc, knowing how Stieglitz had admired the German publication, he implied that Stieglitz now showed poor judgment. But Stieglitz's indignant response may also indicate the shrinking of his commitment to Kandinsky's ideas and his art. He answered: "You amuse me. Why should I be interested in anything as serious as that."[65] While Stieglitz's comment reflected his recent focus on the wit of the Dada aesthetic, many Dada enthusiasts, including the poet and collector Walter Arensberg, were among those who read Kandinsky's treatise.[66] Stieglitz's momentary change of direction did not, however, diminish interest in Kandinsky's art and theory among the first American avant-garde. That had just begun.

1. My essays in this volume are adapted from my doctoral dissertation, "Wassily Kandinsky and the American Avant-Garde, 1912–1950" (Rutgers University, 1976). At the time I began my dissertation, the only consideration of the impact of Kandinsky on American art was "Kandinsky in America," a brief article by Thomas M. Messer, published in "Wassily Kandinsky, 1866–1944: Centenaire de Kandinsky," *XX*^e *Siècle,* no. 27 (December 1966), pp. 111–117; English translation, pp. VIII–X. After my own study had been turned in, Judith K. Zilczer's doctoral dissertation, "The Aesthetic Struggle in America, 1913–1918: Abstract Art and Theory in the Stieglitz Circle" (University of Delaware, 1975), appeared, presenting a concise but excellent treatment of Kandinsky's impact within the context of these first few crucial years for American modernism. In the fifteen years since my dissertation appeared, archives previously restricted have been opened, and unpublished letters and artworks in estates and private collections have come to light. During this period, many scholars have contributed to our understanding of Kandinsky's influence on specific American artists, particularly those figures of the first American avant-garde whose work was previously neglected. Despite limitations of space, I have tried to incorporate the fruits of this new research into this essay and to acknowledge these scholars in the accompanying notes. Marianne Lorenz conceived the idea for this exhibition, one that I had long dreamed of doing. I am grateful that, on discovering my dissertation, she generously invited me to collaborate with her on this project.

2. *Camera Work,* "Extracts from 'The Spiritual in Art,' " no. 39, July 1912, p. 34.

3. Wassily Kandinsky, *The Art of Spiritual Harmony,* trans. Michael T. H. Sadler (Boston: Houghton Mifflin, 1914). Sadler later changed his name to Sadleir, but for consistency he is referred to as "Sadler" in this text. I refer to this edition only when the artist in question would have read it. Otherwise, I use the following translation: Wassily Kandinsky, *On the Spiritual in Art,* trans. Peter Vergo, in Kenneth C. Lindsay and Peter Vergo, eds., *Kandinsky: Complete Writings on Art* (Boston: G. K. Hall, 1982), pp. 114–219.

4. See Martin Birnbaum, *The Last Romantic* (New York: Twayne, 1960), pp. 51–52, and Martin Birnbaum, *Catalogue of an Exhibition of Contemporary German Graphic Art* (New York: Berlin Photographic Company, 1912–13), catalogue no. 121. This woodcut was made after a watercolor with the same motif as the 1911 canvas *Composition IV;* it was intended to be used as the cover for a monograph (which was never published). See Hans K. Roethel and Jean K. Benjamin, *Kandinsky Catalogue Raisonné of the Oil Paintings* (Ithaca, N.Y.: Cornell University Press, 1982), vol. 1, p. 366.

5. W. H. de B. Nelson, "Germanic Art: Berlin Photographic Company," *International Studio* 49 (March 1913), p. xx.

6. Ibid.

7. Birnbaum, Introduction to *Catalogue of an Exhibition of Contemporary German Graphic Art,* p. 18. Birnbaum, *The Last Romantic,* p. 52, reiterates how Kandinsky and other artists "were then treated like anarchists."

8. See Paul Avrich, *The Modern School Movement: Anarchism and Education in the United States* (Princeton, N.J.: Princeton University Press, 1980).

9. Kandinsky, *On the Spiritual in Art,* p. 139. Kandinsky's anarchist beliefs were in keeping with his belief in theosophy, which often led modern artists to "social radicalism through its belief in universal brotherhood." See Donald Drew Egbert, *Social Radicalism and the Arts* (New York: Knopf, 1970), p. 261. See also Rose-Carol Washton Long, "Occultism, Anarchism, and Abstraction: Kandinsky's Art of the Future," *Art Journal* 46 (Spring 1987), pp. 38–45.

10. Wassily Kandinsky, "On the Question of Form," in Klaus Lankheit, ed., *Der Blaue Reiter Almanac, Edited by Wassily Kandinsky and Franz Marc, Documentary Edition* (New York: Viking, 1974), p. 158.

11. Thomas Von Hartmann, "On Anarchy in Music," in Kandinsky and Marc, *The Blue Rider Almanac,* p. 118.

12. Birnbaum, Introduction to *Catalogue of an Exhibition,* p. 20.

13. Ibid.

14. "Berlin Exhibitions," *American Art News* XI (December 14, 1912), p. 6.

15. The painting's list price was $731.25. See Milton W. Brown, *The Story of the Armory Show* (New York: Joseph H. Hirshhorn Foundation, 1963), p. 256.

16. Henry Clifford and Carl Zigrosser, *History of an American Place: "291" and After; Selections from the Stieglitz Collection on Exhibition at the Philadelphia Museum of Art* (Philadelphia: Philadelphia Museum of Art, 1944), p. 16.

17. Brown, *Armory Show,* p. 256.

18. [Israel White], "Arts Trend Is Exhibit Lesson," *Newark Evening News,* February 18, 1913, p. 7.

19. Typescript of a letter from Stieglitz to Israel White, March 18, 1913, the Alfred Stieglitz Archive in the Collection of American Literature, Beinecke Rare Book and Manuscript Library, Yale University, New Haven, Conn.

20. Carbon copy of letter from Stieglitz to Kandinsky dated May 26, 1913, Stieglitz Archive, Yale.

21. "Art Extremists in Broadsides of Lurid Color Invade New York and Capture Armory," *New York Herald,* February 17, 1913, p. 10.

22. Quoted in Meyer Schapiro, "Rebellion in Art," in *America in Crisis,* ed. Daniel Aaron (New York: Knopf, 1952), p. 213.

23. Kandinsky to Stieglitz, letter of April 26, 1913, and an undated letter of 1913, Stieglitz Archive, Yale.

24. Kandinsky to Stieglitz, undated letter from sec-

ond half of 1913, Stieglitz Archive, Yale.

25. "Buy Cubist Pictures While Critics Cavil," *Chicago Record-Herald*, March 26, 1913; article in Museum of Modern Art Armory Show Scrapbook.

26. Ibid.

27. Brown, *Armory Show*, p. 100.

28. Roethel and Benjamin, *Kandinsky Catalogue Raisonné*, list sixteen paintings produced between 1908 and 1914 as having been owned by Eddy.

29. Arthur Jerome Eddy, *Cubists and Post-Impressionism* (Chicago: A. C. McClurg, 1914; rev. ed., 1919).

30. Ibid.

31. " 'I See It,' Says Mayor at Cubists Art Show," *Chicago Record-Herald*, March 28, 1913; article in Museum of Modern Art Armory Show Scrapbook.

32. Eddy to Kandinsky, letter of June 16, 1914, Der Blaue Reiter Archives, Gabriele Münter Foundation, Städtische Galerie, Munich, Germany.

33. Eddy, *Cubists*, p. 116.

34. Ibid., pp. 116–117. This article originally appeared as "The Allied Artists," by Roger Fry, *The Nation* 13 (August 2, 1913), pp. 676–677. The three paintings discussed here by Fry were owned by Eddy.

35. Daniel Catton Rich, *The Arthur Jerome Eddy Collection, Bulletin of the Art Institute of Chicago*, December 1931, 9, p. 5.

36. Ibid.

37. Eddy, *Cubists*, p. 118.

38. Ibid., pp. 125–126.

39. "Cubists, Post-Impressionists, and Other Rebels against the Conventional Painting Analyzed in New Book—Interesting Pages on Cezanne, Van Gogh, and Many More Eccentric Artists," *New York Times*, June 21, 1914, p. 10.

40. "Modern Painting," *New York Times*, February 13, 1916, sec. 6, p. 54. Willard Huntington Wright, *Modern Painting: Its Tendency and Meaning* (New York: John Lane Co., 1915).

41. *New York Times*, June 21, 1914, p. 10.

42. Ibid.

43. *The Little Review*, 1, November 1914, p. 70. Quotation is from Sadler's introduction to *The Art of Spiritual Harmony*, p. xxi.

44. Herman Schuchert, "Harold Bauer in Chicago," *The Little Review*, 1, November 1914, p. 53. Quotations are cited by Kandinsky, who is not further identified.

45. Wright, *Modern Painting*, pp. 263 and 308

46. Ibid., p. 315.

47. Frank Jewett Mather, Jr., "The New Painting and the Musical Fallacy," *The Nation* 99 (November 12, 1914), pp. 588–589.

48. Ibid., p. 589.

49. Ibid.

50. Ibid.

51. See Gail Levin, "Wassily Kandinsky and the American Literary Avant-garde," *Criticism: A Quarterly for Literature and the Arts*, Fall 1979, pp. 347–361.

52. "Books on Art: Its Various Phases by Kadinsky [sic] and others," *New York Times Book Review*, November 15, 1914, p. 500.

53. Ibid.

54. For a discussion of this issue, see Gail Levin, "Die Musik in der frühen amerikanischen Abstraktion," in *Vom Klang der Bilder: Der Musik in der Kunst des 20. Jahrhunderts* (Munich: Prestel Verlag, 1985), pp. 368–373, and Zilcer, "The Aesthetic Struggle in America," Chapter II, pp. 43–110.

55. J. Nilsen Laurvik, *Is It Art?* (New York: International Press, 1913), pp. 25–26.

56. Ibid., p. 26.

57. Lee Simonson, "Panic in Art," *New Republic* I (November 7, 1914), p. 21, reprinted in a collection of Simonson's articles. See Lee Simonson, *Minor Prophecies* (New York: Harcourt Brace, 1927), pp. 49–58.

58. Ibn Gabirol [Alexander S. Kaun], "My Friend the Incurable," *The Little Review*, 1, no. 8 (1914), pp. 43–44. Gertrude Stein, *Tender Buttons* (New York: Claire-Marie, 1914). See Gail Levin, "Wassily Kandinsky and the American Literary Avant-garde," pp. 350–354.

59. Michael Sadleir, *Michael Ernest Sadler (1861–1943): A Memoir* (London: Constable, 1949), p. 240n. Sadler later changed his name to Sadleir, but for consistency, he is referred to as "Sadler" in the text.

60. Sadler, Translator's Introduction to *Art of Spiritual Harmony*, pp. xxv.

61. Ibid., p. xxiv.

62. Ibid., p. x.

63. Sadakichi Hartmann to Alfred Stieglitz, letter of May 20, 1915, Stieglitz Archive, Yale.

64. Ibid. In this same letter, Hartmann elaborated: "I must confess I never expected to see such an accumulation of balderdash, bombast, rodomontade, gallimaufry, salamagundi and 'I scratch you on the back if you tickle me' rant and prattle under one cover."

65. Alfred Stieglitz to Sadakichi Hartmann, letter of May 25, 1915, Stieglitz Archive, Yale.

66. Arensberg's copy of *The Art of Spiritual Harmony* is in the Philadelphia Museum of Art Library. He later purchased several of Kandinsky's paintings.

Kandinsky and the First American Avant-Garde

Gail Levin

By July 1912, when Marsden Hartley wrote from Paris to Alfred Stieglitz in New York, eager to share his enthusiasm for Kandinsky's work, Stieglitz had already discovered the Russian artist. After the July 1912 issue of *Camera Work,* American artists such as Arthur Dove, Abraham Walkowitz, Oscar Bluemner, and others were soon reading both Kandinsky's *Über das Geistige in der Kunst* and the almanac *Der Blaue Reiter.* The almanac, with its illustrations of art from diverse cultures, including many non-European examples and folk objects, prompted many American artists to investigate primitive art and folk art as sources for their own work.[1] They began to look at the tribal art of Native Americans and at local folk art.

Arthur Dove, who first exhibited with Stieglitz in March 1910 and had his first one-man show at 291 from February 27 through March 12, 1912, developed a lasting interest in Kandinsky. Dove owned both a copy of the first German edition of *Über das Geistige in der Kunst* and one of the almanac. The latter is inscribed "Mar. 19, 1913 from Mr. Stieglitz."[2] Dove's son remembers that his father admired Kandinsky's early work.[3] Dove must have communicated his enthusiasm to Stieglitz as well. This would account for Stieglitz's gift to Dove of *Der Blaue Reiter;* it is unlikely that Stieglitz would have given this book to Dove if he had shown no interest in the Russian artist whose work Stieglitz had purchased out of the Armory Show less than two weeks previously.

Dove may have known Kandinsky's art before *Improvisation No. 27* (see fig. 1.1) was exhibited in the Armory Show, as he had traveled to Paris in 1907. In the light of Dove's interest in new directions in art, it seems unlikely that he ignored his fellow artists exhibiting in the Paris salons. He might well have noticed Kandinsky's work in the 1908 and 1909 salons, the second of which included four landscape paintings by the Russian artist. Still in his twenties, Dove managed to exhibit his own work in these same two salons.

After his return from Europe in the spring of 1909, Dove seems to have developed his own abstract style independently of Kandinsky, whose works he later knew well. Indeed, Kandinsky's works of the years 1910 through 1912, when Dove was painting his first abstractions, are often more literal, more clearly representational than Dove's compositions. Both Kandinsky's and Dove's earliest abstract works derived from nature; both artists painted organic shapes and nature's rhythms.

When Dove saw Kandinsky's *Improvisation No. 27* in the Armory Show and later at 291, he must have felt himself to be a kindred spirit to an artist of such a freely expressive abstraction. Initially, however, Dove found Kandinsky's ideas, as expressed in his writing, more appealing than his painting. Dove's unpublished notes contain statements such as this: "We certainly seem to set down a self-portrait of our own inner feelings with everything we do. . . . It is the form that the idea takes in the imagination rather than the form as it exists outside."[4] Here Dove expressed ideas about which he had read in Kandinsky's treatise, such as "a particular state of mind clothed in the forms of nature (which one calls 'mood')."[5] Dove had studied some German and had read his copy of Kandinsky's treatise, in which he made notes on color in English. He undoubtedly read about Kandinsky's theories at length in

Arthur Jerome Eddy's book, which also featured Dove's explanation of his own painting *Based on Leaf Forms and Spaces,* owned by Eddy.[6]

Dove, inspired by Kandinsky's treatise, seems to have focused on the idea of abstraction based on musical analogy, producing, for example, *Music* and *Sentimental Music* in the 1910s. During the 1920s, he was once again moved to explore musical analogy in such works as *Chinese Music; Factory Music, Silver, Yellow, Indian-Red and Blue; George Gershwin—"Rhapsody in Blue" Part I* and *Part II; I'll Build a Stairway to Paradise—George Gershwin* (plate 14); and *Orange Grove in California—Irving Berlin.* The calligraphic style of Dove's *Improvision* of 1927 (plate 15), however, bears the closest resemblance to Kandinsky's painting. Indeed, the title surely derives from Kandinsky's term, *improvisation,* although it also refers to jazz improvisation.[7]

Dove, having become familiar with both "primitive" non-western art and folk art in *Der Blaue Reiter,* made use of both in his own work. For "primitive" art, Dove turned to Native American art which, for example, became the theme of *Indian Spring* of 1925 and *Indian One* of 1943. Dove also employed folk motifs and materials, particularly in his collages such as *Reds* of 1926 with its lock of Helen Torr's red hair or *Grandmother* of 1925 with its pressed flowers and needlepoint.

Another member of the Stieglitz circle interested in Kandinsky was Oscar Bluemner, who discovered the Russian artist's work when he left New York to return to his native Germany in the spring of 1912. Bluemner had immigrated to the United States in 1892, at the age of twenty-five. He was already an accomplished architect when he discovered modern art at the Cézanne watercolor exhibition held in March 1911 at Stieglitz's gallery 291.

Bluemner, having developed his interest in modern art through frequenting Stieglitz's gallery, was undoubtedly eager to see the work of Europe's most avant-garde artists. In May, while Bluemner was in Berlin for an exhibition of his work, artists were talking about the new almanac *Der Blaue Reiter,* just published. Bluemner had many opportunities to learn about Kandinsky and Der Blaue Reiter while he was in Berlin; he probably discovered *Über das Geistige in der Kunst* as well as the almanac during this trip. Bluemner also traveled to Cologne that summer of 1912 to see the International Exhibition of the Sonderbund, the exhibition that influenced the organizers of the Armory Show. The exhibition included two paintings by Kandinsky, one of which was non-objective. Bluemner reviewed this show for a Cologne paper, praising Kandinsky along with Van Gogh, Gauguin, and Matisse and insisting on the necessity "to see nature unphotographically."[8]

Bluemner returned to New York in time to submit his work to the Domestic Committee selecting additional artists for the 1913 Armory Show. Two of his oils and three of his watercolors were shown. He soon began to write articles on the new art for *Camera Work,* in the first of which—"Audiator [sic] et Altera Pars: Some Plain Sense on the Modern Art Movement," which appeared in the June 1913 issue—he demonstrates his keen awareness of just which artists were important. He named Kandinsky among those whom he believed would prove to be most influential in the future: "We have, furthermore, the individual points of view and means of expression, of such radical thinkers as Rodin, Kandinsky, Matisse, and Picasso, who have the strength of mind which is able to repudiate tradition and give us benefits of their analysis in a radical form."[9]

Kandinsky's work continued to challenge Bluemner. In an article in *Camera Work,* he wrote about the Russian-born American artist Abraham Walkowitz, whom he contrasted to Kandinsky, showing his own familiarity with Kandinsky's *Über das Geistige in der Kunst:*

Paint-symbols stand for thought, feeling, in short for idealism. . . . One may assemble those symbols—line, tone, color—in a free way, in any way suited for another purpose than that of copying nature, such as in ornament, decoration—and the true pictorial way is the one by which not semblance to life, but expression of an idea, vision of feeling is conveyed. The symbols may still resemble natural effects; their assemblage is personal: free painting; or on the other hand they may be unimitative, wholly invented. Then painting gets to be abstract, as Kandinsky wants it. But the former way is that of Walkowitz's new work. And he takes that step as he goes toward a more intense and pure recording of his sensations, though they are still derived from reality, as before. Only he sets them free, pictorially; while formerly they remained in the bondage of reality. Walkowitz is impelled by the "inner necessity": Kandinsky, however, like other radicals appears not to proceed gradually and inwardly, but with a mind to create an intellectual feat—which is not art.[10]

Bluemner obviously found much that he agreed with in Kandinsky's treatise, particularly the concept of the artist's "inner necessity." In 1914 he even wrote an essay, intended for *Camera Work,* called "Picasso Picabia Kandinsky," in which he dealt with the issue of "imaginative feeling visions."[11] However, like so many other American artists in the early twentieth century, Bluemner could not accept the result of "unimitative symbols" completely removed from nature—or totally abstract painting, which Kandinsky called "pure abstraction." Bluemner obviously objected to certain statements Kandinsky made in his treatise, such as: "We can maintain that only a few 'hours' separate us from this pure composition."[12] To him, some of Kandinsky's more abstract paintings seemed to represent this "first stage." Indeed, Bluemner probably disapproved of Kandinsky's *Improvisation No. 27.*

Bluemner's comparison of Abraham Walkowitz to Kandinsky suggests not only his own interest in Kandinsky's art and theory, but also Walkowitz's fascination with Kandinsky's ideas. A Siberian-born immigrant, Walkowitz, who arrived in the United States as a young child in 1880, was among the first of America's avant-garde to experiment with radical abstract styles. He discovered the new art during trips abroad. Walkowitz went to Paris in 1906, where he studied at the Académie Julien and saw the Salon d'Automne of 1907, with its great Cézanne memorial exhibition. Also included in the salon that year were four paintings, three drawings, and four woodcuts by Kandinsky.

Upon his return in 1908, Walkowitz managed to convince picture framer Julius Hass to show his work in the basement storerooms of his Madison Avenue shop. Nothing was sold, and Walkowitz later called this show "a success of disesteem."[13] By December 1912, however, Stieglitz gave Walkowitz his first of several exhibitions. Having been thus initiated into the circle of 291, Walkowitz had every opportunity to continue his interest in new artistic directions. He exhibited in the Armory Show, showing five representational oil paintings along with five drawings, a color monotype, and a watercolor.[14]

Walkowitz read the excerpt from Kandinsky's treatise in the July 1912 issue of *Camera Work,* and that same year he obtained a copy of the first German edition of *Über das Geistige in der Kunst,* which he kept for the rest of his life. By the time Stieglitz gave him his second exhibition, in November 1913, Walkowitz was painting mostly abstractions, some deriving from the dramatic New York City skyline. He referred to these as Improvisations, recalling Kandinsky's use of the term. He also gave such titles as *I Glorify New York: A Symphony in Lines* to works that date around 1913, after he had had a chance to read Kandinsky's treatise, in which the artist defined a "symphonic" composition.

Walkowitz's well-worn copy of *Über das Geistige in der Kunst* has survived, complete with his many marginal notes, underlined phrases, and occasional sketches, which suggest that he interpreted each statement literally. For example, on page sixty-three, Walkowitz drew in the margin the scrambled features of a distorted face as a kind of illustration of Kandinsky's text: "If, e.g., facial features or different parts of the body have been dislocated or 'distorted' for artistic reasons, one comes up against not only purely pictorial problems, but also anatomical ones, which confine the scope of the artistic intention, forcing irrelevant considerations upon it."[15] This literal interpretation of Kandinsky's remarks is characteristic not only of Walkowitz, but of other American artists (such as Marsden Hartley) who were among the first to experiment with abstraction.

Walkowitz seems to have paid careful attention to Kandinsky's statements about abstract form, for these sentences are almost entirely underlined. Kandinsky's contention that "form alone, as the representation of an object (whether real or unreal), or as the purely abstract dividing up of a space, of a surface, can exist *per se*" must have seemed like a revelation to Walkowitz, who would follow up this suggestion with experiments in the years ahead.[16] Comparing a typical Walkowitz drawing from this period, such as *City Abstraction*, to Kandinsky's *Improvisation No. 27*, one sees that Walkowitz's use of fluid, wavy lines relates to the energetic freedom of Kandinsky's painting. Walkowitz, who continued to paint city views for several more years, also began to paint pure abstractions. Although some totally abstract watercolors are dated as early as 1909, it seems more likely that these works, some of which are called improvisations, were actually painted after 1913 and predated at a much later date, after the term "improvisation" gained currency with the publication of Kandinsky's treatise.

Walkowitz was particularly fond of his *Improvisations of New York*, and he had his friend Haldeman-Julius publish a book with this same title, reproducing many of these works, in 1948. Walkowitz gave an autographed copy of this book to his younger friend and fellow painter, Jackson Pollock. Walkowitz's abstract watercolor *Creation* of 1914 (fig. 2.1) was included by Sidney Janis in the 1944 book *Abstract and Surrealist Art in America*, along with the art of many younger artists, including Pollock. Janis commented: "Walkowitz's *Creation*, nonfigurative, is part of a series started in 1914 and akin to the sensibility of Kandinsky done in the same period."[17] Janis also quoted Walkowitz on abstraction: "Pure abstract art is wholly independent of picturization in any form or of any object. It has a universal language, and dwells in the realm of music with an equivalent emotion. Its melody is attuned to the receptive eye as music is to the ear."[18]

Here Walkowitz was influenced by Kandinsky's treatise, though he was able to reshape aspects of it for his own use. Most of Walkowitz's marginal notes consist only of translated words and phrases, or of phrases repeated for emphasis. Yet he clearly read Kandinsky's book with the enthusiasm and diligence of an eager student. Undoubtedly, Walkowitz was among the first American artists not only to recognize the possibilities presented by Kandinsky, but also to develop a personal, lyrical abstract style based on these principles. Walkowitz suggests continuity between the first American avant-garde and the Abstract Expressionists, some of whom shared his enthusiasm for Kandinsky's work.

Georgia O'Keeffe, the artist most closely associated with Stieglitz, also found much of value in Kandinsky's writing and painting. Known for her reluctance to disclose anything about herself and her sources, O'Keeffe has recently been characterized as maintaining a "secretiveness . . . that as she got deeper into old age . . . intensified until it verged on para-

Fig. 2.1 Abraham Walkowitz. *CREATION*, 1914.
Eight drawings, mounted together, 35⁵⁄₁₆ × 45¹³⁄₁₆″ (90.54 × 117.47 cm) overall
Metropolitan Museum of Art, New York, Alfred Stieglitz Collection, 1949

noia."[19] Despite such reticence, when, nearly two decades ago, I wrote to ask her about Stieglitz's interest in Kandinsky, she, then eighty-seven, responded with a surprising assertiveness and was uncharacteristically forthcoming about herself, volunteering: "I was very interested in Kandinsky's book *Spiritual Harmony in Art,* and liked his paintings."[20] Clearly, O'Keeffe considered that Kandinsky had played an important role in her artistic development and wanted me to recognize that fact.

O'Keeffe's intense early interest in Kandinsky is now well documented in her 1915 correspondence with her art school friend Anita Pollitzer. By June, when their extant letters begin, Pollitzer is writing about Arthur Jerome Eddy's book.[21] By the end of July, she casually tells O'Keeffe: "I wish Kandinsky taught in New York," making it quite clear that her friend knew to whom she was referring.[22] It was through Eddy's book that O'Keeffe first came into contact with Kandinsky's work, as she had not yet read *Camera Work,* since, as late as that June, she asked Anita to lend her the first back issue that she had just acquired. Years later, O'Keeffe recalled that it was Alon Bement, with whom she studied and then worked as a teaching assistant at the University of Virginia, who first recommended that she get Eddy's book "to look at the pictures" and read "Kandinsky, 'On The Spiritual in Art.' "[23] In late August 1915, when Georgia responded to Anita's comment that she "had Jerome Eddy & Kandinsky" and that "there's something new in Kandinsky everytime I look at it," she assured her friend, "I got Jerome Eddy a long time ago—and sent to The Masses for Kandinsky but haven't been able to get it. They said they couldn't find out who published it."[24] It is noteworthy that O'Keeffe associated Kandinsky with the radical politics of the journal *The Masses,* just as Martin Birnbaum had associated Kandinsky with anarchism in his 1912 catalogue introduction.

Pollitzer wrote in September, informing O'Keeffe that "Kandinsky's 'Art of Spiritual Harmony' is published by Houghton Mifflin Company—Boston & N.Y.," and commenting, "It gets better with each rereading—I've really digested most of it—now—it's good. . . . I'm doing a picture—it's quite symbolic & I'm working it out in colors which have meanings."[25] Later that month, O'Keeffe comments: "Kandinsky is reading much better this time than last time too."[26] Now, she, too, was ready to experiment with Kandinsky's ideas in her work. She knew the Russian artist's painting from reproductions in Eddy's book and in *The Art of Spiritual Harmony.* By 1915, O'Keeffe was experimenting with organic abstraction in charcoal drawings. Similar to Kandinsky's early abstractions, O'Keeffe's abstract works derive from landscape and other nature imagery.

In 1916, O'Keeffe painted Palo Duro Canyon in Texas, which she called *Painting No. 21* (plate 19).[27] Her composition borders on abstraction, with only a small patch of blue sky among the black lines and orange and yellow forms to suggest that this is a landscape. She may have been influenced by Kandinsky's *Improvisation No. 27,* which she could have seen at 291 when she visited the gallery during 1914–1915, the period when she was studying at Teachers College in New York. That same year, she was painting abstractly, particularly in a series of mellifluous blue watercolors. Her choice of color must reflect her reading of Kandinsky, who stressed how "colour is a power which directly influences the soul" and referred to blue as "the typical heavenly colour," comparing it to various musical instruments from flutes to an organ, depending on its tonality.[28]

O'Keeffe, like Dove, Hartley, and other American modernists of her generation, responded to Kandinsky's emphasis on the link of abstraction to music. Kandinsky wrote in *The Art of Spiritual Harmony:* "Music is the best teacher. . . . A painter, who finds no satisfaction in mere representation, however artistic, in his longing to express his inner life, cannot but envy the ease with which music, the most non-material of the arts today, achieves this end. He naturally seeks to apply the methods of music to his own art."[29] According to Kandinsky, this led to desires for rhythm and abstract construction in painting, and placing "color in motion." Of course, there were many earlier sources prompting artists' interest in musical analogy, from Baudelaire and Mallarmé to Whistler.[30] In O'Keeffe's case, her teacher, Arthur Wesley Dow, stressed that seeing visual relations was equivalent to hearing music. Dow also shared Kandinsky's concern with the spiritual in art, but he did not believe that Kandinsky's work equaled that of the great Japanese artists. O'Keeffe may have read Dow's article "Modernism in Art," published in 1917 in the *Magazine of Art,* in which he insisted: "I saw in Germany and France great numbers of prints of brushwork by modernists, mostly in big wide black lines. . . . Kandinsky does not equal Keisai Yeisen."[31] By this time, however, she had already read Kandinsky's treatise.

Although O'Keeffe's interest in music had preceded her knowledge of Kandinsky, reading his treatise encouraged her to pursue what later prompted Stieglitz to describe her art as "color music."[32] This preoccupation with musical analogy is apparent in O'Keeffe's paintings such as *Blue and Green Music* (fig. 2.2) or *Music—Pink and Blue, I* and *II,* all of 1919. O'Keeffe's musical themes were discussed by critics during the early 1920s, especially Herbert Seligmann and Paul Rosenfeld, who also wrote on music.[33]

Another of the first-generation American modernists to discover Kandinsky's work was Konrad Cramer, who, at the age of twenty-three, emigrated from Germany to the United States. Arriving in New York the autumn of 1911, Cramer soon found that his enthusiasm for Kandinsky and the almanac *Der Blaue Reiter* was shared by those in the Stieglitz circle. After studying art in Karlsruhe, Cramer had arrived in Munich in 1910, probably in time to see the second show of the New Artists' Association, which opened at the Neue Galerie Thannhauser in September 1910. International in scope, this exhibition included many artists in addition to the association's members and gave the cubists ample exposure.

It was also in Munich, in February 1911, that Cramer met the American artist Florence Ballin, whom he married in June of that year. In October, the two artists left Europe for the United States, where they settled in Woodstock, New York. Cramer became a pioneer American modernist, painting pure abstractions before the Armory Show took place in 1913. Although his art was not included in the Armory Show, he first exhibited six of his abstract paintings at the MacDowell Club in New York City in November 1913, in what was one of the earliest exhibitions of non-representational art painted in America. He called several of his abstractions in this show "improvisations."

Cramer had arrived in Munich open to the new aesthetic experiments causing controversy there. It was the year preceding the breakup of the New Artists' Association, in December 1911, when Kandinsky, Gabriele Münter, Franz Marc, and Alfred Kubin withdrew. The main issue of disagreement among the association's members was Kandinsky's belief in "inner necessity" and his attempts to paint freely without clearly representing objects in his pictures.

On March 14, 1911, Cramer and Ballin visited the Neue Münchner Verein and the studios of both Adolf Erbslöh and Franz Marc, which Ballin described as "very interesting and enjoyable."[34] Since this visit took place just before Kandinsky and Marc began working on the almanac *Der Blaue Reiter,* Cramer and Ballin certainly must have heard about Kandinsky, although there is no evidence that they met him. Word of the projected almanac probably spread quickly in Munich as other artists were invited to participate as contributors. Although

Fig. 2.2 Georgia O'Keeffe. *BLUE AND GREEN MUSIC,* 1919. Oil on canvas, 23 × 19'' (59 × 48.7 cm) The Art Institute of Chicago, Alfred Stieglitz Collection, Gift of Georgia O'Keeffe, 1969.835 (Photograph © 1992 The Art Institute of Chicago. All rights reserved.)

Cramer departed before the first exhibition of Der Blaue Reiter was held at the Moderne Galerie Thannhäuser in December 1911, he was in Munich long enough to become interested in the creative vitality of the artists who were to participate.[35] Of these artists, Kandinsky, of course, exerted the largest influence in liberating his fellow artists from the weight of tradition. Before Cramer left Munich in 1911, he had grasped the importance of Kandinsky and the emerging group Der Blaue Reiter.

In Woodstock, Cramer communicated his imported ideas about abstraction to the other local artists. He reportedly "sowed the first seeds of discord in the ranks of the Woodstock painters" and participated in forming an art gallery in the dining room of Rosie McGee's boarding house, which at the time was the local gathering place for artists.[36] This group of artists chose as their motto "Modern Art or Die!"

Before long, Cramer also had become acquainted with Alfred Stieglitz and the circle of 291 in New York City. By 1914 Stieglitz had photographed Cramer, who had written a letter in answer to Stieglitz's query, "What is 291?," which he circulated to many in his circle. Cramer's reply, subsequently published with many others in *Camera Work,* was appropriately abstract:

> It is like a straight line rising, a line of living red, rising above gray formlessness, and other straight lines run towards the big, straight, rising line at many angles. Some almost run parallel, others melt gradually into it: some meet it at right angles; others cross it like the slash of a sword. Towards the bottom, some undefined lines of insipid colors, but only a few. But all is rising, is straight—but not the line of least resistance.[37]

Cramer is perhaps influenced here by Kandinsky's language in the essay "On the Question of Form," published in *Der Blaue Reiter.* Cramer had obtained his copy of the almanac after he had arrived in the United States. Kandinsky had written of the straight line in a different sense: "The viewer can and must follow the artist, and he should not be afraid of being misguided. Man cannot move in a straight line physically . . . much less spiritually. And on spiritual paths especially, the straight line is often the longest because it is false, and the apparently false path is often the right one."[38] In another sense, Cramer may have been describing 291 in terms of the abstract forms and lines of his own non-representational paintings.

Cramer's interest in Kandinsky's art is demonstrated in his painting *Improvisation,* probably finished in late 1911 or early 1912. Related to any of a number of paintings by Kandinsky of 1910, such as *Improvisation No. 9* or *Church in the Mountains,* Cramer's *Improvisation* retains aspects of landscape although it approaches pure abstraction with its rhythmic curves of green heavily outlined in black. Low pink hills across the bottom of the composition, before a yellow highlighted mountain peak, remind one that this painting still suggests a landscape— and is not just an arrangement of forms and colors. Cramer's palette is also close to Kandinsky's work of 1910, with rich purples and deep greens predominating amid dramatic insertions of yellow, orange, and pink strategically placed. Cramer was moving rapidly toward pure abstraction. He first emulated Kandinsky's landscapes and improvisations, then read the Russian painter's theories in *Der Blaue Reiter* (and probably in *Über das Geistige in der Kunst*), and finally developed purely abstract compositions of his own.

An example of Cramer's most abstract painting is *Improvisation No. 1* (1912). With this title Cramer is once again paying homage to Kandinsky by choosing one of the three categories the Russian artist used to describe his own paintings. Kandinsky defined an "improvisation" as "chiefly unconscious for the most part suddenly arising expressions of events of an inner character, hence impressions of 'internal nature.' "[39] Cramer's picture, devoid of reference to any particular material object, recalls as well Kandinsky's statement in *Der Blaue Reiter:* "In a painting, when a line is freed from delineating a thing and functions as a thing in itself, its inner sound is not weakened by minor functions, and it receives its full inner power."[40]

Strife (1913; plate 20), another of Cramer's most abstract paintings, is strikingly close to Kandinsky's work of 1911, the year Cramer left Germany. Cramer absorbed Kandinsky's style with great facility. His colors are rich and bright with soft edges merging into one another in the manner of the fluid colors in the background of Kandinsky's *Improvisation No. 19* of 1911. The heavy black lines that Cramer superimposed over the liquid color in *Strife* are typical of Kandinsky's work in 1911. Most of the black lines in Kandinsky's *Composition No. 4,* for example, are utilized on a diagonal and serve to create a sensation of movement, a mannerism that Cramer has adapted in *Strife.* Indeed, even as an abstract composition, *Strife* expresses a sense of the fleeting moment.

The title *Strife* perhaps reflects Kandinsky's remark about "a particular state of mind clothed in the forms of nature (which one calls 'mood')."[41] The "strife" referred to here might echo Cramer's own inner struggle to come to grips with abstraction. This avant-garde development evidently created an aesthetic conflict for Cramer, whose wholehearted espousal of purely abstract art was short-lived. Years later, Cramer stated: "In the beginning, I consciously broke away from painting 'reality' in order to explore the extent to which communication between painter and beholder could be maintained when painting became more and more abstract."[42] In both *Improvisation No. 1* and *Strife,* Cramer had attempted just this.

Yet Cramer also added, "When the point of contact with the beholder was lost entirely, the painting itself seemed to become sterile." This statement reflects his shift by the 1920s from the radical non-representational art of his youthful improvisations to mildly abstract landscapes and still lifes. The lesson from *Der Blaue Reiter* that remained with him was a fascination with folk art. Yet before Cramer replaced his early enthusiasm for Kandinsky's theories, he managed to interest others in them, including his friend and fellow painter in Woodstock, Andrew Dasburg, who painted a series of abstract "improvisations" about 1916.[43]

Just seven years after Kandinsky's first painting exhibited in America had been seen, scorned, and sold at the 1913 Armory Show, Katherine Sophie Dreier and Marcel Duchamp founded Société Anonyme, Inc., with the published aim of being an "International Organization for the Promotion of the Study in America of the Progressive in Art."[44] The Société Anonyme, whose first exhibition opened on April 30, 1920, at 19 East 47th Street in New York, with just sixteen paintings, continued the tradition of Stieglitz's first tiny gallery, 291, which had closed just three years earlier, in 1917. The Société Anonyme perpetuated Stieglitz's proselytizing zeal for the acceptance of modernism by organizing traveling loan exhibitions and a variety of lectures, some complete with lantern slide shows.

In the fifth exhibition held at the Galleries of the Société Anonyme, from November 1 through December 15, 1920, Kandinsky's work was shown with the work of the Americans Marsden Hartley, Man Ray, Joseph Stella, and Abraham Walkowitz, as well as that of other European artists. Fifteen months after his debut with Société Anonyme, Kandinsky was given his first American one-man exhibition in the Galleries of the Société Anonyme from March 23 through May 4, 1923. At this time Kandinsky was made first vice-president of the Société Anonyme, a largely honorary position (since he never visited the United States) that he held until his death in 1944.

For Kandinsky's first American exhibition, Katherine Dreier published a monograph, *Kandinsky,* with a cover in red and black designed by the artist himself.[45] Kandinsky wrote to Dreier, thanking her for the catalogue, but pointing out that she had reproduced his drawing on its side; he also requested that *The Art of Spiritual Harmony* be sold at the exhibition.[46] Four years later, Dreier purchased the right to translate into English and publish Kandinsky's *Punkt und Linie zu Fläche.* Although Dreier finished a rough translation, her version was never published. *Point and Line to Plane* finally appeared in English in 1947, translated by Howard Dearstyne and Hilla Rebay, to whom Dreier sold the rights.[47]

Katherine Dreier, who chose to dedicate her time and financial resources to the promotion of modern art in America, was also a painter. That she chose to bestow on Kandinsky the honor of being vice-president of the Société Anonyme indicates her high regard for the Russian painter and the strength of his reputation among the American avant-garde. Her fascination with Kandinsky's work was undoubtedly tied up with her attraction to German culture and to their mutual interest in theosophy. The daughter of German immigrants, Dreier had frequently visited Germany as a child and was fluent in German.

Like Bluemner, Dreier saw Kandinsky's work at the Cologne Sonderbund Exhibition during the summer of 1912, where she was particularly attracted to Van Gogh's painting. Returning to America, she exhibited two of her paintings in the Armory Show, where once again she saw Kandinsky's work. That year, Dreier read Kandinsky's *Über das Geistige in der Kunst,* and it was probably then that she acquired copies of *Der Blaue Reiter* and the catalogue of Kandinsky's exhibition at the Berlin gallery Der Sturm. In her own painting, Dreier turned to abstraction in 1918.[48] For her abstract compositions such as *The Garden* (plate 22) and *Unknown Forces* (plate 23), she was inspired by Kandinsky's paintings, which she also began to collect. She came to view Kandinsky as "trying to establish the beginning of a science of art."[49]

1. For examples of American modernists' use of primitive art, see Gail Levin, "American Art," in William Rubin, ed., *"Primitivism" in 20th Century Art: Affinity of the Tribal and the Modern* (New York: Museum of Modern Art, 1984), pp. 453–469.

2. Collection of William Dove, the artist's son.

3. William Dove, letter to the author, February 15, 1975.

4. Quoted in Barbara Haskell, *Arthur Dove* (Boston: San Francisco Museum of Modern Art, 1974), p. 8.

5. Wassily Kandinsky, *On the Spiritual in Art,* trans. Peter Vergo, in Kenneth C. Lindsay and Peter Vergo, eds., *Kandinsky: Complete Writings on Art* (Boston: G. K. Hall, 1982), p. 129.

6. Arthur Jerome Eddy, *Cubists and Post-Impressionism* (Chicago: A. C. McClurg, 1914; rev. ed., 1919), pp. 48 and 116–137.

7. Opinion is divided on whether Dove's title was inadvertently misspelled in the 1927 Intimate Gallery catalogue or whether he chose to create a new word out of the elision of "improvise" and "vision."

8. Quoted in Jeffrey R. Hayes, "Oscar Bluemner—Romantic Modern," in *Oscar Bluemner: A Retrospective Exhibition* (New York: Barbara Mathes Gallery, 1985), n.p.

9. Oscar Bluemner, "Audiator [sic] et Altera Pars: Some Plain Sense on the Modern Art Movement," *Camera Work,* special number (June 1913), p. 32.

10. Oscar Bluemner, " 'Walkowitz' (extracted from 'Kandinsky and Walkowitz,' an essay which will be published in a later issue)," *Camera Work,* no. 44 (October 1913; published March 1914), p. 26. The later essay did not appear.

11. Quoted in Jeffrey R. Hayes, *Oscar Bluemner: Landscapes of Sorrow and Joy* (Washington, D.C.: Corcoran Gallery, 1988), p. xi. Typescript of June 24, 1914, Oscar Bluemner Papers, Archives of American Art, Smithsonian Institution, N737: 544–545.

12. Kandinsky, *On the Spiritual in Art,* p. 197.

13. Quoted in Rudi Blesh, *Modern Art U.S.A.: Men, Rebellion, Conquest, 1900–1956* (New York: Knopf, 1956), p. 34.

14. Milton W. Brown, *The Story of the Armory Show* (New York: Joseph H. Hirshhorn Foundation, 1963), p. 297.

15. Kandinsky, *On the Spiritual in Art,* p. 171.

16. Ibid., p. 162 (German edition, p. 51).

17. Sidney Janis, *Abstract and Surrealist Art in America* (New York: Reynal and Hitchcock, 1944), p. 33.

18. Ibid., p. 44; statement by Walkowitz in 1944.

19. Sarah Whitaker Peters, *Becoming O'Keeffe* (New York: Abbeville, 1991), p. 13. This comprehensive study of O'Keeffe's early work and her sources was published just as this book was going to press. It considers Kandinsky's impact on O'Keeffe in a broader context than permitted here; see pp. 95–102.

20. Georgia O'Keeffe to Gail Levin, letter of November 22, 1974. She refused to comment on Stieglitz's interest in Kandinsky.

21. Clive Giboire, ed., *Lovingly, Georgia: The Complete Correspondence of Georgia O'Keeffe and Anita Pollitzer* (New York: Simon and Schuster, 1990), p. 4. Pollitzer's biography of O'Keeffe was posthumously published as *A Woman on Paper: Georgia O'Keeffe* (New York: Simon and Schuster, 1988).

22. Giboire, *Lovingly, Georgia,* p. 8, letter of July 26, 1915.

23. Georgia O'Keeffe, *Georgia O'Keeffe* (New York: Viking, 1976), n.p., adjacent plate 12.

24. Giboire, *Lovingly, Georgia,* pp. 10 and 15.

25. Ibid., p. 19.

26. Ibid., p. 24.

27. In Jack Cowart and Juan Hamilton, *Georgia O'Keeffe Art and Letters* (Washington, D.C.: National Gallery of Art, 1988), plate 11, this work is identified as *Special No. 21.*

28. Wassily Kandinsky, *The Art of Spiritual Harmony,* trans. Michael T. H. Sadler (Boston: Houghton Mifflin, 1914), pp. 38 and 58.

29. Ibid., p. 19.

30. See Gail Levin, "Die Musik in der frühen amerikanischen Abstraktion," in *Vom Klang der Bilder: Der Musik in der Kunst des 20. Jahrhunderts* (Munich: Prestel Verlag, 1985), pp. 368–373.

31. Arthur W. Dow, "Modernism in Art," *Magazine of Art,* VIII, January 1917, p. 116.

32. Barbara Buhler Lynes, *O'Keeffe, Stieglitz and the Critics, 1916–1929* (Ann Arbor: UMI Research Press, 1989), p. 18.

33. Ibid., pp. 197 and 204–209.

34. Florence Ballin, unpublished diary, Cramer family collection.

35. See Sarah Greenough and Juan Hamilton, *Alfred Stieglitz: Photographs & Writings* (Washington, D.C.: National Gallery of Art, 1983), p. 31. Although Greenough claims that Cramer knew Kandinsky personally and that he was still in Munich in December 1911, when *Über das Geistige in der Kunst* was published, she offers no documentation for these assertions. Indeed, there is no proof that it was Cramer who gave Stieglitz his copy of Kandinsky's treatise.

36. "Konrad Cramer," *The Overlook,* June 25, 1932, p. 7.

37. Konrad Cramer, "What is 291?," *Camera Work,* no. 47 (July 1914, published in January 1915), p. 33.

38. Wassily Kandinsky, "On the Question of Form," in Klaus Lankheit, ed., *Der Blaue Reiter Almanac, Edited by Wassily Kandinsky and Franz Marc, Documentary Edition* (New York: Viking, 1974), p. 157.

39. Kandinsky, *On the Spiritual in Art,* p. 218.

40. Kandinsky, "Question," in *Der Blaue Reiter,* p. 168.

41. Kandinsky, *On the Spiritual in Art,* p. 128.

42. Quoted in Konrad Cramer, *Konrad Cramer,* Brooklyn Center, Long Island University, May 1958.

The next quotation is also from this source.

43. See Gail Levin, "Andrew Dasburg: Recollections of the Avant-Garde," *Arts Magazine,* April 1979, pp. 102–106.

44. *Collection of the Société Anonyme, Museum of Modern Art, 1920* (New Haven: Yale University Art Gallery, 1950), p. xx.

45. Katherine S. Dreier, *Kandinsky,* (New York: Société Anonyme, 1923). Reprinted in *Selected Publications Société Anonyme (the First Museum of Modern Art: 1920–1944)* (New York: Arno, 1972), vol. 3.

46. Kandinsky to Dreier, letter of May 15, 1923. Société Anonyme Collection Beinecke Rare Book and Manuscript Library, Yale. Dreier's letters to Kandinsky are in the Fonds Kandinsky, Centre Nationale d'Art et de Culture, Centre Georges Pompidou, Paris.

47. Wassily Kandinsky, *Point and Plane to Line* (New York: Solomon R. Guggenheim Foundation, 1947). Rebay to Dreier, letter of July 28, 1945, Société Anonyme Collection, Yale.

48. Dreier to Frank Merchant of *The Literary Digest,* June 8, 1936, Société Anonyme Collection, Yale, states: "I have . . . painted Abstract Art since 1918."

49. Dreier to Marcel Duchamp, undated letter of about July 1928, Société Anonyme Collection, Yale.

Plate 1
Vassily Kandinsky
STUDY FOR IMPROVISATION 7, 1910
Yale University Art Gallery, New Haven, CT
Gift of Collection Société Anonyme,
New York
Photo credit: Joseph Szaszfai

Plate 2
Vassily Kandinsky
AUTUMN II, 1912
The Phillips Collection, Washington, D.C.

Plate 3
Vassily Kandinsky
FRAGMENT 1 FOR COMPOSITION 7
(*Center*), 1913
Milwaukee Art Museum

Plate 4
Vassily Kandinsky
*SKETCH FOR PAINTING WITH WHITE
BORDER (MOSCOW),* 1913
The Phillips Collection, Washington, D.C.
Bequest of Katherine S. Dreier, 1953

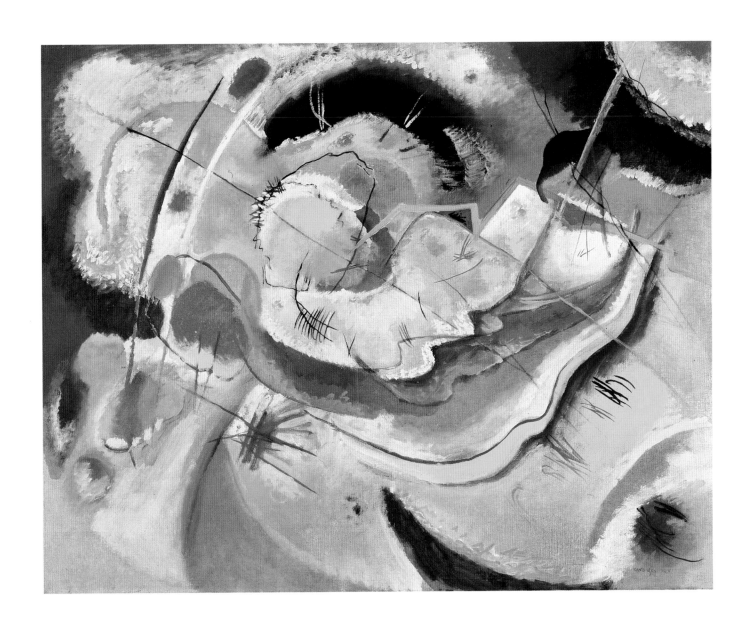

Plate 5
Vassily Kandinsky
LITTLE PAINTING WITH YELLOW, 1914
Philadelphia Museum of Art, The Louise and
Walter Arensberg Collection

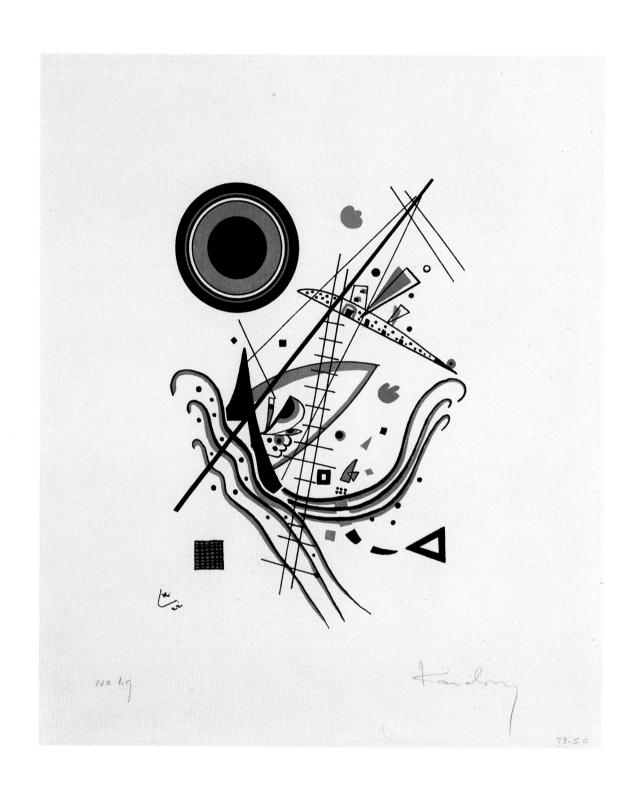

Plate 6
Vassily Kandinsky
BLUE LITHOGRAPH, 1922
Long Beach Museum of Art, Long Beach, CA

Plate 7
Vassily Kandinsky
BLACK LINES, 1924
Long Beach Museum of Art, Long Beach, CA

Plate 8
Vassily Kandinsky
BLUE PAINTING, 1924
Solomon R. Guggenheim Museum, New York
Gift of Fuller Foundation, Inc., 1976

Plate 9
Vassily Kandinsky
ABOVE AND LEFT, 1925
Collection of the Modern Art Museum of Fort
Worth, TX, made possible by a donation from
Mr. and Mrs. J. Lee Johnson III

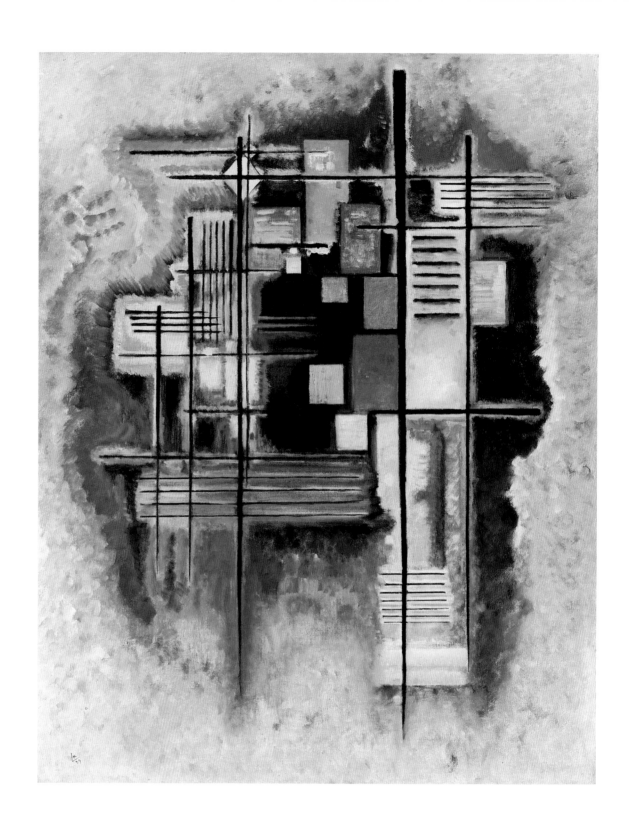

Plate 10
Vassily Kandinsky
CONDENSATION, 1929
The University of Iowa Museum of Art,
Iowa City
Gift of Owen and Leone Elliott
Photo credit: Randall Tosh

Plate 11
Vassily Kandinsky
SOFT PRESSURE, 1931
Collection, The Museum of Modern Art,
New York
The Riklis Collection of McCrory Corporation
(fractional gift)

Plate 12
Vassily Kandinsky
SUCCESSION, 1935
The Phillips Collection, Washington, D.C.

44

Plate 13
Vassily Kandinsky
POINTS, 1935
Long Beach Museum of Art, Long Beach, CA

Plate 14
Arthur Dove
I'LL BUILD A STAIRWAY TO
PARADISE—GEORGE GERSHWIN, 1927
Gift of the William H. Lane Foundation
Courtesy of Museum of Fine Arts, Boston

Plate 15
Arthur Dove
IMPROVISION, 1927
Lucile and Donald Graham Collection, Denver

Plate 16
Arthur Dove
ABSTRACTION, 1929
Collection of Lee Ehrenworth
Photo credit: Ed Watkins, New York

Marsden Hartley, Albert Bloch, and Kandinsky in Europe

Gail Levin

Marsden Hartley

By the time Marsden Hartley arrived in Paris for the first time, in April 1912, he was already well acquainted with the work of Cézanne, Matisse, and Picasso, the three artists most admired by the French avant-garde. Not only had Hartley been able to see examples of their work at Stieglitz's 291, but reproductions were also available to him in *Camera Work* and other art magazines. The financial aid that he received from Stieglitz and the painter Arthur B. Davies enabled Hartley, at the age of thirty-five, to make this first trip to Europe.

In Paris, Hartley lost no time in getting invited to Gertrude and Leo Stein's studio at 27 rue de Fleurus, where their art collection included the work of Renoir, Cézanne, Matisse, and Picasso. Introduced as a friend of Lee Simonson, Hartley first made the acquaintance of Gertrude Stein during the late spring of 1912. During the summer of that year, while Stein was in Spain, Hartley became friendly with a German crowd (that frequented the Restaurant Thomas on the Boulevard Raspail) that included Arnold Rönnebeck and a handsome young German officer, Rönnebeck's cousin, Karl von Freyburg, who later became the "subject" of several of Hartley's abstract paintings.[1]

Hartley also discovered a new direction in modern art with which the Stieglitz circle was not yet acquainted when he left New York for Paris. He wrote to Stieglitz in July 1912 about *Rhythm,* a little English magazine published in Paris, where John Duncan Fergusson was art editor:

> In one of the last numbers of Rhythm is a treatise on Gauguin's influence in which Kandinsky is talked of among others. He is evidently one of Gauguin's pupils and is I believe a modern light in Berlin or Munich—He has lately brought out a new magazine called *Die* [sic] *Blaue Reiter* which I shall look up—Very likely they talk much of modernism—and god knows they talk much about everything here.[2]

By the time Hartley's letter arrived, however, Stieglitz had already discovered Kandinsky and had published a passage from *Über das Geistige in der Kunst* in the July 1912 issue of *Camera Work,* which Hartley had not yet received in Paris. The same issue of *Rhythm,* which was sold in Brentano's bookstore in New York's Union Square, may also have been the source of Stieglitz's discovery of Kandinsky.

Rhythm was initiated and published by Middleton Murry and none other than Michael Sadler, the future translator of Kandinsky's *Über das Geistige in der Kunst.* It was Sadler's article, "After Gauguin," that described Kandinsky as "a Polish artist" who was one of Gauguin's disciples.[3] Sadler labeled these artists "neo-primitives, because they have arrived in their search for expression at a technique reminiscent of primitive and savage art." Sadler also discussed Kandinsky's desire "to harmonize the innerer Klang of external nature with that of humanity" and explained that the artist's expression of "the inner soul" would result in an art that will be definitely "unnaturalistic, anti-materialistic."

At this time Hartley also came into contact with Jacob Epstein, the American-born sculptor who had moved to England. Epstein was in Paris during the summer and fall of 1912 in conjunction with the placement of his controversial tomb monument to Oscar Wilde. It was probably both Sadler's article and Epstein's influence, as well as the almanac *Der Blaue Reiter,* that prompted Hartley to visit the Trocadero Museum with its famous collection of African and other tribal art. Hartley's reaction to primitive art was immediate, as he wrote to Stieglitz: "Yes we can always find the real thing at Trocadero. These people had no mean ambition. They created out of spiritual necessity."[4]

Hartley's use of the phrase "spiritual necessity" reflects his growing interest in Kandinsky's treatise, which he had purchased along with *Der Blaue Reiter* at Clovis Sagot's art gallery. Hartley wrote to Stieglitz:

> Saw Miss Rhoades for a few minutes and she is to take a fine book to you—a copy of Kandinsky's Die [sic] Blaue Reiter—which has turned out to be a fine thing. It is expensive but necessary for you to have over there and for me to have too—as I am taking a very sudden turn in a big direction owing to a recent visit to the Trocadero. One can no longer remain the same in the presence of these mighty children who get so close to the universal idea. . . . These revolts must come and until they come one can only proceed according to one's artistic conscience. They must be revolts of the soul itself if they are to mean anything other than intellectual imitation. . . .[5]

Hartley wrote to Stieglitz again about *Der Blaue Reiter* on September 27, 1912: "By this time you will have the Blaue Reiter. It has a good character."[6] Hartley's initial interest in *Der Blaue Reiter* is apparent in some of the still lifes he painted in 1912, in which he depicted primitive art objects. *Indian Pottery (Jar and Idol)* also suggest a comparison with Gabriele Münter's *Still Life* of 1911, which was reproduced in *Der Blaue Reiter.*

After making a brief trip to London at Epstein's suggestion, Hartley wrote to Stieglitz about his latest work, explaining that he had departed from still lifes "in favor of intuitive abstraction," which he insisted was "not like anything here. It is not like Picasso—it is not like Kandinsky not like any 'cubism.' It is what I call for want of a better name subliminal or cosmic cubism." Hartley admitted making this departure "as a result of spiritual illuminations" and claimed:

> I am convinced that it is my true and real utterance. It combines a varied sense of form with my own sense of color which I believe has never needed stimulation. . . . My first impulses came from the new suggestion of Kandinsky's book the Spiritual in Art. Naturally I cannot tell what his theories are completely but the mere title opened up the sensation for me, and from this I proceeded. In Kandinsky's own work I do not find the same convincing beauty as his theories hold. He seems to be fine theorist first and a good painter after.[7]

Hartley probably learned more about Kandinsky and Der Blaue Reiter when he visited Robert Delaunay, who had exhibited with this group in Munich and was included in the almanac. Hartley told Stieglitz that his friend Rönnebeck generously translated many things for him, both from French and German.[8] Reporting on showing his work to a "German painter from Munich . . . working on the musical principle," who commented on Hartley's expression of "pure mysticism" in the modern idiom, he insisted:

> I am probably the first to express pure mysticism in this modern tendency. . . . I am making every effort by way of concentration and faith toward going to Berlin early in January and if it is in any way possible to come back by way of Munich, as I would like to meet Kandinsky and size up the Blaue Reiter group and its activity there.[9]

The encounter Hartley described coincides with the visit to Paris of Franz Marc and August Macke to meet Robert Delaunay in October 1912. Just about this time, Hartley began his series of Musical Theme paintings, which was the body of work he described as "intuitive abstraction" in his letter to Stieglitz. Some of these paintings were originally known as *Bach: Prelude and Fugue,* and one painting even includes this phrase as a part of the composition. Of course, Hartley had probably seen František Kupka's purely abstract *Amphora, Fugue à deux couleurs* of 1912, exhibited in the recent Salon d'Automne.

Hartley's first trip to Germany, in January 1913, was brief, only about three weeks in all, but important in its impact. The single most important event was his trip with Rönnebeck to meet Vassily Kandinsky. Writing to Stieglitz from Paris just days after his return, Hartley's enthusiasm was unbounded. He felt that he had now entered his really creative period: "I have something personal to say—and that no one else is saying just this thing—It all comes out of a new growth in my life—a culmination of inward desires of longstanding—I went with my friend to see Kandinsky whom I found to be a splendid man and a most generous and constructive attitude toward art."[10] Hartley also told how Kandinsky had asked that they exchange photographs of their work. He announced his intention to go to Germany to live and work as soon as he could make arrangements: "It is more constructive and I am weary of this French nervosité."[11]

According to Hartley, it was Rönnebeck who described to Kandinsky the new work that Hartley was doing, prompting Kandinsky to suggest exchanging photographs of their work. Both Hartley and Rönnebeck were captivated by Kandinsky's collection of Bavarian glass pictures, old Chinese wood sculptures from Siberia, and Russian folk art.[12] Hartley told Stieglitz that he would like Kandinsky, exclaiming: "I have never been in the presence of an artist like him—so free of convention with a hatred of all the traditions that cling to art—bohemianism, uncleanness, lack of mental order—this chaos which makes Paris so charming to those who like looseness—For myself I am weary of it."[13]

Hartley had in common with Kandinsky his interest in the spiritual. He stressed to Stieglitz how he had discovered himself through sources such as William James's pragmatism, Henri Bergson, and more directly "the fragments of mysticism" that he had found in Boehme, Eckhardt, Tauler, Suso, Ruysbroek, and the Bhagavad-Gita. Hartley's interest in James had been stimulated by his discussions with Gertrude Stein, who had studied with William James while at Harvard. "I found myself going into the subjective," he proudly told Stieglitz of his new series of paintings, which he claimed some said were "the first expression of mysticism in modern art." "No one," he insisted, "has presented just this aspect in the modern tendency—Kandinsky is theosophic—Marc is extremely psychic in his rendering of the soul of animals. It is this which constitutes the most modern tendency which without knowing until I had been to Munich I find myself directly associated."

Only by labeling Kandinsky "theosophic" and Marc "extremely psychic" did Hartley feel that he was able to claim to be the first to express mysticism in modern art. Although Kandinsky wrote in *Concerning the Spiritual in Art* of the Theosophical Society as the "material form [of] . . . one of the greatest spiritual movements" and of his admiration for Madame Helena Petrova Blavatsky's views on India and for Rudolph Steiner's writing, he also referred frequently to "mystical inner content" and "mystical necessity."[14] Kandinsky's interest in theosophy was actually a facet of his interest in mysticism.

Hartley had, in fact, been drawn to the art of the American mystic painter Albert Pinkham Ryder long before he had ever heard of Kandinsky. Hartley reminded Stieglitz that Arthur B. Davies had declared that the essence of his first landscapes was American mysticism. He wrote that he was confident that Kandinsky would respond favorably to his art: "I know that what I have to express coincides perfectly with his notion of Das Geistige in der Kunst."

Although Hartley dismissed Kandinsky's interest in theosophy as totally different from his own interest in mysticism, there are indications that he did find certain aspects of theosophy of interest. Kandinsky had written of Madame Blavatsky's many years in India and that she was the first person "to see a connection between these 'savages' and our 'civilization.' "[15] In her book *Isis Unveiled,* Blavatsky sought to establish that the one source of all wisdom of the past is India.[16] Hindu mysticism was certainly an important influence on both Madame Blavatsky and Rudolph Steiner. As theosophists, they would have been interested in Meister Eckhardt, whose notion of the Godhead as a dark and formless essence is a favorite thesis of theosophy, and in Jacob Boehme, whose thought had been influenced by Eckhardt and his younger contemporary Johannes Tauler. These are the same mystical texts about which Hartley expressed enthusiasm to Stieglitz. In fact, Hartley shared many interests with the theosophists, and though he admitted he had been curious about Boehme for several years, some of his enthusiasm for mysticism resulted from his reading of Kandinsky's treatise.[17]

In late May 1913, Hartley had written to Stieglitz from Berlin that he expected to meet Rudolph Steiner and Eduard Schuré, whom he described as "occults."[18] Yet Hartley, while stressing his personal mystical outlook, again insisted that he was ignorant of such ideas. By October 1913, Hartley's interest in the spiritual had reached its peak. He wrote to Stieglitz that he had read such books as Richard Maurice Bucke's *Cosmic Consciousness* and William James's *Varieties of Religious Experience.*[19]

In the upper right corner of Hartley's *Musical Theme (Oriental Symphony)* (1912–13; plate 24), a figure of Buddha, with his legs crossed in a lotus position, is shown meditating. The figure rests beneath an exotic arch, and another evocative "oriental" arch is found in the top center above three hands raised toward the sun. These hands give the *abhaya mudra,* or the hand sign typically found in Indian religion, which indicates "have no fear." Beneath the hands is a circle that probably represents another heavenly body—the moon. Indeed, the language of the theosophists includes references to astral bodies. Eight-pointed stars are also found across the top half of this painting—as if it is the "heavenly realm." These same stars are frequently present in other versions of Hartley's musical themes. In a letter to Stieglitz of August 1913, Hartley described the mystical significance of these stars as:

> A mystical presentation of the number 8 as I get it from everywhere in Berlin. Of course you know that mysticism was very strong in Germany—and the element remains although not as strongly as once. One instance is that everywhere in Berlin one sees the eight pointed star—all the kings wore it over their heart—the soldier on the forehead—I find also the same stars in the Italian primitives—This is a real reason for all these signs but it remains mystical—and explanations are not necessary.[20]

Hartley's remark that he also found the eight-pointed stars in the Italian primitives suggests the actual source of his stars. In the almanac *Der Blaue Reiter,* Hartley found inspiration in a primitive painting by an unknown Italian or Spanish master. In addition to Hartley's revered eight-pointed stars sprinkled liberally across the background, this primitive may also have suggested the strange scalloped arches in *Oriental Symphony.* Hartley may even have borrowed the idea of the interlocking circles found in the center of *Oriental Symphony* from the circular shapes of these overlapping haloes. Hartley's creation of abstract forms out of traditional images is also apparent in other paintings he made that relate to illustrations in *Der Blaue Reiter.* In this one primitive painting, Hartley found both the spirituality and the abstract shapes and patterns he sought for his own mystical paintings.

Hartley's choice of a musical theme for these paintings is a significant one. Like so many of his contemporaries who read Kandinsky's *Über das Geistige in der Kunst,* where he wrote of artists comparing "their own elements with those of other arts," Hartley agreed with Kandinsky's idea that "the inner life of the artist" could be assisted by music, "the least material of the arts today."[21] In his conclusion to his treatise, Kandinsky defined what he called symphonic composition as opposed to simple and obvious form composition, which he called melodic: "complex composition, consisting of several forms, again subordinated to an obvious or concealed principal form. This principal form may externally be very hard to find, whereby the inner basis assumes a particularly powerful tone."[22] Hartley's interest in this particular aspect of Kandinsky's theories may have been encouraged by his contact with Kupka, in the company of the musician Walter Rummel, who first introduced Kupka to the ideas of Kandinsky. The impetus for Hartley's abstract Musical Theme series can be placed securely within the ambience of Kandinsky and *Der Blaue Reiter.*

Writing to Kandinsky and Münter after his first visit with them, Hartley exclaimed that it was "a great pleasure to me always to know real artists, those who know the real meaning of art—I and my friend Rönnebeck speak of you both—and we are just now engaged in a strong defense of Herr Kandinsky's principles."[23] Hartley expressed his eagerness to have Kandinsky and Münter see his paintings, which he would be sending to the Galerie Goltz in Munich. Although Münter, who had lived in the United States between 1898 and 1900, spoke excellent English, Hartley urged Kandinsky to write to him in German, noting that Rönnebeck would translate for him.

Since Hartley described himself as "a convert to the field of imagination into which I was born," Kandinsky's definition of form as "the external expression of inner meaning" and his emphasis on the principle of "inner necessity" must have been especially significant to him.[24] Kandinsky's references to the "three mystical necessities" and "in the root of roots—in the mystical content of art" would have struck a receptive chord in Hartley, who, as he had written to Stieglitz, felt he had discovered his essential self through intellectual and spiritual freedom that resulted from his search among the mystics' writings.[25]

Around the middle of April 1913, Hartley left for an extended stay in Germany. Stopping in Munich on his way to Berlin, Hartley lost no time renewing his earlier acquaintance with the artists of Der Blaue Reiter. Having corresponded with Kandinsky, Münter, and Marc from Paris, Hartley arranged to have these artists, as well as Albert Bloch, the only American contributor to the almanac, gather at the Galerie Goltz to see his "intuitive abstractions."[26] These included paintings such as *Pre-war Pageant* with its apparent symbolism around groups of three—the aureoles in three colors, the connected medallions.[27] Marc sent a postcard to Kandinsky to arrange this meeting, demonstrating friendly interest in Hartley. He invited Kandinsky and Münter to join them for an hour at the Goltz gallery and suggested that they could all go out to eat afterward.[28] Hartley wrote to Stieglitz at length about his reaction to this momentous encounter.

After the meeting, Hartley immediately began to express growing reservations about Kandinsky's work. To Stieglitz he explained: "Kandinsky volunteered a discourse on the law of form—that of the individual as applied to the universal . . . which however left me unmoved."[29] Hartley, who described Kandinsky as "a complete logician trying so earnestly to dispense with logic" and himself as a "simple one and without logic having an implicit faith in what is higher than all intellectual solutions," commented:

After experimenting in the direction of the emotional lyricism and fluid abstraction of Kandinsky in *Abstraction* and other works of 1913, Hartley chose to tighten his abstract images into more personal hard-edged emblems. By 1914–1915 Hartley often appears to have paid more attention to what Kandinsky advocated in his writings than to what he was actually painting, but in 1913, he could not ignore the images that Kandinsky produced.

Lee Simonson, an artist close to Hartley at this time, observed his friend's infatuation with Kandinsky and Germany. Simonson affectionately recorded his observation in a watercolor, *Caricature of Hartley,* which he presented to the artist in September 1913. Simonson depicted a blond Hartley (with his characteristic aquiline nose) in the dress of a Prussian soldier marching, flag in hand, before a scene of Berlin in the distance. Hartley's flag is composed of colorful triangles and abstract shapes with the letters K A N D I N S K Y superimposed in an abstract way. Hartley's uniform is emblazoned with the numbers 2 9 1 on both his hat and epaulets, representing his first allegiance to Stieglitz, whose letter Simonson quotes in the top left of the caricature: "Hartley has about made up his mind to become a permanent citizen of Germany." Simonson's caption reads: "Marsden adopts Germany to the tune of 'Ich bin ein Preusser. Kennt ihr meine Farben,' etc." [I am a Prussian. Do you know my colors, etc.] Hartley's love of life in Germany is shown by the fact that in his other hand he holds a beer tankard containing his paintbrush. In this charming manner, Simonson recorded the tremendous impact of Kandinsky on the impressionable Hartley.

During this period, Hartley was interested to convey what he referred to as his "spiritual enthusiasm." He often incorporated an abundance of "abstract entities" in his works such as *Abstraction with Flowers* (plate 25) and *Painting No. 48,* including the mandorla, the triangle, and the circle. The use of these forms recalls Kandinsky's concern with "pure abstract entities" and the "pointlessness (in art) of aimlessly copying the object."[33]

Hartley's mysticism may have provided him with solace, but it could not help him out of his dire financial situation. By October 1913, he was forced to take Stieglitz's advice and return to New York, bringing his paintings with him in order to try to raise additional funds. When Hartley arrived in New York in late November 1913, he had with him his collection of Bavarian glass paintings similar to the *Hinterglasmalerei* that Kandinsky had collected and published in *Der Blaue Reiter.*[34] He remained there until March 1914. After an exhibition at 291, Hartley had arranged enough additional funding to enable him to return to Germany. On his way back to Berlin, he stayed briefly in London and in Paris, returning to Berlin by late April. In late May or early June 1914, Hartley wrote to Stieglitz that Kandinsky's book was now out in English as *The Art of Spiritual Harmony.* Hartley admitted that "it reads well" but felt that it was a book for the unsophisticated in such private matters as spiritual thoughts.[35] Indeed, Hartley, now more critical of Kandinsky, maintained that such a subject was very personal, one for discussion only in the home.

Despite the signs of impending disaster, Hartley chose to stay on in Germany after the declaration of war in August 1914. His good friends Arnold Rönnebeck and Karl von Freyburg were Prussian officers. Rönnebeck was wounded during the winter of 1914–15, but his cousin, Karl von Freyburg, was killed in action in France on October 7, 1914.[36] At this time, Hartley stopped working on his Amerika, or Indian-theme, paintings, which may have been prompted by his trip home, and began a series of emblematic military pictures, some of which are a direct tribute to his dead friend.[37]

Forced to return to America in December 1915, Hartley moved about, staying in New

Fig. 3.3 Marsden Hartley.
EL SANTO, 1918.
Oil on canvas, 36 × 32″
(92.3 × 82.1 cm)
Courtesy Museum of New
Mexico, Santa Fe

York, Provincetown, and Bermuda. During the summer of 1917, he went to Maine, staying in Ogunquit at the art colony founded by collector, writer, painter, and patron Hamilton Easter Field.[38] There Hartley produced a number of paintings on glass. Although some have argued that his paintings on glass were simply the result of his interest in the early American folk art of saloon-window painting, the evidence indicates that the impetus to look at American glass painting and folk art came earlier, from Kandinsky.[39] Glass paintings by the artists of Der Blaue Reiter, including Kandinsky, Münter, Marc, Klee, and Macke, and the folk *Hinterglasmalerei* reproduced in the almanac influenced not only Hartley's glass paintings, but also his other paintings of the period 1913 to 1920.

When he traveled to New Mexico in 1918, Hartley gave up the difficult technique of glass painting to work first in pastels and on drawings, then in oil on canvas. Although he had given up the practice of working the fragile medium, the memory of Kandinsky's glass paintings and the Bavarian primitives he collected must have remained with Hartley as late as 1918, when he began to paint the primitive New Mexican Santos. At first glance, Hartley's *El Santo* (fig. 3.3), for example, reflects only his western surroundings, including a desert plant, an Indian blanket, and one of the Santos, or images of saints that Hartley saw in New Mexico. The evocative spiritual quality of the painter's Santos is reminiscent of the Bavarian glass paintings that he had admired and collected in Germany. In another painting, *Blessing the Melon* (1918; fig. 3.4), Hartley presented the Virgin Mary holding a bouquet of flowers flanked by both candles and pulled-back curtains. This figure, centrally placed in a symmetrical arrangement, resembles a glass painting called *Sancta Francisca* (fig. 3.5), painted by Kandinsky in 1911, which has a very similar curtain effect framing the centrally placed saint. When Hartley first saw the primitive Santos in New Mexico, he must have recalled similar folk religious images painted on glass as well as those by Kandinsky that he had admired several years earlier in Germany.

Hartley's association with Kandinsky and the other painters of Der Blaue Reiter was an important phase in his artistic development. He produced many strong abstract paintings during these years that stand out among the best work done by America's first avant-garde artists. Several writers on Hartley have emphasized a statement he made in reference to the influence of Kandinsky on his work, in which Hartley is credited as having said that he was "happy that he never did slide down the Kandinsky kaleidoscope."[40] In fact this was a sentence taken out of context from a letter that Hartley wrote in 1929 from Paris to his friend, the painter Rebecca Salsbury Strand. In the letter, Hartley revealed that his reason for wanting to have an exhibition of his work in Paris was to demonstrate that he "did not slide down the Kandinsky kaleidoscope."[41]

Actually, the acerbity of Hartley's remarks was provoked by a statement made by his old friend Lee Simonson in the foreword he had written for the catalogue of Hartley's 1929 show at Stieglitz's Intimate Gallery in New York. Simonson had written: "In the interval between Maine and Aix-en-Provence, Hartley did, like Alice thru the looking glass, seem to disappear for a while down Kandinsky's kaleidoscope and be lost among its colored fragments. Fortunately he has come thru the other end. . . ."[42] In this context, Hartley's defensive response is understandable. Nevertheless, the few years during which Hartley worked in the ambience of Der Blaue Reiter resulted in his best abstract paintings.

Fig. 3.4 Marsden Hartley. *BLESSING THE MELON: THE INDIANS BRING THE HARVEST TO CHRISTIAN MARY FOR HER BLESSING,* 1918. Oil on board, 32½ × 23⅞" (83.3 × 61.2 cm) Philadelphia Museum of Art, Alfred Stieglitz Collection

Albert Bloch

Fig. 3.5 Vassily Kandinsky. *SANCTA FRANCISCA*, 1911. Hinterglasbild, 6 × 4⅗″ (15.6 × 11.8 cm) Solomon R. Guggenheim Museum, New York

Albert Bloch is the only American artist whose work was included in the almanac *Der Blaue Reiter* and in the group's two exhibitions. Bloch, who left his native St. Louis for Europe in 1908, while still a young man in his twenties and, except for occasional visits to the United States, remained abroad until 1921, had been living in Munich for several years when Marsden Hartley arrived. Although never a part of the Stieglitz circle, Bloch had visited 291 in April 1908, where he saw the first Matisse exhibition in the United States. In the first exhibition of Der Blaue Reiter, chosen by Kandinsky and Marc and held at the Thannhäuser Gallery in Munich in December 1911, Bloch showed six paintings. Bloch had studied in the art school in his home town and then worked as a free-lance draftsman in New York and St. Louis.[43] William Marion Reedy, who published Bloch's caricatures in his political and literary periodical known as *The Mirror,* encouraged Bloch to travel abroad to advance his career and gave him financial support for a time. In return, Bloch contributed articles and reports on the new European movements in literature and painting.

In 1934, when Hartley's friend Arnold Rönnebeck was director of the Denver Art Museum, he invited Bloch, whom he and Hartley had first met in Munich in 1913, to lecture there. In his talk, entitled "Kandinsky, Marc, Klee: Criticism and Reminiscence," Bloch recalled his first meeting with Kandinsky in 1910, after a visitor to his studio had suggested that he invite Kandinsky and his associates to have a look at his work. Kandinsky, he remembered, "was glad to come, and when he did come—well, the upshot was, that I was invited to cast my lot with him and his friends."[44]

Although he had not sought membership in this group, in retrospect, Bloch considered that his joining Kandinsky and Marc had been entirely logical: "What wonder, then, that an obscure newcomer like me, still in his twenties who had until then shown only an occasional picture or two at the jury-shows of the Berlin and Munich Secessions, should feel delighted and flattered to be asked by two such men to join them in their planned enterprise of Der Blaue Reiter."[45] Bloch claimed that at the time he was not very interested "despite my awareness (or suspicion) that the group or rather the team of Marc and Kandinsky was to make Central European art history."

After Bloch returned to America, he had an exhibition in November 1921 at the Daniel Gallery in New York and taught for a year at the Academy of Fine Arts in Chicago. In 1923 he accepted an offer to head the Department of Drawing and Painting at the University of Kansas and continued to live in Lawrence, Kansas, after his retirement in 1947, until his death in 1961. Living in Kansas, Bloch managed to ignore any new trends in art; he exhibited only on invitation and seemed satisfied to remain aloof from the limelight of the faraway developments of the avant-garde, both in the United States and abroad. This distance, both philosophical and physical, resulted in near obscurity for an American artist who had been among the first Americans to participate in the events of the early twentieth-century avant-garde in Europe.

In spite of Bloch's self-imposed artistic isolationism, he wanted the facts to be known, insisting that "neither [Alexey von] Jawlensky nor [Marianne von] Werefkin ever showed their work with Der Blaue Reiter, nor did poor Marsden Hartley or Lyonel Feininger, as the catalogue of a recent Blaue Reiter exhibition in New York erroneously asserts, with no shadow of excuse for the assertion."[46] Bloch claimed that he was uncertain whether Feininger, whom he viewed as deserving, was ever asked to join Der Blaue Reiter, but said that though they were friends, Feininger had never mentioned it. Bloch proudly asserted that after he returned to America, he "never made a point of mentioning, let alone advertising, my connection with Marc and Kandinsky." Still, he pointed out that he "was never left out of any of their shows" and acknowledged his gratitude to both, "for the tremendous stimulus which association with them brought me."

Bloch was correct that Hartley and Feininger never showed with Kandinsky, Marc, Bloch, and other members of Der Blaue Reiter in Munich, although they did participate in Herwarth Walden's first Herbstsalon in Berlin in 1913, a large international exhibition that included artists as diverse as the Italian futurists and Piet Mondrian.[47] Though Bloch had a rather patronizing attitude toward "poor Marsden Hartley," the two artists often shared similar views. Like Hartley, Bloch professed to admire the work of the American mystic painter Albert Ryder. Bloch recalled that he had liked Kandinsky's paintings better without the elaborate explanations the painter gave about them: "I had understood and admired his work from the beginning without feeling the need for any kind of explanation. I could delight in his pictures for what they were—for what I was, for what they gave back to me of myself, since finally, we can take away from a work of art only what we bring to it."[48]

This statement is reminiscent of Hartley's view that Kandinsky was an "aesthetic philosoph."[49] Whereas Hartley tended to view Kandinsky's painting as too theoretical and without "spiritual enthusiasm," Bloch "deplored the general tendency to theorize, and in particular he felt that Kandinsky was approaching dogma."[50] Bloch and Hartley differed, however, in their attitudes toward abstraction. While Hartley, for a brief period, experimented with the abstract painting of pure form, Bloch could not accept Kandinsky's idea that painting could omit all representational elements. In his Denver lecture, Bloch emphasized that he did not agree with Kandinsky's idea that "the painter, like the musician, should create, in each work, a new world of pure form, sprung each time out of his consciousness fullborn and functioning."[51] Yet while Hartley later tried to deny having been influenced by Kandinsky, Bloch was much more generous:

> It is to be remembered, whatever my critical reservations regarding the actual *work* of Kandinsky, that never had I listened to such inspired and inspiring talk upon the subjects which interested me most and that I had never failed in those days to find his work most stimulating. He was bursting with ideas, and his work between 1909–1914 showed this in every canvas, every scrap of paper. He had thought long and earnestly, often fruitfully, upon all aspects of the subject which so engaged my own thought. How could a receptive hearer sixteen years younger, fail to learn from a man like that, who was not trying to teach?[52]

Like Hartley, Bloch was better acquainted with Franz Marc than with Kandinsky. Bloch described Marc as "the deepest spirit of them all and beyond dispute the very greatest genius that German painting has produced in many generations."[53] Marc obviously admired Bloch as well, for not only had he helped to select his work for the exhibitions of Der Blaue Reiter, but he had even corresponded with Bloch from the trenches during the war that took his life in 1916. Marc also owned at least one of Bloch's paintings, which he displayed in his home. Bloch praised Marc's work, yet its influence on his own work is mainly limited to a shared enthusiasm for the angular, prismatic planes of Robert Delaunay.

Despite his friendship with Marc and his acquaintance with Paul Klee, Bloch was most profoundly affected by Kandinsky. Immediately after Marc and Kandinsky visited his studio in 1910, Bloch came under Kandinsky's influence. Bloch would later disagree with some of Kandinsky's ideas in the as yet unpublished *Über das Geistige in der Kunst,* but in 1910 and in 1911, he must have been studying his paintings rather closely. One finds an emotional religious theme similar to those in Kandinsky's *Hinterglasmalerei* in Bloch's *Procession of the Cross (Kreuztragung)*, painted in September 1911 and shown in the first exhibition of Der Blaue Reiter. For the setting of the bearing of the cross, Bloch has painted rolling hills with a high horizon line like that in landscape paintings by Kandinsky such as *Church in the Mountains* of around 1910. Several of Bloch's figures recall those in Kandinsky's 1911 glass painting *All Saints' Day*.

During the few years that Bloch was close to Kandinsky, he must have painted even more abstract work that reflected his fascination with the Russian artist's art and his own youthful will to experiment. Bloch's paintings were described in 1913 as having "misshapen, embryonic creatures . . . intense postures of love or yearning" with "all material depiction" torn away.[54] Many of these, and the paintings that came before them, unfortunately would have been destroyed by the artist himself, who later in his life asserted: "In the course of this career of mine I have destroyed far more pictures than I was ever able to complete or save."[55]

Among the paintings that have survived Bloch's self-censorship are several that reflect Munich's symbolist milieu, the same cultural currents that significantly affected Kandinsky.[56] *Harlequinade* of 1911 (plate 26) and *Harlequin with Three Pierrots* of 1914 recall Paul Verlaine's collection *Fête Galantes*, with poems like "Pantomime" and "Colombine."[57] Verlaine's poetry was part of the cultural currency in Munich then, familiar to those in the circle of the poet Stefan George, including Kandinsky.[58] *Harlequinade* was exhibited in the first Blaue Reiter exhibition and reproduced in the catalogue.

Bloch also felt the influence of the composer, painter, and writer Arnold Schönberg, who was also in the Stefan George circle. Schönberg was represented in the almanac *Der Blaue Reiter* by a *Lied,* a theoretical article on music, and three of his paintings. Some of the titles that Bloch gave to his paintings completed in the years just after the almanac's publication, such as *Lied I* (plate 28), suggest Schönberg's influence. Schönberg composed his melodrama *Pierrot Lunaire* [*Moonstruck Pierrot*] in 1912.

Behind the figures in *Harlequin with Three Pierrots,* Bloch has painted a landscape of rolling hills that demonstrates his admiration of Kandinsky's paintings. Kandinsky's *Improvisation No. 19* (1911) has a similar group of elongated figures set in a colorful fluid landscape, although they are more abstract than Bloch's figures. Bloch adapted the heavy black vertical lines found across the center of his painting from Kandinsky's *Composition No. 4,* familiar through a study for it that was reproduced in the almanac. Bloch's use of rich color and confetti-like dabs of paint is also characteristic of Kandinsky. Bloch celebrates his own subject matter with a use of line and color similar to that of Kandinsky. The result is his own personal style, advanced for 1914, but not so radical in retrospect.

Bloch's own reservations about Kandinsky's move toward total abstraction are expressed in an article on Bloch's work by Murray Sheehan that appeared in Reedy's magazine, *The Mirror.* Before writing his article in Munich, Sheehan, who had communicated with Bloch, claimed that the artist's work was largely subjective and explained:

> Subjective painting strives to free us altogether from the limitations of camera-art by presenting merely the feelings which are provoked by a certain subject. They would introduce the pure lyric into painting. Of course, the danger then arises of their giving us all the feelings without giving us the key as to what they are about. That is the trouble with Kandinsky. Too frequently he gives but a puzzle-picture of emotions, and leaves you to figure out what it is all about.[59]

In spite of any reservations that Bloch may have held about his ideas, Kandinsky liked

Bloch, as is demonstrated by his mention of the young American artist in a letter written to Arthur Jerome Eddy during October 1913: "He works most energetically, accomplishes much, makes fine progress, and constantly gains in the form of his inner expression. Him, too, I can recommend warmly."[60] On the basis of this letter from Kandinsky, some photographs of Bloch's work, and his own correspondence with the artist, Eddy mentioned him in the first edition of *Cubists and Post-Impressionism.*[61]

Eddy also began to collect Bloch's paintings, continued to correspond with the artist, and was instrumental in arranging for Bloch's one-man exhibition at the Chicago Art Institute during the summer of 1915. The exhibition, which included twenty-five of Bloch's paintings, was also shown at the City Art Museum in St. Louis. The catalogue essay, written by Eddy, claims that "it would be difficult to conceive pictures more unlike than Bloch's and Kandinsky's, while those of Franz Marc, a brilliant member of the group, are still different."[62] Eddy also wrote:

> These paintings are in no sense cubist. Neither are they futurist. What are they then? Compositional painting is the best term for them. That is what Kandinsky calls his work: compositional painting in precisely the same sense that music is compositional sound. . . . There is music that is cheaply realistic, and there is music so pure and abstract that one loses all sense of realities. The new men are attempting to do with line and color what great composers have done for centuries with sound—to make compositions of line and color beautiful in themselves.[63]

By the time Bloch returned to live in the United States in 1921, Stieglitz had closed 291 and was not to open his second gallery, the Intimate Gallery, until 1925. While Stieglitz might have been receptive to Bloch's work, the opportunity did not present itself. Bloch's first exhibition on returning was held in New York in 1921 at the Daniel Gallery. At the time, Bloch, who had a wife and two children to support, chose the financial security of a teaching position in the artistically conservative Midwest. The result, however, was Bloch's separation from the rest of America's avant-garde. In Kansas, Bloch, working in isolation, created much more introspective, often haunting, pictures, allowing his former association with Kandinsky and Der Blaue Reiter to become only a memory.

1. Hartley to Stieglitz, letter of July 1912. All of the Hartley-Stieglitz correspondence referred to in this text is preserved in the Alfred Stieglitz Archives in the Collection of American Literature, Yale University. My original study of Hartley, Bloch, and Kandinsky appears here in an abbreviated form due to limitations of space. See Sandra Gail Levin, "Wassily Kandinsky and the American Avant-Garde, 1912–1950," doctoral dissertation, Rutgers University, 1976, pp. 79–140.

2. Hartley to Stieglitz, letter of July 1912. Michael Sadler, "After Gauguin," *Rhythm, Art, Music, Literature* 1, Spring 1912, pp. 23–29.

3. Sadler, "After Gauguin." The following quotations in this paragraph are also from this source.

4. Hartley to Stieglitz, postcard of October 9, 1912.

5. Hartley to Stieglitz, series of three undated postcards from early September 1912.

6. Hartley to Stieglitz, postcard of September 1912.

7. Hartley to Stieglitz, letter of December 30, 1912.

8. Hartley to Stieglitz, letter of December 1912.

9. Hartley to Stieglitz, letter of December 20, 1912.

10. Hartley to Stieglitz, postcard of February 1, 1913.

11. Ibid.

12. Arnold Rönnebeck, unpublished diary, Yale.

13. Hartley to Stieglitz, letter of February 1913. Following references to this trip are also from this letter.

14. Wassily Kandinsky, *On the Spiritual in Art,* trans. Peter Vergo, in Kenneth C. Lindsay and Peter Vergo, eds., *Kandinsky: Complete Writings on Art* (Boston: G. K. Hall, 1982), pp. 143 and 174–176.

15. Ibid., p. 32.

16. Helena Petrova Blavatsky, *Isis Unveiled: A Master-key to the Mysteries of Ancient and Modern Science and Theology* (New York: Bouton, 1877).

17. Hartley to Stieglitz, letter of December 20, 1912.

18. Hartley to Stieglitz, letter of May 1913.

19. Hartley to Stieglitz, letter of October 22, 1913. Richard Maurice Bucke, *Cosmic Consciousness: A Study in the Evolution of the Human Mind* (Philadelphia, 1901; facsimile reprint, New York: Causeway Books, 1974).

20. Hartley to Stieglitz, letter of August 1913.

21. Kandinsky, *On the Spiritual in Art,* p. 154.

22. Ibid., p. 215.

23. Marsden Hartley to Gabriele Münter, letter of c. February 1913, in the Franz Marc papers, Archiv für Bildende Kunst, Germanisches Nationalmuseum, Nuremberg, Germany. Hartley's letters to Münter, Marc, and Kandinsky are published in full in Patricia McDonnell, "Marsden Hartley's Letters to Franz Marc and Wassily Kandinsky, 1913–1914," *Archives of American Art Journal,* 29, nos. 1 and 2 (1989), pp. 35–44.

24. Hartley, autobiographical notes, in *Marsden Hartley* (New York: Museum of Modern Art, 1944); Kandinsky, *Concerning,* pp. 52–53.

25. Kandinsky, *On the Spiritual in Art,* pp. 174–175.

26. Hartley to Stieglitz, letter of March 13, 1913.

27. See Gail Levin, "Marsden Hartley and Mysticism," *Arts Magazine* 60, November 1985, pp. 16–21.

28. Marc to Kandinsky, postcard of April 1913, Gabriele Münter Siftung, 726, Städtische Galerie, Munich.

29. Hartley to Stieglitz, undated letter of late May 1913; the following quotations are also from this letter.

30. Quoted in Donald Gallup, "The Weaving of a Pattern: Marsden Hartley and Gertrude Stein," *Magazine of Art,* November 1948, pp. 256–261.

31. Ibid., p. 256.

32. Hartley to Stieglitz, letter of August 1913. The following quotations are also from this letter.

33. Kandinsky, *On the Spiritual in Art,* pp. 165–166.

34. Hartley to Stieglitz, letter of October 31, 1913.

35. Hartley to Stieglitz, letter of June 12, 1914.

36. Hartley to Stieglitz, letter of October 23, 1913.

37. See Gail Levin, "Hidden Symbolism in Marsden Hartley's Military Pictures," *Arts Magazine* 54, October 1979, pp. 154–158.

38. See Doreen Bolger, "Hamilton Easter Field and His Contribution to American Modernism," *The American Art Journal,* XX, no. 2 (1988), pp. 78–107; *Hamilton Easter Field Art Foundation Collection* (Ogunquit, Me.: Barn Gallery Associates, 1966).

39. Elizabeth McCausland, *Marsden Hartley* (Minneapolis: University of Minnesota Press, 1952), p. 32.

40. McCausland, *Marsden Hartley,* p. 21; Jerome Mellquist, "Marsden Hartley," *Perspectives U.S.A.,* Summer 1953, p. 71.

41. Hartley to Strand, letter of January 26, 1929, Yale.

42. Lee Simonson, Foreword to *Marsden Hartley* (New York: Intimate Gallery, January 1929), n.p.

43. Bloch studied with Dawson-Watson at the art school of Washington University.

44. Transcript of Bloch's lecture in the Städtische Galerie, Munich; reprinted in part in Hans Konrad Roethel, *The Blue Rider* (New York: Praeger, 1971), p. 38. The lecture was delivered on December 13, 1934.

45. Bloch to Edward A. Maser, letter of June 20, 1955; reprinted in Ernest Scheyer, *Albert Bloch: An Exhibition of Watercolors, Drawings, and Drypoints* (Lawrence, Kan.: University of Kansas Museum of Art, 1963). The next quotation in this paragraph is from this letter.

46. Ibid. The following quotations in this paragraph are also from this letter.

47. Peter Selz, *German Expressionist Painting* (Berkeley: University of California Press, 1957), p. 266.

48. Quoted in Donald G. Humphrey, *Albert Bloch: A Retrospective Exhibition of His Work from 1911 to 1956* (Tulsa, Okla.: Philbrook Art Center, 1961), n.p.

49. Hartley to Stieglitz, letter of May 1913.

50. Humphrey, *Albert Bloch,* from the Denver lecture, n.p.

51. Ibid.

52. Ibid.

53. Ibid. The lecture is also the source for the following information about Marc and Bloch.

54. Murray Sheehan, "The New Art, a propos the Work of Albert Bloch," *The Mirror,* 22, April 11, 1913, p. 6.

55. Bloch to Maser, June 20, 1955.

56. See Peg Weiss, *Kandinsky in Munich: The Formative Jugendstil Years* (Princeton, N.J.: Princeton University Press, 1979), especially pp. 81–91.

57. Paul Verlaine, *Fêtes Galantes* (Paris, 1869; Paris: Flammarion, 1976).

58. See Weiss, *Kandinsky in Munich,* pp. 81–84.

59. Sheehan, "The New Art," p. 6.

60. Arthur Jerome Eddy, *Cubists and Post-Impressionism* (Chicago: A. C. McClurg, 1914; rev. ed. 1919), p. 200.

61. Ibid.

62. Arthur Jerome Eddy, *Catalogue of Paintings by Albert Bloch* (St. Louis: St. Louis Art Museum, 1915), p. 4.

63. Ibid., pp. 6–7.

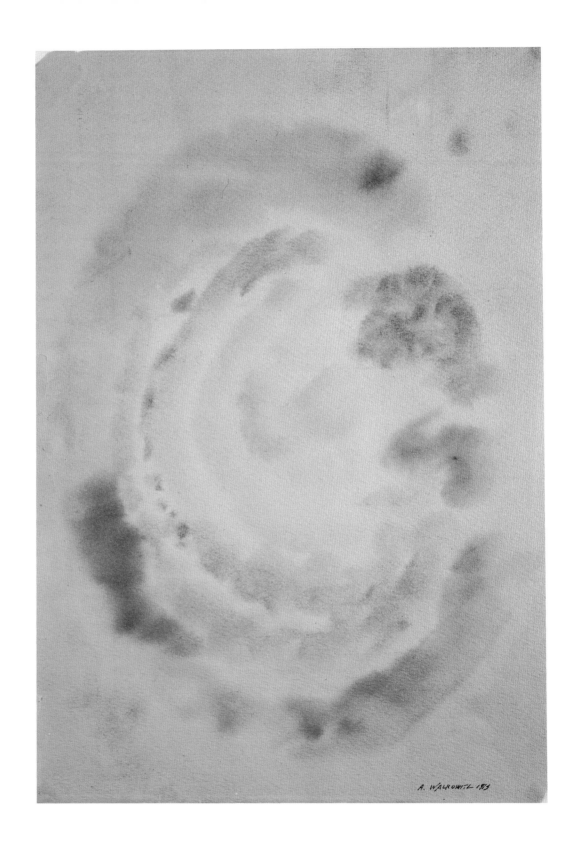

Plate 17
Abraham Walkowitz
ABSTRACTION, n.d.
Zabriskie Gallery, New York

65

Plate 18
Abraham Walkowitz
ABSTRACTION, 1913
Zabriskie Gallery, New York

Plate 19
Georgia O'Keeffe
SPECIAL 21, 1916
The Georgia O'Keeffe Foundation
Photo credit: Malcolm Varon, New York

Plate 20
Konrad Cramer
STRIFE, c. 1912
Hirshhorn Museum and Sculpture Garden
Smithsonian Institution, Washington, D.C.
The Joseph H. Hirshhorn Bequest, 1981
Photo credit: Lee Stalsworth

Plate 21
Konrad Cramer
IMPROVISATION, c. 1913
Pinnacle West Capital Corporation

Plate 22
Katherine S. Dreier
THE GARDEN, 1918
Collection of The Newark Museum,
Newark, NJ
Gift of Mrs. Charmion Von Wiegand, 1958
Photo credit: Sarah Wells

Plate 23
Katherine S. Dreier
UNKNOWN FORCES, before 1934
Brooklyn Museum

Plate 24
Marsden Hartley
*MUSICAL THEME (ORIENTAL
SYMPHONY)*, 1912–13
Rose Art Museum, Brandeis University,
Waltham, MA
Gift of Samuel Lustgarten

Plate 25
Marsden Hartley
ABSTRACTION WITH FLOWERS, 1913
Collection University Art Museum, University
of Minnesota, Minneapolis
Bequest of Hudson Walker from the Ione and
Hudson Walker Collection

73

Plate 26
Albert Bloch
HARLEQUINADE, 1911
Collection, The Museum of Modern Art,
New York
Given anonymously

Plate 27
Albert Bloch
WORKING DRAWING FOR HARLEQUIN
WITH 3 PIERROTS, 1913
Courtesy Sid Deutsch Gallery, New York
Photo credit: Jim Enyeart

Plate 28
Albert Bloch
LIED I, November 1913–April 1914
The Snite Museum of Art, University of Notre
Dame, Notre Dame, IN
Gift of Mr. Robert Shapiro

Plate 29
Albert Bloch
DIE HÖHEN, 1914
Krannert Art Museum and Kinkead Pavilion
University of Illinois

Plate 30
William Schwartz
SYMPHONIC FORMS, NO. 18, c. 1935
Courtesy private Texas collection

78

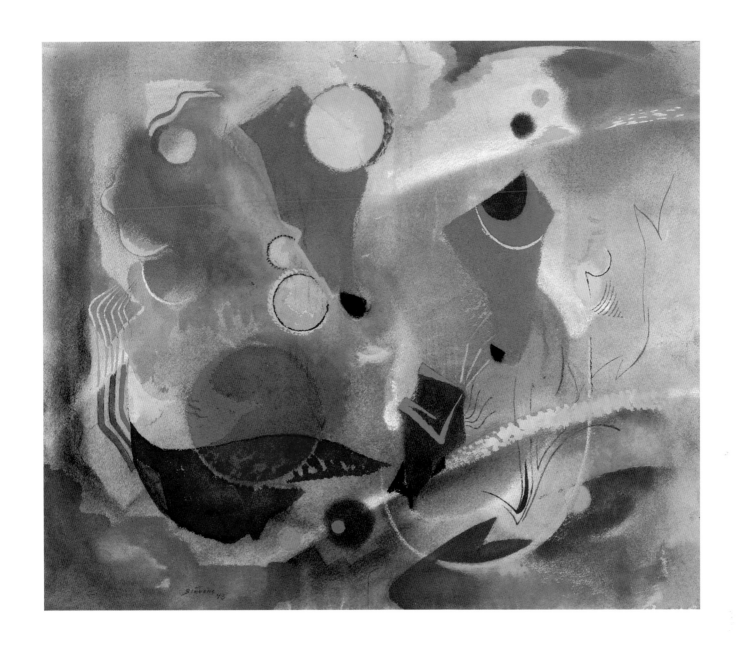

Plate 31
Will Henry Stevens
SPATIAL ABSTRACTION, 1943
Richard York Gallery, New York

Plate 32
Will Henry Stevens
UNTITLED ABSTRACTION, 1945
Blue Spiral 1, Asheville, NC

Kandinsky and Regional America

Marianne Lorenz

The geographical breadth of Kandinsky's impact on American painting can be seen as one examines the development of abstract art in regional America. The 1930s saw a proliferation of exhibitions, publications, and lectures that featured Kandinsky and made his work accessible to artists in the Midwest, the South, the Southwest, and the western United States. In Chicago, Arthur Jerome Eddy's collection, which contained nine Kandinsky paintings, was seen by a whole generation of artists in the late 1920s and 1930s. The Solomon R. Guggenheim Collection of Non-Objective Painting mounted extensive exhibitions of its collection of Kandinsky and Rudolf Bauer in the late 1930s in Charleston, Philadelphia, and Baltimore, and published and disseminated nationwide a deluxe catalogue of the collection. In California, Galka Scheyer exhibited and promoted Kandinsky as a member of the Blue Four. Finally, artists hailing from New York, Chicago, and Toronto brought their knowledge of Kandinsky's work to other artists and the public in New Mexico. Kandinsky's presence was neither isolated nor uniform; it crossed regional lines and was transmitted through a variety of media. While many of the artists discussed here came into contact with Kandinsky's work and ideas in the 1920s, his impact on their work was not fully in evidence until the following decade.

Chicago

In Chicago, where the introduction and assimilation of modernism was subject to numerous cultural and geographic barriers, a thorough appreciation of Kandinsky's art came slowly.[1] In addition to what has been called "an unusually francophile view of international modernism that until the mid–1930s . . . paid only scant attention to the various schools of German expressionism,"[2] Chicago was governed by traditional tastes that favored concrete, if idealized images and known quantities. The Art Institute of Chicago, whose students supposedly hung Matisse in effigy when his works were shown at the Armory Show in 1913, was a bastion of academism and made little concerted effort to engage students in modernist ideas.[3]

Though young Chicago artists interested in the new forms of expression emanating from Europe were at a significant disadvantage, there were opportunities for those willing to pursue avant-garde ideas. Manierre Dawson, for example, visited the Armory Show and formed his own judgments, which ran contrary to the prevailing negative attitudes. Feeling as though he had "been thru a dream," Dawson found the works of Matisse and Kandinsky "extremely important in breaking open the avenues of freedom of expression."[4] While there is no evidence Dawson had seen Kandinsky's work prior to 1913 (despite a trip to Munich in 1910), works such as *Prognostic* (1910; fig. 4.1) reveal the fact that Dawson's thinking paralleled that of Kandinsky and other European modernists. If one accepts the 1910 date of *Prognostic,* then Dawson prefigured Kandinsky's Improvisations of about 1913.[5] Dawson, like Kandinsky, believed that "great art must come from within"[6] and that "transcendental feelings about shapes, attitudes and relations must be signified by the forms given out by the artist."[7] Ironically, then, in the heart of Chicago's conservative artistic climate, one of its native sons

81

Fig. 4.1 Manierre Dawson. *PROGNOSTIC*, 1910. Oil on canvas, 33¾ × 35¾'' (86.54 × 91.66 cm) Milwaukee Art Museum Collection, Purchase, Acquisition Fund

was breaking ground similar to that which Kandinsky himself was exploring during the same years.

Dawson's example notwithstanding, Chicago retained its orthodox artistic outlook throughout the 1920s and 1930s. Even European guests denounced extreme abstraction. In 1928 the German art critic Julius Meier-Graefe visited the Eddy home, and while he took some interest in the work of Albert Bloch, Kandinsky held "no appeal"[8] for the distinguished Cézanne scholar. C. J. Bulliet, writing in 1930, remarked that "with all its reputation for gun-play and gangsterism, Chicago observes better the traditions and amenities."[9] Chastising Chicago for living too comfortably in its conventions, Bulliet sought to identify Chicago modernists and patrons of modernism to compete with those of New York. Holding up as exemplars artists such as Rudolph Weisenborn ("commander of the rebel forces"), Stanislaus Szukalski, and William S. Schwartz, Bulliet argued that to fight their art was akin to "Tennessee's gallant fight against Darwinism."[10] One particularly unforgettable example of Chicago's conservatism can be seen in the case of Mrs. Josephine Hancock Logan. Mrs. Logan and her husband, who since 1917 had been donors of the Logan Prize Fund at the Art Institute, established in 1937 a society bearing the name Sanity in Art. Calling most modernist artists "astigmatic," Mrs. Logan advocated a return to logic and accuracy in painting. The *Chicago Herald and Examiner,* in its report on Logan's activities, reproduced Kandinsky's *Improvisation No. 30 (Cannons)* (see fig. 3.1) with a caption that read, "Modernistic paintings like these are the kind under the fire of Mrs. Josephine."[11]

In 1933, J. Z. Jacobson published his catalogue of progressive art, *Art of Today: Chicago, 1933.* Of the over fifty contemporary artists included in the book, Jacobson noted that they are all "representatives of living art and as such they have something pertinent to say to all of us who are up with the times intellectually and spiritually."[12] That Jacobson was familiar with Kandinsky's writings is also made clear from the following statement:

> Truly enough the skyscrapers are an expression of Chicago, as are the elevated trains, and the Board of Trade, and the overflowing stream of humanity on State Street. But esthetically, and metaphysically, and spiritually considered these are merely phases of the outer form of the inner principle.[13]

The vocabulary used by Jacobson ("outer form of the inner principle") may have been drawn from his reading of Eddy's *Cubists and Post-Impressionism,* in which Eddy quotes an article by Kandinsky in *Der Sturm.* There Kandinsky states: "The 'vital,' the 'determining' element is the 'inner,' that controls the outer form, even as the idea in the mind determines the words we use, and not the words the idea."[14]

By the early 1930s, then, despite Chicago's reluctance to embrace modernism as exemplified by Kandinsky and other members of the European avant-garde, the message had been received and assimilated by some. This resulted in part from a mild loosening in attitude at the Art Institute of Chicago itself under the influence of Robert B. Harshe and Daniel Catton Rich. In 1926 the Art Institute organized exhibitions of the Eddy Collection (Kandinsky, Marc, Brancusi, Picasso, Duchamp, and Picabia) and that of Arthur B. Davies (Matisse, Picasso, Rousseau, and Cézanne), and in 1929 Odilon Redon was given a one-man exhibition. The Arts Club of Chicago also played a major role in bringing the work of Braque, Rodin, Brancusi, and Matisse to Chicago in the late 1920s. In the spring of 1932 the Arts Club presented an exhibition of the Blue Four (Kandinsky, Klee, Feininger, and Jawlensky). C. J. Bulliet reviewed the show in the *Chicago Evening Post,* and Kandinsky's *Circles in a Circle* (fig. 4.2) was reproduced. Bulliet, who was favorably disposed to modern German art

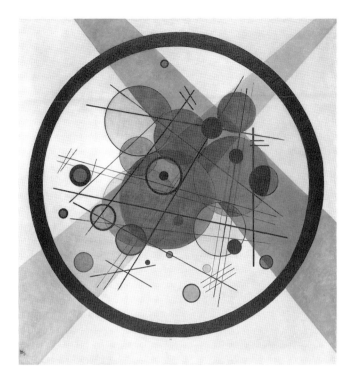

Fig. 4.2 Vassily Kandinsky. *CIRCLES IN A CIRCLE,* 1923. Oil on canvas, 38¾ × 37⅝'' (99.4 × 96.5 cm) Philadelphia Museum of Art, Louise and Walter Arensberg Collection

and should be given a great deal of the credit for educating Chicago audiences about Kandinsky and other modernists, said the show was composed of outstanding work by "four geniuses." Urging the audience to absorb "Kandinsky, Kleee [sic] and half the canvases of Jawlensky as you would a rainbow or a Salt Lake sunset," Bulliet stressed the nonintellectual nature of the work: "Just forget that these things are something to be 'understood' and try to experience them as something to be felt emotionally." Kandinsky's "soap bubbles" were highly praised for their "soul" and "dazzle."[15] Galka Scheyer gave a lecture in conjunction with the exhibition and reported back to the Blue Four that they had "won over the heart of Chicago."[16]

William S. Schwartz

The Art Institute of Chicago mounted its second exhibition of the Eddy Collection (the first had occurred in 1922) from December 22, 1931, to January 17, 1932. This exhibition commemorated the gift of Eddy's collection to the Art Institute by his widow and son. Bulliet's review of the show detailed Kandinsky's life and work and went so far as to quote at length passages from Eddy's discussion of Kandinsky in *Cubists and Post-Impressionism.* Kandinsky's *Improvisation No. 30 (Cannons),* which was given a 5- by 6-inch reproduction in the review, was, according to Bulliet, "destined to be one of the Art Institute's masterpieces." Other artists, including André Derain, Winslow Homer, Manet, Whistler, Rodin, and Vlaminck, are cursorily mentioned.[17]

The Chicago artistic community could not have ignored Bulliet's enthusiasm for the work of Kandinsky and his tacit acknowledgment that the most important works in the Eddy Collection were those of Kandinsky. The brochure that accompanied the exhibition indicates that four Kandinskys were displayed: *Painting with Troika* (1911), *Landscape with Two Poplars* (1912), *Painting with Green Center* (1913), and *Improvisation No. 30 (Cannons)*. All but *Painting with Green Center* were illustrated in the brochure, which also discussed Kandinsky's ideas as they related to his art:

> The paintings of Kandinsky are the products of a special aesthetic cult closely allied with theosophy, the artist's religion. Refusing "story-telling" art and conventional beauty, Kandinsky creates abstract canvases, which are supposed to spring from the "inner need" seeking expression in outer form. The "soul" is the centre of creation; color, forms, compositions spring from "inner harmonies" and set up "spiritual vibrations." Color, line and form are not ends in themselves; they are incidental to the artist's expression of his "soul states." The analogy to music is constantly stressed.[18]

While the allusion to a "special aesthetic cult" and "theosophy" might repel Chicago's more literal-minded, the description of an art grounded in the spiritual and internal was certain to find favor among many. For Chicago artist and operatic tenor William S. Schwartz, the musical analogy to painting would have had particular resonance. Schwartz, born in Russia in 1896, emigrated to New York in 1913. After a brief stay in Omaha, Nebraska, Schwartz arrived in Chicago in 1916 and entered the Art Institute.[19] While it is likely that Schwartz was exposed to the work of Kandinsky and other modernists at the Art Institute, his work remained acceptable to the school's more conservative attitudes and he graduated with honors in 1917. Thereafter, he produced a body of painting that, while sympathetic to modernism, remained firmly within naturalistic boundaries and focused on allegorical and symbolic themes. In the late twenties Schwartz began works demonstrating his interest in the American scene.

According to Manuel Chapman's 1930 monograph on Schwartz, three years after becoming a student at the Art Institute Schwartz began to rebel against the "impervious tradition" of the school. Fashioning a nude in blue and green, Schwartz reportedly justified his action to his colleagues and instructors by saying that the composition demanded such colors, as "only those colors responded to his own inner necessity."[20] Chapman's quote indicates that Schwartz was familiar with Kandinsky's concept of inner necessity very early in his career.

Schwartz was identified as a modernist painter—and one whose work struck a resemblance to Russian modernism. In 1929 J. Z. Jacobson remarked that Schwartz's work leaned "toward constructivism," a trait he associated with "Russianism."[21] Another reviewer writing in 1929 also detected Schwartz's Russian character as well as his avant-garde techniques:

> William Schwartz is Russian enough so that his works express the strong qualities of the Russian mind. And, being a singer by vocation, he forms symphonic compositions of color whose effect of harmony is always interesting and usually pleasing. The use of the curved and straight lines of the cubistic school he employs for the sake of beauty rather than for the achievement of striking results.[22]

Schwartz's style, then, was identified not only with modernism, but with Russian modernism, which during this period in Chicago allied it unmistakably with Kandinsky.

In 1924, Schwartz began a series of abstract canvases exploring the relationship between music and painting. The sixty-six Symphonic Forms paintings, done between 1924 and 1967, sought to fuse Schwartz's interest in landscape with his musical affinities.[23] This series is unique in Schwartz's oeuvre in the extent to which natural forms were abstracted, allowing the painter to approach an art of non-objectivity. Schwartz saw the process of painting these works as that of a composer setting down musical notations:

Viewing these paintings is like listening to music, but it is the spectator who "makes" the music. The painter has set down the notation, like any composer, using the whole vocabulary of the graphic arts as a medium. But just as the score of a symphony is not a symphony, so the separate forms on each canvas are not the painting.

In combining these forms into harmonious compositions I am giving life to the score, and the result is a symphony of forms.[24]

That Schwartz had used Kandinsky as a model in the original formulation of the series seems undeniable, despite Daniel Catton Rich's statement that the paintings were "independent" of such sources.[25] Schwartz would have seen the Kandinskys on view in 1922 as part of the A. J. Eddy Memorial Exhibition at the Art Institute of Chicago, and he would by then no doubt have been familiar with Eddy's *Cubists and Post-Impressionism*. In the 1933 Century of Progress Exhibition of Paintings and Sculpture at the Art Institute, both Schwartz and Kandinsky were included, Schwartz with a 1932 Chicago river harbor scene and Kandinsky with *Improvisation No. 30 (Cannons), Painting with Green Center,* and *Landscape with Two Poplars.* Kandinsky's work was available to Schwartz prior to and during the very period in which he developed the Symphonic Forms.

Symphonic Forms No. 18 (plate 30), executed before 1935, exemplifies the series as a whole. The large, melodic areas of color and form, which fuse with one another and are accented by parallel waved lines, are a compacted, simplified recapitulation of Kandinskys that Schwartz would have seen, such as *Improvisation No. 30 (Cannons).* Figurative and narrative works done parallel to the Symphonic Forms series rely on a tightly ordered Cézannesque substructure, which is to be differentiated from the freely conceived, fused areas of color and form of the Symphonic Forms. Schwartz's conception of the process also reflects Eddy's comments in *Cubists and Post-Impressionism* as he describes the effect of those Improvisations: "With no word of explanation one of Kandinsky's Improvisations does seem—*at first glance*—the last word in extravagance; on fourth or fifth glance it appears to have a charm of color that is fascinating; on *study* it begins to *sound* like color music."[26]

Even more compelling are Kandinsky's own words from the concluding chapter of *The Art of Spiritual Harmony*. Describing the history of painting as parallel to that of music, Kandinsky speaks of more highly developed compositions as symphonic and places his own work in that category: "Complex composition, [consists] of various forms, subjected more or less completely to a principal form. Probably the principal form may be hard to grasp outwardly, and for that reason possessed of a strong inner value. This kind of composition I call the *symphonic.*"[27]

Schwartz himself described his art in terms similar to those Kandinsky used. His emphasis on the inner, personal motivation for his art hints unmistakably at Kandinsky:

In art, among the old masters as well as among contemporary artists, harmony may be of three sorts—of color, of form and of line. In looking at nature, therefore, I search for materials which may be interpreted and manipulated until they become unified wholes and reveal the harmony . . . representative of my own personality— my thoughts and my feelings.[28]

Schwartz's example serves well in illustrating the impact Kandinsky had in Chicago in the 1920s and 1930s. Other artists, such as Raymond Jonson and Ed Garman, discussed later in this chapter, were also first exposed to Kandinsky while living in or visiting Chicago. Even in seemingly hostile territory, Kandinsky's work made significant inroads and contributed to the development of abstraction in Chicago.

The South

Fig. 4.3 Vassily Kandinsky.
ROUND AND POINTED,
1930.
Oil on cardboard, 19⅛ ×
27⅜'' (49 × 70 cm)
Courtesy Kunsthalle, Mannheim

The dissemination of Kandinsky's work and ideas in the South occurred on a more limited and sporadic basis than it did in other parts of the country. In March 1936 the Solomon R. Guggenheim Collection of Non-Objective Paintings was given a major showing at the Gibbes Memorial Art Gallery in Charleston, South Carolina, where Guggenheim maintained a winter home. The exhibit had been proposed as early as 1933, but financial worries forced a postponement.[29] In January 1935 Hilla Rebay, Guggenheim's curator and avid proponent of Kandinsky's work, had been given a show at the gallery, and on February 1 she delivered a lecture entitled "Art Is Intuition Made Visible." Using a chalkboard to explain the development from objective to non-objective art, Rebay began with a discussion of Greece and Rome and followed the path to Kandinsky, who, as the newspaper reported it the next day, "made the decisive step into the absolute, having courage to give up entirely the idea of reproducing nature." The lecture, which was given to a "large and appreciative audience" encouraged Charleston viewers of non-objective art to "forget to look for a subject and look as you would look at the stars in the sky."[30]

Thus, the Charleston audience was prepared in some measure for the large exhibition of Kandinsky and other non-objective artists in 1936. *Art Digest* covered the Charleston exhibition and included comments by two California art writers on what the response to the collection might be. Junius Cravens of the *San Francisco News* noted the relatively "late date" for this introduction of non-objective art to the South and thought it "interesting to speculate on how a community that is famous for cherishing the traditions of a conservative past will receive it."[31] Interestingly, no great furor—positive or negative—was created by this or the second exhibition of the collection in March 1938. The *Charleston Evening Post* concentrated on an interview with Rebay herself, in which she praised Charleston and referred to Kandinsky and Rudolf Bauer (a non-objective artist and intimate of Rebay) as "masters." Another article sympathetically reproduced a non-objective work by a fourteen-year-old local girl, who found the Guggenheim collection "highly interesting and stimulating."[32] The reticence of the press may have been in deference to Guggenheim, who was, after all, a part-time resident of the city, but it is equally likely that the relatively sophisticated inhabitants indeed found nothing threatening about the works on display.

The Charleston showing included some twenty-eight Kandinsky works,[33] and the catalogue reproduced *Pointed and Round* (1925) and *Black Lines I* (1913; see fig. 3.2) in color. Rebay's catalogue essay, "Definition of Non-Objective Painting," is an impassioned apologia for non-objective painting as a whole and mentions Kandinsky (along with Bauer) only once. At the same time, however, her essay is interwoven with melioristic references to a new spiritual age, analogies between music and painting, and the leadership role of the artist—all ideas and themes derived from Kandinsky's *Über das Geistige in der Kunst.*

Will Henry Stevens

The two showings of the Guggenheim collection in Charleston did not appear to have a direct or immediate impact on specific artists working in the South. Indeed, Will Henry Stevens, the one southern artist who was demonstrably interested in Kandinsky's non-objective style, most likely was exposed to it not in Charleston, but in New York at a much earlier date. Stevens was born in 1881 in Vevay, Indiana, and educated at the Cincinnati Art Academy. Leaving the academy around 1906, he went to New York, where he studied with

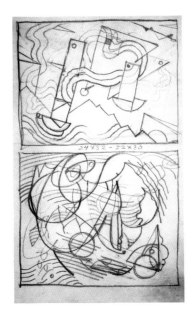

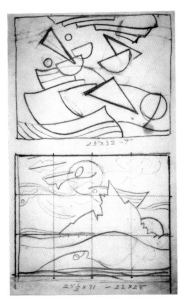

Fig. 4.4 William Henry
Stevens. Two pages of
drawings, c. 1935 (?)
Pencil on paper.
William Henry Stevens Papers,
Archives of American Art
Smithsonian Institution,
Washington, D.C.

landscape artists Jonas Lie and Van Dearing Perrine. During this and subsequent trips to New York, Stevens came into contact with various artists and artistic currents—William Merritt Chase, Albert Pinkham Ryder, Robert Henri, Alfred Maurer, and William Glackens were all friends or acquaintances at one time or another. In the early teens, Stevens returned to Vevay and began a rather peripatetic existence—regular visits to North Carolina and New York and a teaching position in Louisville, Kentucky, punctuated his life during these years. In 1921 he accepted a permanent teaching position at Tulane University in New Orleans, where he remained until retirement in 1948. During this period Stevens continued to travel and had regular exhibitions of his work throughout the Midwest and the South and in New York.[34]

Stevens was a landscape painter. Using the rich, verdant surroundings of his Indiana home and the southern landscape where he lived and vacationed, he concentrated on locating spiritual values in natural forms. An early and avid reader of Emerson, Whitman, and Thoreau, supplemented by such esoteric writers as P. D. Ouspensky and Lao-tzu, Stevens sought to convey his sense of oneness with nature in his work:

> The best thing a human can do in life is to get rid of his separateness or selfness and hand himself over to the nature of things—to this mysterious thing called the Universal Order, that any artist must sense. . . . In human nature we are *consciously* trying to achieve an order. And we are distressed by it, by the task of patterning it on an Order that is not personal or human—that is what I call spiritual.[35]

Stevens's work of the teens and twenties is replete with carefully rendered, realistic landscapes, which show an unusual sensitivity to color and light effects. But by the 1930s he began to experiment with non-objective forms and compositions. Bernard Lemann has noted that in the early 1930s, when he visited Stevens in New York, the artist showed him a series of small drawings he had done in pencil. Lemann describes Stevens's process thus:

> He began with three or four plane geometric forms: lines, circles or various triangles and simple polygons. They were to be organized within small rectangular enframements about the size of a thumb-nail sketch. . . . Later certain ones would be chosen for their essential rightness and perhaps developed. These studies were an early step toward the practice that he speaks of, for "attaining that impersonal state of consciousness."[36]

The sketches that Lemann refers to were undoubtedly of the type illustrated here (fig. 4.4) and are clearly related to Stevens's interest in Kandinsky's non-objective language. Stevens had ample opportunity to see Kandinsky's work during his frequent trips to New York. It is possible, although undocumented, that Stevens attended one of the Société Anonyme exhibitions that included Kandinsky. Lemann recalls that both he and Stevens saw a large collection of Kandinsky and Bauer in New York in 1927 or 1928.[37] The 1932 Valentine Gallery show, which Stevens may have seen, contained works such as *Round and Pointed* (1930; fig. 4.3) and *Rose in Grey* (1926), which can be compared to Stevens's abstractions (plates 31 and 32). While it remains uncertain as to exactly when or where Stevens first was exposed to Kandinsky, by the mid–1930s he was producing fully realized non-objective works that clearly demonstrate that he had "gotten much out of studying the work of Kandinsky."[38] In 1938 Stevens was familiar enough with the Guggenheim collection and Hilla Rebay's activities to ask his friend Onya LaTour to show some of his larger paintings to Rebay.[39] Stevens was a frequent visitor to the Museum of Non-Objective Painting (MNOP) after it opened in 1939.

of Picasso and Braque . . . from this time on painting became more abstract till painters asked themselves if there was not a place for painting entirely divorced from realism, basing itself in mental concepts. Kandinsky and the Blue Rider Group of Munich formed in 1912 gave the answer. . . . It is the hope of the recently formed Transcendental Painting Group to become an integral force in the rapidly developing aesthetic awarness [sic] of this country. To do this the group feels that they must leave past traditions and embark on new concepts of consciousness . . . of paths there are many: it is for the individual to chose the road that satisfies the requirements of his inner vision."[50]

Kandinsky was seen as the group's immediate antecedent and thus provided an important springboard for a new art based on inner vision. Raymond Jonson was even more explicit about the importance of Kandinsky to the group when he spoke at the Martha White Memorial Gallery in Santa Fe, where his work was on view in 1942. Alfred Morang summarized Jonson's comments for the *Santa Fe New Mexican:*

Jonson placed Picasso and Kandinsky as the two major forces in the beginnings of abstract and non-representative art. . . . His analysis of Kandinsky's place in the field of the non-representative was unusually clear, and this painter whose work presents the most involved painting problems emerged for what he is: the greatest non-representative artist so far to evolve from the tradition of art.[51]

Jonson's assessment of Kandinsky as the most important of non-representative artists was undoubtedly shared by other members of the group. For those who sought a means to carry "painting beyond the appearance of the physical world, through new concepts of space, color and design, to imaginative realms that are idealistic and spiritual,"[52] Kandinsky was the most logical exemplar. It was not long before others outside New Mexico who were interested in a non-objective art based on Kandinsky's precepts recognized the importance of the Transcendental Painting Group to the American avant-garde. In May and June 1940, the Museum of Non-Objective Painting mounted the exhibition Twelve American Non-Objective Painters, which included works by Robert Gribbroek, Lawren Harris, Agnes Pelton, Raymond Jonson, and Stuart Walker.[53] According to Dr. Charles Morris, a friend of Jonson's who helped arrange for the exhibition and who, unlike Jonson himself, visited the museum and discussed the paintings with the now director Hilla Rebay, the works were not hung as a group, but rather were interspersed with the works of other artists in the exhibition. Morris described the effect in a letter to Jonson: "It does seem to me unfortunate that she [Rebay] broke the exhibition up: it would have made a more compact and integral impression if it had been kept as a whole with its own name."[54]

Significantly, the fact that the MNOP show did not acknowledge the artists as a group was not a major concern to Jonson and his colleagues. Despite the visible signs of organization and the numerous efforts to inform the public about its exhibitions and activities, the Transcendental Painting Group was, in actuality, a serendipitous alliance of convenience. For the most part, the members neither sought nor found in the group an essential source of creative or intellectual stimulation and growth. All but the youngest (Garman, Miller, and Pierce) were artists in full maturity whose basic ways of thinking and working were already developed. As Garman described the situation, "I don't think the connection was ideological. I think it was sheer practicality, needing space and wanting to exhibit, so that they could have their say. And, of course, they reinforced themselves any way they could with other painters."[55] The common commitment to non-objectivity and a shared interest in the ideas of Kandinsky as well as other mystical thinkers and writers provided the group with the glue that held it together between its founding in 1938 and its de facto disbanding in 1940–41.[56]

Raymond Jonson

For Jonson, as for most of the other Transcendental Painting Group artists, the interest in and influence of Kandinsky had begun long before the summer of 1938. Born in 1891 in Lucas County, Iowa, Jonson spent a peripatetic youth following his Baptist minister father through Minnesota, Wyoming, Colorado, and Kansas, finally settling in 1902 in Portland, Oregon. In 1909 he enrolled at the Portland Museum Art School and studied under Kate Cameron Simmons, who had in turn been a student of Arthur Wesley Dow. By 1910 Jonson had arrived in Chicago to study art. A year later, he had a "spiritual experience" that led him to the conclusion that his life was to be dedicated to art. An early predisposition to mystical, spiritual experiences (he had his first in 1902) was with him throughout his life. His brother Arthur later reported: "The whole mystical background of religion is part of Raymond's background. The 'experience' is something he has known. It has affected his work."[57]

Although he moved to Chicago to study commercial art at the Chicago Academy of Fine Arts, Jonson quickly acquainted himself with Chicago's avant-garde milieu. He enrolled in night classes at the Art Institute and began a long and fruitful contact with his teacher at the academy, B. J. O. Nordfeldt.

On March 24, 1913, Jonson wrote to his parents about his visit to the Armory Show, which opened that day in Chicago:

> Today the big International Exhibit opened with a reception. Of course I was there. And such an exhibit. You must have heard about it—the Cubists, Futurists, Extremeists, etc. Well, it's some exhibit. Some is rotten if there is such a distinction. There are no rules in art, so the sanest way is to say that each man may paint as to express himself or to express a sensation or experience. In other words, to show or express the way one feels."[58]

If Jonson took note of Kandinsky's *Improvisation No. 27* (see fig. 1.1), which was included in the Armory Show, he made no mention of it, although his use of the word "extremeist" indicates he was familiar with the New York press's description of Kandinsky in such terms. Indeed, Jonson's work during this period is that of the competent student—sketches done from the model or conservative paintings from nature—and shows little influence of European modernism. But Jonson's emphasis on an internal, personal approach to painting was to set the tone for all his subsequent work and explains his later interest in Kandinsky as a guide to fulfilling his ambition to produce an art that results "because of the idealistic concept of the force, essence and rhythm of matter and spirit."[59]

During this period Jonson undoubtedly also read A. J. Eddy's *Cubists and Post-Impressionism,* published in 1914. There he would have found illustrations of Kandinsky's *Improvisation No. 30 (Cannons), Improvisation No. 29, Murnau-Village Street,* and *Landscape with Two Poplars.* Eddy's text oriented Jonson to the issues and distinctions in abstract and non-objective art. Jonson was to repeat Eddy's analysis of the essential differences between Kandinsky and Picasso in 1936 when he contrasted cubism ("abstract but arrived at through the abstraction of the object") and Kandinsky's work ("not developed from the object but purely arbitrary and drawn from some storehouse of the subconscious"). Eddy, who like Jonson saw cubism as an artistic dead end, extols Kandinsky's "pure art."[60]

In the ensuing years, Jonson's search for an art of inner essences continued. Writing in his diary in 1918, he states: "Can't one go deeper than just surface. Won't paint as a color and material if properly used if the mind sees light do what nothing else can do—create the spirit of emotion that is felt and therefore created by the creator."[61] Jonson's ideas about the future direction of his painting—a direction that would first wed inner with outer sensation and then ultimately express inner sensations through absolute means—evolved at a rapid pace. In July 1919 he wrote in his diary: "There is a fine relation between the inner and outer—to grasp these all important characteristics and weave them into a rhythmic whole which moves and calls forth the spirit of each object used is the proper conception of composition."[62] By the following summer, he was contemplating completely abstract compositions: "I've been thinking that the creation of an entirely abstract composition would be an excellent thing. Why shouldn't planes of colour in gradation properly arranged make beauty."[63]

In July 1921, Jonson mentions Kandinsky for the first time in his diary:

Yesterday was a great day and a hard one—a group of Cor Ardens visited the Eddy collection. It is a strain to experience such intenseness. Bloch and Kandinsky are the two who impressed me the most. . . . Kandinsky I comprehend, admire but am not disturbed. I feel it is difficult to enter his world—that if one could it would be a great experience. I find it hard to do so under the conditions of their present environment. Sooner or later we must all accept his attitude. Now I am going for a walk![64]

Jonson's hesitation before Kandinsky is curious. While he embraced Kandinsky's attitude, his inability to "enter his world" indicates that Jonson, who at the time was methodically and carefully working to imbue the physical with the metaphysical, had not sufficiently developed his own ideas about the potential of abstraction to be able to relate fully to what must have seemed very radical work. Jonson's preferred artists at the time were Albert Bloch and Nicholas Roerich, both of whom continued to seek and find the spiritual in the physical.[65] It appears that Jonson, for whom Kandinsky's work represented a logical, yet seemingly extreme and radical, evolution from his own artistic concerns at the time, found it difficult to integrate Kandinsky with his immediate interests—namely, Bloch and Roerich. Whatever his intellectual aspirations, his work of this period was still firmly grounded in nature. But Jonson's thinking progressed rapidly from this point on. In April 1921, he wrote:

I find that the work that is simply for itself and not a design for something else is by far the most complete and satisfying. Here we have the ultimate use of art. The work for itself—to stand as the expression of an emotion, the abstract spiritual ego of the individual . . . it can have no use outside of feeding the spirit.[66]

At this point, Sheldon Cheney gave Jonson a copy of Kandinsky's *Art of Spiritual Harmony,* published in 1914.[67] As Garman expressed it, "here was an artist who had pondered deeply on the very subject to which [Jonson's] own thoughts had been turning."[68] Jonson wrote:

I have spent the last two entire days reading and digesting Kandinsky's "The Art of Spiritual Harmony." It is the greatest book concerning art I have ever read. It is immense. One cannot, if one be wise, but accept and believe the truth he put forth. It is a task to take in the significance of it all. I believe we must sooner or later know him to be right, at least in theory—and that is the point—theory. And then what about practice? Of course one works for emancipation from material. To be able to live and actually work in the spiritual is of course a great ideal and one to hope and work for."[69]

His reading of Kandinsky created immediate challenges for Jonson. Finding the figure composition (*Autumn*) he was currently working on "lacking in spirit," he removed the paint. He proceeded to make various sketches for other ideas and then destroyed them all.[70] Feeling that such work had become "trite" or "just a story or illustration—it seems small and narrow," Jonson began work on a new composition that he considered to be his best work to date, *Life* (1921).

> In design and rhythm this is the best thing I've done. Everything in the composition seems right to me—consistent. I consider this decidedly from the standpoint of expressing an idea or thought and feelings in form, colour and design. . . . Why I have used the particular arrangement I cannot say except that as it seems right. I feel I have expressed my feelings in regards to life. . . . I've tried to build a composition that gives the sense of movement, struggle, light—and therefore life. Not by the object used as much as by the arrangement and range of forms and colours. I hope I have given the sensation of something and not an illusion.[71]

These words echo those of Kandinsky in *The Art of Spiritual Harmony:* "The composition arising from this harmony is a mingling of colour and form each with its separate existence, but each blended into a common life which is called a picture by the force of the inner need."[72] It is obvious that in this composition Jonson has begun to work with the emotive and visual properties of the colors yellow and blue. Kandinsky discusses these colors at length in *The Art of Spiritual Harmony.* Yellow and blue are notable for their spiritual qualities: blue is the "typically heavenly colour" and creates a feeling of "supernatural rest." As blue approaches black, it "echoes a grief that is hardly human" and the deeper the blue the stronger its inner appeal. Yellow, an eccentric color, moves out from the center, reflecting human energy and "bursts forth aimlessly in every direction."[73] *Life* calls forth a number of Kandinsky's ideas and weds them with symbolic or landscape elements found in the work of Roerich and late nineteenth-century European symbolism.[74]

Jonson was late in responding to Kandinsky's improvisational techniques and loose automatism due to his own ideas about structure and design. Feeling that there should be "a governing sense of arrangement" and "order" in painting, Jonson continued to conceive his works carefully, almost intellectually, although he imbued them with a spiritual, emotional symbolism.[75] In this, Jonson reflected the ideas of Sheldon Cheney, who wrote in 1924: "In general there is a wandering, soft, unstructural quality about them [Kandinsky's purely abstract pictures] which seems to me to be a denial of something important to painting. . . . His present compositions are at best spineless, at worst chaotic. They lack 'form' in the structural and voluminous sense."[76]

Jonson later acknowledged that his work took a different turn after 1921. In 1928 he explained to philosopher and friend Charles Morris that his canvases beginning in 1922 were "primarily of the abstract":

> It has been my hope to so purify, simplify and organize a work that it expresses completely my reaction, or emotion, or sensation, in regard to nature, life, and in fact, to any object, even to the things that are not visible but have a profound emotional reaction upon me. I feel that it is the inner significance of things that

counts, and that is a quality that is abstract. It is the abstract that so interests me at present. It seems to be the life and soul of painting. I do feel, though, that it is to a certain extent connected with the actual . . . a work results from some actual experience. From that point it becomes pure creation. . . . I believe all emotions, if pure enough, are abstract. . . . This is really as far as I have gone. Absolute abstraction I have not accomplished.[77]

Jonson's emphasis on "inner significance" and his desire to express "things that are not visible" mirror Kandinsky's admiration of art that divines the "inner life in everything"[78] and that replaces the material and objective truth with inner, spiritual truth.[79]

In 1924 Jonson left Chicago to settle permanently in Santa Fe. During his initial years there, Jonson became increasingly interested in cubist-derived forms as evidenced in his Earth Rhythms series (1923–1927). These tightly structured works would be followed in the early 1930's by a general loosening of space and a more open approach to composition that approximates that advocated by Kandinsky.

In 1925, Jonson met Arnold Rönnebeck, who visited Mabel Dodge Luhan in Taos in 1924 and 1925. Calling Rönnebeck the "one person who gets what I'm aiming at,"[80] Jonson found in him a kindred spirit and source of first-hand information on Kandinsky as well as Hartley. Hartley himself had lived in New Mexico from 1918 to 1921, producing there a number of landscapes and still lifes, such as *El Santo* (1918; see fig. 3.3). That Jonson was occupied during this period by Hartley's Kandinsky-inspired Berlin work can be seen in his own 1928 *El Santo* (fig. 4.6), which reveals his interest in indigenous art forms and Cézanne's still lifes while at the same time paying homage to Hartley's Berlin-period German officer paintings. The curtain on the right of the painting with its stripes and checks is clearly a reference to Hartley works such as *Portrait of a German Officer* and *Berlin Abstraction,* both of 1914. Jonson's *El Santo* not only reflects his interest in Cézannesque interiors (which was consistent with his cubist experimentations in the Earth Rhythms series) but also demonstrates that Rönnebeck may have made him familiar with the *Blaue Reiter* almanac and its concentration on folk and naïve art. Kandinsky was ever close at hand.

Another, even more serendipitous, meeting for Jonson also came in 1925, this time with Galka Scheyer, who was responsible for bringing exhibitions of the Blue Four to the United States. On a train trip from New York to California, the summer following the Blue Four's debut exhibition at the Daniel Gallery in New York, Scheyer and Angelica Archipenko made a stopover in Santa Fe. When an acquaintance failed to pick them up at the station, they hired a car whose driver claimed to "know every artist" in Santa Fe. Miraculously, he drove them straight to Jonson's home, "yellow like sand, flat roof with atelier," where they were received most hospitably. According to Scheyer, Jonson painted "abstract romantic landscapes" and "knew of my Blue Four."[81] The visit appears to have been brief, perhaps only an overnight stay, but once more Jonson was provided with a direct link to Kandinsky and those who knew his work well. Jonson does not write of Scheyer's visit, but later letters show that he had not forgotten her or the Blue Four. In 1931, Jonson's brother Arthur sent him a catalogue of the Blue Four (perhaps from the 1927 exhibition in Portland and Spokane) and discussed why Scheyer "didn't like" Jonson's work:

> It isn't that she is particularly interested in the abstract—as she said she was—for there is nothing of the abstract in Klee's dawdlings. . . . The true reason for her attitude is this: she wants violent color relationships, sharp discords of color. . . . Composition, structure, rhythm, everything is . . . subordinated to the achievement

of a clash between dirty red and dirty green. So Scheyer will not like you so long as you understand what happens to red when it is next to green.[82]

Later, when Jonson was doing completely non-objective paintings that reflected more closely Kandinsky's work and Scheyer's taste, Scheyer responded more favorably. In 1934, Jonson wrote to Charles Morris, who was planning a European tour:

> If you get anywhere near Wassily Kandinsky try and see him. You have in America a fine friend who is an [sic] painter and a great admirer of him. This painter is a good friend of Madame Galka E. Scheyer. That name Scheyer might be a perfect pass word for you as far as all the Blue Four are concerned. . . . I think Kandinsky is in Weimar (Dessau) at the State Bauhaus. At least he was.[83]

Thus, while Jonson's life in Santa Fe may have separated him physically from the major art centers of the country, he was kept abreast of important exhibitions, publications, and ideas through an extensive network of friends, relatives (his brother Arthur was particularly important in this regard), former students, and acquaintances in the art world. Jonson's work was exhibited in Seattle, Los Angeles, and Tucson in 1928, and he had a one-man exhibition at the Delphic Studios in New York in 1931. In 1932 Jonson's *Time Cycle: Morning, Noon, Night* was included in a group exhibition at the Renaissance Society at the University of Chicago, which also included two Kandinskys. (Trude Morris, Charles's wife, reported in a letter to Jonson: "With the exception of two Kandinskys, your three pictures just walk away with the show."[84]) Jonson knew Sheldon Cheney, who reproduced his work in *Expressionism in Art,* and his friendship with Charles Morris provided him not only with support for his art but also with news of both the Chicago and New York art scene. (Morris became acquainted with Laszlo Moholy-Nagy in 1937, while Moholy was involved with the Chicago Bauhaus, and showed Jonson's *Suspended Ovals* to Moholy, who reportedly liked it "very much." As noted above, Morris was instrumental in the exhibition of works by several members of the Transcendental Painting Group at the Museum of Non-Objective Painting.) But Jonson was aware that he was on a very personal journey as far as his art was concerned. In a 1928 letter to Morris he described his situation as an artist: "It has not been my intention to make pictures of places and things, but rather an effort to work out my own salvation. That, you know, was one reason for our coming out here—to be by one's self, working away at the job."[85]

But there was also a price to pay for working alone on personal salvation. Jonson's isolation in Santa Fe was most acutely felt with regard to showing his work in major art centers. He was, of course, aware of Stieglitz's group and often regretted the fact that Stieglitz took no interest in his work.

It might be argued that Jonson's relative obscurity in American art circles—his failure to win the complete support and admiration of such opinion-makers as Scheyer and Stieglitz—was due not only to his reticence and geographical isolation, but also to the distinct and highly individual nature of his art. Not content (or comfortable) with merely assimilating and then capitalizing on other artists' discoveries, Jonson laboriously worked through each artistic and philosophical problem on his own, slowly and methodically exploring and finding his own voice. Quite frequently, this meant that his paintings had a somewhat *retardataire* quality. Nicolai Cikovsky, Jr., alluded to this aspect of Jonson's career when he commented that, despite Jonson's obvious and stated interest in modernist artistic ideas, "the process of their maturation into works of explicitly modernist character and conviction was a slow one."[86] While Jonson might have been on the "cutting edge" intellectually and philosoph-

Fig. 4.6 Raymond Jonson.
EL SANTO, 1928.
Oil on canvas, 40 × 28″
(102.6 × 71.8 cm)
Roswell Museum and Art Center,
Roswell, New Mexico

ically, his careful pioneering of these ideas and their application to his own oeuvre was done as though he were the first and only artist to work through them. His work shows no sudden and radical transformations, only a slow and methodical process of self-discovery. Finally, although no records reveal precisely how O'Keeffe or Scheyer or Stieglitz evaluated Jonson's work, it could well be that they sensed there a slight timidity coupled with an emphasis on pattern that ran counter to their more virile ideals of modernism. Philosophically and constitutionally unable to throw himself into the regionalist/traditionalist camp and personally and artistically unwilling to produce works of stunning unorthodoxy, Jonson appears to have fallen between every critical crack. These same qualities, however, make him one of the most singular artists of the period and account for the fact that his work, although influenced by Kandinsky, was never derivative.

The 1930s brought Jonson closer to an art that was "purely imaginative where no religious subject, no occult symbolism, and no abstraction is used—in short the absolute."[87] Absolute painting would require that Jonson give up not only the motifs—landscape, portraiture, still life, symbols—that had occupied his work up to that time, but also all artistic subjectivity. The process of eliminating subject from his work was done in Jonson's own meticulous fashion. He began several series of paintings (Growth Variants, 1929–1935; Digits, 1929–1930; Variations on a Rhythm, 1930–1936) that allowed him to invent forms and create harmony, rhythm, and unity unfettered by the demands of a motif. Pictorial organization would be based on the requirements of the elements and media of painting itself rather than subject matter or emotion. This paring down to essentials can be seen clearly in works such as *Variations on a Rhythm-B* (1931; plate 33). Here, as Garman points out, the subject is the "rhythmic force" derived from the shapes of the letters.[88] The billowing, linear curves of the letter *B* echo one another, setting up a rhythmic cadence against a series of thrusting planes accented by small points of color. Kandinsky's basic elements of painting as outlined in *Point and Line to Plane* are united according to the "rhythmic law of constructive counterpoint."[89]

Point and Line to Plane (originally published in German as *Punkt und Linie zu Fläche* in 1926) was the ninth in a series of fourteen Bauhaus books edited by Walter Gropius and Laszlo Moholy-Nagy. It did not appear in English translation until 1947, when the Solomon R. Guggenheim Foundation for the Museum of Non-Objective Painting published it in a translation by Howard Dearstyne and Hilla Rebay. Jonson, however, must have been aware of much of the book's contents through Charles Morris, who furnished him with New Bauhaus circulars from Moholy-Nagy as early as 1937. In a 1938 outline of a book, never published, on Jonson, Morris mentions that he intends to discuss Jonson's work in relation not only to his own *Foundations of the Theory of Signs,* but also to Kandinsky's *Über das Geistige in der Kunst* and *Punkt und Linie zu Fläche.*[90] By the mid-thirties, Hilla Rebay's activities at the Museum of Non-Objective Painting were accelerating, and she published a series of books, pamphlets, and other materials, which Jonson collected. The ideas outlined by Kandinsky in *Point and Line to Plane* were important in the development of Jonson's work during the 1930s, for that work occurred in the context of Jonson's interest in Kandinsky's Bauhaus painting and reflects Kandinsky's thinking in *Point and Line to Plane.*

Following a 1933 visit to Chicago's Century of Progress Exposition, Jonson began a series of murals for the library of the University of New Mexico entitled *Cycle of Science.* Jonson had been impressed at the exposition by an exhibition based on mathematical equations in the Hall of Science.[91] Consisting of six works, *Mathematics* (plate 34), *Biology, Astronomy, Engineering, Chemistry,* and *Physics,* Jonson's series also demonstrates his increasing interest

Plate 33
Raymond Jonson
VARIATIONS ON A RHYTHM-B, 1931
Lee Ehrenworth
Photo credit: Ed Watkins, New York

Plate 34
Raymond Jonson
CYCLE OF SCIENCE: MATHEMATICS,
1934
Jonson Gallery of the University Art Museum
University of New Mexico, Albuquerque

Plate 35
Raymond Jonson
INTERLOCKED FORMS—ERUPTED, 1936
Jonson Gallery of the University Art Museum
University of New Mexico, Albuquerque

Plate 36
Raymond Jonson
WATERCOLOR NO. 9, 1938
Jonson Gallery of the University Art Museum
University of New Mexico, Albuquerque

Plate 37
Lawren Harris
ABSTRACT, c. 1939
Private collection

Plate 38
Lawren Harris
UNTITLED, 1939
Collection of Georgia de Havenon

Plate 39
Dane Rudhyar
STORM GODS, 1938
Courtesy of Leyla Rudhyar Hill

103

Plate 42
Ed Garman
UNTITLED, ORANGE TRIANGLE (NO.
220), 1941
Michael Rosenfeld Gallery, New York

Plate 43
Ed Garman
UNTITLED, RED CIRCLE ON BLACK
(NO. 297), 1942
Michael Rosenfeld Gallery, New York

Plate 44
Emil Bisttram
PULSATION, 1938
Lee Ehrenworth
Photo credit: Ed Watkins, New York

Plate 45
Emil Bisttram
CACTUS, 1938
Lee Ehrenworth
Photo credit: Ed Watkins, New York

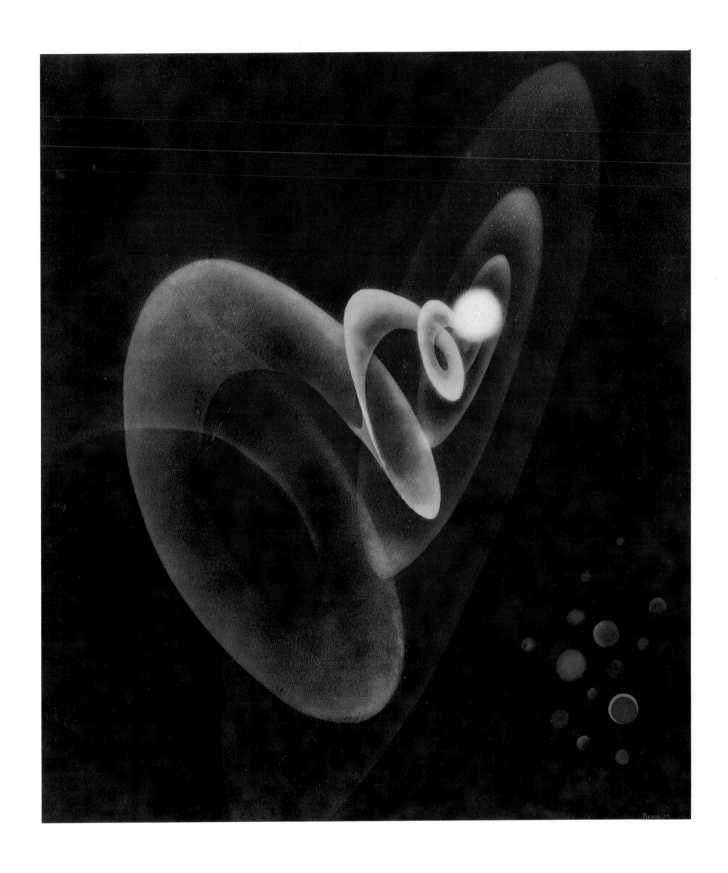

Plate 46
Horace Pierce
KEY DRAWING FROM MOVEMENT 1,
1939
Collection of Georgia de Havenon

Plate 47
Florence Pierce
RISING RED, 1942
Collection of Jane and Ron Lerner

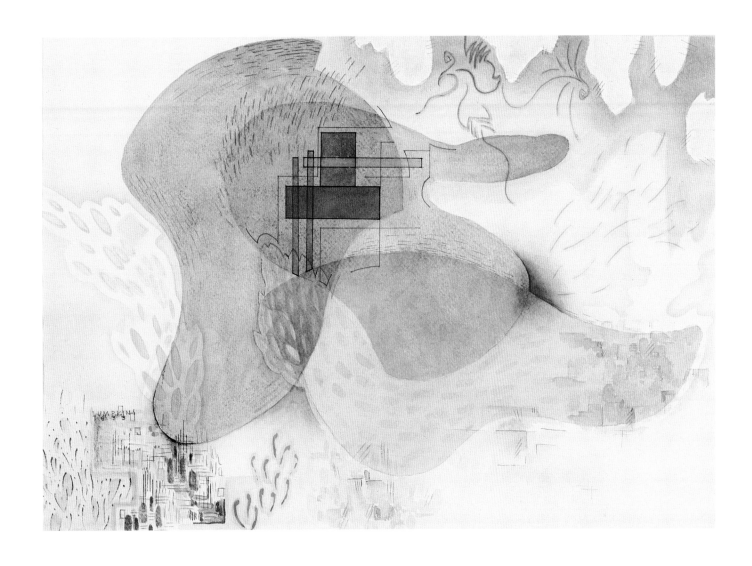

Plate 48
William Lumpkins
TRANSPARENCY, 1933
Hal Sonderegger Collection

Plate 49
Stuart Walker
COMPOSITION 65, 1934
Collection of Georgia de Havenon

112

in Kandinsky's vocabulary of abstract line, form, color, and compositional elements. In 1935 his wife, Vera, gave him a copy of *Axis* magazine (No. 1, January 1935) with a lead article on Kandinsky and reproductions of the following Kandinsky works: *Drawing* (1924), *Each for Itself* (1934), *Circles in a Circle* (1923), *White—Soft and Hard* (1932), *Points in the Arc* (1927), and *Composition No. 7* (1913). These works contain many of the elements Jonson incorporated into his cycle: whiplash curves, intersecting lines, points of color, and triangular planes. Given Jonson's keen interest in and familiarity with Kandinsky's work by this time, he undoubtedly had access to other images as well. During the Christmas holiday of 1935–36 Jonson and Vera visited the Walter Arensbergs in California, who owned several Kandinskys, including *Circles in a Circle,* which had been sold to them by Galka Scheyer in 1931.[92] While based on specific subjects, the cycle works clearly mark a separation between those subjects and the expressive elements used to describe them. Indeed, Jonson may have been attracted to science as a subject due to its inherently abstract nature. Most interesting in this respect is *Mathematics,* in which Jonson uses Kandinsky's points and force lines to create a non-objective universe. His comments on the *Cycle of Science* underscore his goal of using absolute means to convey a subject:

> My aim and hope in these works has been to present a series of compositions that expresses my emotional concept of a plastic idea based on the particular subjects that came to mind. . . . Each composition is the result of a definite concept of a color harmony in relation to the form and design. I think of them as symphonic compositions consistent with my medium and honest to the highest ideal I stand for.[93]

In addition to larger works done during this period, Jonson completed a number of watercolors, drawings, and small paintings inspired by Kandinsky's absolute language. Works such as *Ascending Circle* (1933) and *Interlocked Forms* (1936) demonstrate his use of non-objective motifs set forth by Kandinsky. Comparing Kandinsky's *Contrast with Accompaniment* (1935; fig. 4.7) (shown in the 1936 Museum of Non-Objective Painting exhibition in Charleston and illustrated in the catalogue, which Jonson owned) to Jonson's *Interlocked Forms—Erupted* (1936; plate 35) makes clear Jonson's reliance on Kandinsky at the time.

With his turn toward non-objectivity in the 1930s, Jonson undoubtedly hoped his work would find a place in the Guggenheim collection of non-objective art. But to do so, of course, meant finding favor and acceptance with Hilla Rebay—a task Jonson ultimately found impossible. In the spring of 1937, Jonson sent his brother a copy of the "Guggenheim book" (the exhibition catalogue for the 1936 Solomon R. Guggenheim Collection of Non-Objective Paintings exhibition at the Gibbes Memorial Art Gallery in Charleston). Arthur responded that "these people ought to be interested in your work, particularly the latest."[94] But Arthur perhaps correctly evaluated Rebay's biases when he wrote that Rebay's catalogue essay speaks more of "hero worship" (particularly in the case of Bauer) than of a rational exegesis of non-objective painting. He also states that Rebay and Bauer rely "too heavily on music." In discussing the works in the exhibition, Arthur commented that many of them did not stand up to Rebay's criteria for "absolute painting": Kandinsky's *Black Lines* (1913) was essentially a "still life," and Bauer's *Blue Balls* (1934–35) was indeed a painting of blue balls and "requires no intuition to see them, just memory and association." From Arthur's point of view, painting should "express what can be expressed no other way . . . in a way that I can only feel and can't describe because it has nothing to do with words or literature." Jonson's work appealed to Arthur because it gave him the "sort of feeling that nothing else [i.e., music or literature] can give."[95] Jonson's response to these comments amount to a modest

Fig. 4.7 Vassily Kandinsky. *CONTRAST WITH ACCOMPANIMENT,* 1935. Mixed media on canvas, 37⅖ × 63⅕″ (97 × 162 cm) Solomon R. Guggenheim Museum, New York

apologia for the Guggenheim works, as well as Rebay's interpretation of them:

> Remember we have no vocabulary equal to music when it comes to talking or writing or titling purely abstract or non-objective works in painting. Neither Kandinsky or Bauer I am sure make any effort or are interested in painting music. Their interest, as well as mine even tho it is different, is to have in painting a release from representation and be able to paint as "purely" as is possible to compose in music.[96]

Regarding Arthur's comments that what were purportedly non-objective works actually contained a great many references to nature, Jonson commented that, as far as he was concerned,

> the cube, triangle and circle are not nature forms. (The sun and planets of course are circles.) If you will not accept that idea it becomes impossible to see non-objective works as such. They will always look like something else and that is just as bad as connecting them with music. . . . By intuition Rebay obviously means something other than the usual meaning or use of the word. Remember this work has nothing to compare it with. There is no still life set up or any other objects and so I imagine what she means is that intuition tells one whether the component parts are related in order to carry out the singleness of meaning, etc.[97]

While Jonson's comments demonstrate that by 1937 he was very far along in his understanding of and commitment to non-objective principles as espoused by Kandinsky, Bauer, and Rebay, he also noted a distinction between his interests and theirs. Although the work of Kandinsky and Bauer was "geometrical," his own present work was a combination of geometrical and non-geometrical.[98] Jonson clearly did not feel that he had sufficiently worked through or worked out his reliance on figurative motifs and allusions to subject to abandon them completely for an art based on and limited to circles, lines, squares, and triangles. Indeed, he questioned whether or not a completely geometrical approach would produce the effects he desired. This was reinforced when in December 1937 he visited Chicago and saw an Alexander Archipenko exhibition. He wrote:

> I am getting much from this trip. I hope to feel that a fresh impulse will result. The geometrical painters such as Albers, Moholy-Nagy, Helion, etc. have gone so much farther in the purity of form that my exhibit [a one-man exhibition at Tulsa Art Center] will probably look a little academic! But I do not quite agree with the geometrical approach and feel confident that my own can go farther in the end than the other. But at present . . . it is farther along the path than the thing I am after.[99]

Jonson's rejection of the "geometrical approach" would not necessarily include Kandinsky's work of the period, which was replete with biomorphic shapes and curvilinear accents. It may well be that what Jonson felt was lacking in a purely geometric approach was the lyricism through which he attained the emotional and spiritual effect of his art. The cool intellectuality of Josef Albers and the strict geometry of Rudolf Bauer and even of some of Kandinsky's Bauhaus work may have operated contrary to Jonson's ongoing interest in transcendental expression. If Jonson was to put this new vocabulary to work toward his essentially romantic, emotional, and spiritual vision, he would need more latitude than that offered by Albers and Moholy, whose approach, though pure, was limiting.

There can be little question that it is in his transcendental works that Jonson relied most heavily on Kandinsky's painting as opposed to his philosophies. The experiments with Kandinsky's non-objective vocabulary of the early 1930s were applied in a more rigorous and cohesive body of work during his association with the Transcendental Painting Group.

Respected artists such as Emil Bisttram and Lawren Harris, whose own interest in non-objective painting had begun in the 1930s and whose philosophies of painting Jonson shared, underscored his commitment. In 1938, the same year he began using the airbrush, Jonson began a series of "improvisations." For Kandinsky, an improvisation was "a largely unconscious spontaneous expression of inner character, the non-material nature."[100] In *Watercolor No. 9* (plate 36) Jonson, like Kandinsky, sought to "bombard the eye by a spontaneity of direct execution either in a calm or an active environment as the case may be."[101] Jonson's Improvisations of the late 1930s and early 1940s demonstrate the new freedom for spontaneity that the airbrush provided and are the painter's works closest in spirit to Kandinsky's own Improvisations. *Watercolor No. 9* shows particularly well Jonson's adaptation of Kandinsky's straight lines, triangles, and squares in a seemingly random fashion. Although Jonson had undoubtedly considered Kandinsky's improvisational style in earlier readings and illustrations, it was not until the late 1930s that he felt sure enough of his inner vision and abstract language to experiment with improvisational techniques. Even here, however, Jonson's tight organization and control over form are in evidence.

Jonson's hopes of gaining acceptance with Rebay and the Guggenheim MNOP were dashed with the exhibition of the Transcendental Painting Group's works at the museum in 1940. Charles Morris was actually responsible for much of the coordination with Rebay concerning the exhibition, while Jonson chose the works to be sent. By the time of the exhibition, Jonson seems to have realized the vagaries of Rebay's taste and temperament, particularly regarding her predilection for the work of Rudolf Bauer:

> I feel she [Rebay] has gone too far in the extreme statements pertaining to the collection and especially Bauer. If he is the greatest painter of spiritual values that has ever lived well and good but I draw the line absolutely as far as anyone being the greatest that ever will live. That stops the great movement of art in the upward journey. One of the great contributions a great artist gives is the step added to the infinite ladder of art. He adds something and therefore it becomes possible to add still another and another ad infinitum. Anyhow I rather suspect Kandinsky is the man who has added the step and not Bauer.[102]

Jonson's echoing of Kandinsky's language in *The Art of Spiritual Harmony* ("The spiritual triangle, slowly but surely, with irresistible strength, moves onwards and upwards")[103] is telling here as he comes down clearly in Kandinsky's camp.

While he gladly accepted and hoped to find a place in the history of non-objective painting, Jonson's temperament was unsuited to the role of follower or member of any artistic coterie. Jonson's chief concern was not Rebay's negative judgment of his work (of the three works he sent to the 1940 exhibition, she included only *Watercolor No. 9*), but rather that "a prejudice is being established instead of interest in the so-called non-objective painting."[104] At the same time, Jonson was reinforced in his direction by Galka Scheyer, who had visited him in the fall of 1940. Jonson reported that "at least she is in favor of what I am doing. This means much to me, as I feel she knows what it's all about." During her visit, Scheyer and Jonson chose a number of his works to include in an exhibition Scheyer was to arrange in Los Angeles "sometime later."[105] The exhibition never took place.

After 1941, Jonson's work continued to develop along geometric lines accented with linear arabesques and often displaying overlapping planes of color or form. His enduring belief in the value of tight composition and hard-edged design was in increasing evidence in his later works. Jonson's interest in Kandinsky endured as well, but no longer played an active role in the progression of his art. Kandinsky, at first a stimulant to Jonson's concept of painting and then a visual exemplar as Jonson made the transition between figuration and non-objectivity, was an important catalyst during a crucial period in Jonson's development.

Lawren Harris

Lawren Harris's affiliation with the Transcendental Painting Group resulted from sheer fortuity. As Jonson recounted it:

> One day, it must have been in early 1938, we saw a stunning looking couple walking past our home and studio in Santa Fe. I went out and introduced myself to them and they to us. . . . I was delighted at our meeting for I knew of Lawren Harris as I had seen an exhibition of his work at the Roerich Museum (afterwards the Riverside Museum) in New York in late 1931 or early 1932. It was a beautiful and wonderful exhibition and impressed me tremendously. . . . A close friendship resulted and we saw each other as much as possible.[106]

The two artists held in common a great deal of artistic ground. Both were deeply committed to spiritual values and had evoked those values in dramatic landscape painting. The desire to create an art based on universals but which was also expressive of their respective nations was shared by Harris and Jonson. At the same time both artists were vitally interested in European modernist developments and followed those developments closely. Their meeting in 1938 came at a time when both were actively involved in the search for non-objectivity with Kandinsky as a philosophical and artistic model.

Like Jonson, Harris's interest in Kandinsky had been long-standing. Harris was born in Brantford, Ontario, in 1885 to a wealthy family, which provided him with the means to support himself as an artist throughout his lifetime. Also like Jonson, he came from a family of ministers: his grandfather and two of his uncles were ministers, and his mother was a committed Christian Scientist. He attended high school in Toronto, and after one semester at the university, he went to Germany, where he studied art from 1904 to 1907. While there, Harris met the German landscape painter Adolph Thiem, who introduced him to a variety of "unorthodox" religious ideas, including theosophy.[107] After a brief stint as an illustrator for *Harper's Weekly* in the Middle East, he returned to Canada in 1908. In that same year, Harris developed a friendship with Roy Mitchell, an active theosophist who later became secretary and then vice president of the Toronto Theosophical Society. Harris was increasingly involved in this group, becoming a member-at-large of the International Society before becoming a member of the local Canadian section in March 1924.[108]

By 1913, Harris had met and begun sketching trips with J. E. H. MacDonald, Tom Thomson, Arthur Lismer, and other members of what was to become the Group of Seven. The Group of Seven drew their inspiration from the dramatic and untamed Canadian landscape.[109] Harris embraced the idea of a uniquely Canadian painting with great enthusiasm: "When I returned from Germany and commenced to paint in Canada my whole interest was in the Canadian scene. It was, in truth, as though I had never been to Europe. Any paintings, drawings, or sketches I saw with a Canadian tang excited me more than anything I had seen in Europe."[110]

The group was not concerned, however, with mere topography or postcard imagery. Its aim was to capture or re-create the essence and spirit of the North:

Our sole concern was to paint Canadian themes in search of their informing spirit. This became a close functioning interplay between the character, moods and spirit of the country and the working momentum and devotion it evoked. . . . Each one of us painted hundreds of sketches. The whole series of each of these represented a long communion with nature and a continuous endeavour to paint the different parts of the country according to what a scene or subject itself dictated. This endeavour inevitably invokes an inner vision, which is the only way an artist can respond to the dictates of a scene or subject in terms of its spirit, which alone can give a painting any enduring life. This is the creative interplay between the artist's observation and his developing inner life of aesthetic and spiritual response.[111]

Harris's spiritual leanings were thus developed and nourished from the very onset of his career. The Group of Seven's early exhibitions were held in 1920, 1921, 1922, 1925, 1926, 1928, and 1930. Reviews of Harris's work in these exhibitions allude to the transcendent, universal aspects of his art. F. B. Housser, himself a theosophist, wrote in 1928: "Lawren Harris continues his search for ultimate values. His results are not 'Canadian' they are beyond Canada and today."[112] Augustus Briddle, writing for the *Toronto Star*, called Harris's art "transcendentalism . . . despairingly beautiful and inhuman."[113]

Harris's association with the International Theosophical Society provided him not only with an ongoing source of ideas and inspiration for his painting but also with an outlet for his own thoughts on theosophy and art. He was a frequent contributor to *The Canadian Theosophist*, writing articles such as "Science and The Soul" and "Revelation of Art in Canada."[114] These writings reveal that Harris was conversant with the major theosophical treatises of P. D. Ouspensky, Mme. Blavatsky, Annie Besant, and C. W. Leadbeater. Harris, then, like other members of the Transcendental Painting Group, such as Dane Rudhyar, Agnes Pelton, and Emil Bisttram, was on intimate terms with the authors who were also Kandinsky's sources.[115] As such, the direct influence of Kandinsky on Harris's principles and practice of art is more difficult to discern. But, as with Jonson, it is likely that Harris utilized Kandinsky's concepts many years prior to his adoption of a non-objective idiom. Jeremy Adamson has noted that Harris's use of color, for example, was probably indebted to Kandinsky rather than Mme. Blavatsky and other theosophists.[116] The icy whites of Harris's Arctic landscapes of 1930 relate to Kandinsky's view that "white . . . acts upon our psyche as a great, absolute silence. . . . White has the appeal of nothingness that is before birth, of the world in the ice age."[117]

It is not clear exactly when Harris came to read *The Art of Spiritual Harmony*, but given its mystical overtones and Harris's involvement in theosophical theory and avant-garde developments, it was likely sometime in the early 1920s. He was most certainly conversant with the book by 1927, when he was instrumental in bringing a portion of the Société Anonyme's Brooklyn exhibition to the Art Gallery of Toronto in April of that year.[118] Katherine Dreier had seen Harris's work for the first time through her involvement in the sesquicentennial exhibition in Philadelphia in 1926, for which she wrote the catalogue. Harris had exhibited two paintings, *North Shore, Lake Superior* and *Ontario Hill Town*, and Dreier was impressed enough to invite him to participate in the Brooklyn exhibition. Harris and Dreier shared common backgrounds of economic privilege and an interest in theosophy. Dreier had practically cut her intellectual teeth on mystical thought, and with the formation of the Société Anonyme in 1920 she hoped to promulgate an art based on spiritual principles; Kandinsky was made honorary vice president of the Société in 1923, and the catalogue for the Brooklyn exhibition was dedicated to him.[119] On seeing Harris's art, Dreier must have recognized a kindred spirit. When he visited the exhibition in Brooklyn and met Dreier, Harris decided that a showing in Toronto "would do wonders for our young people."[120] Harris was able, through a combination of charm and influence, to convince the Art Gallery of Toronto to mount the exhibition. This would be the first comprehensive exhibition of modern art to be seen in Canada. Although the Brooklyn showing contained six Kandinskys— *White Point* (1925), *Small Yellow* (1926), *Abstract Interpretation* (1925), *Capricious Line* (1924), *Cheerful* (1924), and *Red Depth* (1925)—the exhibition in Toronto contained only *Capricious Line, Cheerful,* and *Red Depth.* In a review of the exhibition for the *Canadian Forum,* Harris articulated his views on the new art. Although he did not mention specific artists or artwork, his sympathies for the artists working abstractly were clear. Also clear is the fact that Harris saw in much of the work the same qualities he valued in the Group of Seven, namely, a spiritual component:

> The idiom is too new, is still too much in the experimental stages to look for but a few devotional works. The range of ideas it is suited to may synchronize with a new idea of devotion peculiar to the coming generations. That to us now its appearance is mechanistic says nothing. Behind and within, and yet an integral part of this appearance, is a life peculiarly moving and containing its own possibilities of devotional expression perhaps as great as any we have had. . . . The most convincing pictures were directly created from an inner seeing and conveyed a sense of order in a purged, pervading vitality that was purely spiritual.[121]

Harris also recognized that a new vocabulary of expression was being used in the abstractions—a vocabulary that might appear to the onlooker "like charts, as if they were arrived at by mathematical calculation or by the use of the engineering draughtsman's instruments." Here, he may well have been referring to works such as Kandinsky's *Cheerful* or *Red Depth,* which, in their strict geometry of triangles, circles, and squares, could have been done largely with a protractor and ruler. But Harris finds there a "concentration of feeling" and "spiritual ideas, crystal clear, powerful, and poised."[122] Finally, in words that echo those Kandinsky used in *The Art of Spiritual Harmony* to describe the vanguard role of the artist, Harris argues for the rightness of an art of inner integrity regardless of negative public response:

> Every new development in the arts has had a handful of adherents merely, and hosts of opponents. This is ever the test. If it has sufficient vitality, inner life to withstand the repugnance and recrimination of the conservatives, it persists, and the temporary fuss and animosity subside. If it has no real life but is the product of cheapness or conceit, it disappears. The truth is that works of art test the spectator much more than the spectator tests them. Great art is never kept alive by the masses of men, but by the perceiving, by those who are sufficiently affected to bother about it. It is in the vanguard of life not in the main body.[123]

Thus, as Harris, who as yet had not adopted a non-objective approach in his own work, defended those who had, he called upon Kandinsky's idealistic view of the artist and his role as leader toward an age of spiritual expression.

Dreier traveled with the exhibition to Toronto, gave two lectures at the museum, and then made an informal presentation to local artists at Harris's studio.[124] Through Dreier, Harris must have gained a wealth of information about Kandinsky and other abstract artists.

Dreier had chosen Harris's *Ontario Hill Town* and *Mountain Forms* for the Brooklyn exhibition. These two works were not included in the Toronto showing. *Mountain Forms* (fig.

Fig. 4.8 Lawren Harris. *MOUNTAIN FORMS*, 1928. Oil on canvas, 60 × 70″ (152.4 × 177.8 cm) Location unknown; photograph courtesy Art Gallery of Ontario

4.8) in particular shows Harris's march toward an art that "leaves behind the heavy drag of alien possessions and thus attains moments of release from transitory earthly bonds."[125] Like many of his landscapes of the late 1920s and early 1930s, *Mountain Forms* is an iconic rendering of a mountain using a series of triangular forms. Jeremy Adamson has noted that both the theosophists and Kandinsky saw the triangle in a particularly spiritual way: "For the theosophists the triangle represented spirit force and matter; for Kandinsky it was an expression of the 'life of the spirit.'"[126] For Harris it became a means through which he could wed spiritual symbol and natural form.

While Harris's art of the late 1920s and early 1930s reveals an increasing simplification and geometrization, it remained firmly rooted in the landscape of the North. His contact with Kandinsky and other non-objective artists did not result in any immediate experimentation with non-objective language. The reasons for this can at least partially be attributed to Harris's strong identification of his art with a national Canadian expression.[127] The Group of Seven had gained considerable acceptance in Canada, and his works were already in important private collections and public institutions. As leader of the Group of Seven, Harris had also established himself as a spokesman for Canadian art. Arguing that "a new vision is coming into art in Canada," Harris wrote of the distinctiveness that could be found in the new Canadian art based on the comparative cleanliness of "the psychic atmosphere," the personality of the people, and the "cleansing rhythms" of the great North.[128] As such, Canadian art would always distinguish itself from the art of its southern neighbors. His review of the Société Anonyme exhibition in 1927 further clarified and expanded on this notion of a national expression, one that by now allowed for the development of abstract art:

> Many people deeply interested in the future of Canadian Art feared that the direction shown in the exhibition might lure some Canadian artists from their path. That seems very unlikely . . . it would be almost impossible now for any real Canadian artist to imitate any European artist. Our way is not that of Europe, and when we evolve abstractions, the approach, direction and spirit will be somewhat different.[129]

Thus, Harris did not see abstraction and a uniquely Canadian art as mutually exclusive options. But he did still view art as an expression of a nationalist, rather than universal, impulse. If Canadians were to paint abstractions, they would be somehow nationalist in spirit. This, of course, was somewhat at odds with Harris's ongoing and strong interest in theosophy, which strives outward toward universal and cosmic concepts. Harris would have to find a way to reconcile his two artistic concerns—nationalism and universalism.

By 1928–1929, however, Harris was willing to go beyond his earlier formulations concerning Canadian art and began to concentrate on art's potential to express the universal:

> Today the artist moves toward purer creative expression, wherein he changes the outward aspect of Nature, alters colours, and, by changing and re-shaping forms, intensifies the austerity and beauty of formal relationships and so creates a somewhat new world from the aspect of the world we commonly see; and thus he comes appreciably nearer a pure work of art and the expression has been a steady, slow and natural growth through much work, much inner eliciting experience.[130]

In a letter written to fellow Canadian artist Emily Carr during a trip to Europe in June 1930, Harris expressed some reservations about abstractions that were not tied in some way to natural phenomena:

> I have seen almost no abstract things that have that deep resonance that stirs and answers and satisfies the soul. . . . But that does not say that some painter may not

work "varies between ice-like planes and forms that seem related to organic shapes that have been re-assembled after some disturbance of atomic energy and are endeavoring to force themselves into a new yet animated entity."[148]

Harris traveled to Charleston to see the Guggenheim exhibition at the Gibbes Memorial Art Gallery in March 1938.[149] In addition to *Bright Unity,* among the twenty-eight Kandinskys on view were *Pointed and Round* (1925) and *Composition Eight* (1923). It is entirely possible that Harris was aware of the exhibition in 1936, prior to his arrival in Santa Fe. (If not, he undoubtedly would have seen Jonson's copy of the exhibition catalogue.) In any case, Rebay's introduction to the 1938 exhibition catalogue would have been resonant for Harris. There she states that "pure forms like the triangle, square, and circle are used for their own beauty in shape, and combined with balance of space interval to such perfection that spiritual life is originated to elevate our minds beyond earthly reminiscence. Creation of spiritual life is their essential message. This life is missing in earthly reproductions and also in abstractions of nature."[150] Harris's exposure to this collection at the height of his interest in Kandinsky's work clearly contributed to the vocabulary and syntax of his non-objective work of the period. Indeed, so closely did he associate the Guggenheim collection with the work being done by the members of the Transcendental Painting Group that he arranged to have the group represented at the Golden Gate International Exposition in San Francisco in 1939.[151]

Dane Rudhyar

Like Harris, the musician, writer, and painter Dane Rudhyar had a thorough grounding in theosophy before becoming involved in the Transcendental Painting Group. Born in Paris, Rudhyar immigrated to New York in 1916, where he became a Zen master and began a lifelong interest in theosophy, astrology, and the occult.[152] His remarkably active life, filled with composing, writing, lecturing, and publishing, took him at various times to California, Chicago, and New York.[153] In 1933 and 1934 he lived in New Mexico, delivering some thirty lectures in Santa Fe and Taos and spending a summer at Mabel Dodge Luhan's ranch. During this period he became acquainted with Raymond Jonson, to whom he gave an inscribed copy of his 1930 work *Art as Release of Power.*[154] In 1938 Rudhyar returned to Santa Fe, met members of the Transcendental Painting Group, became the foundation's vice president, and began to paint. Rudhyar was instrumental in the naming of the group, and he and Jonson were the primary authors of the group's published manifesto, although he did not actually belong to the group, probably because at the time of the group's formation he was not yet a painter in his own right.

A mutual interest in theosophy and other mystical tenets undoubtedly was an important bond between Rudhyar and Harris. The Transcendental Painting Group's manifesto, which called for artists to "carry painting beyond the appearance of the physical world, through new concepts of space, color, light and design, to imaginative realms that are idealistic and spiritual,"[155] stated a goal that Harris and Rudhyar shared.

In *Art as Release of Power,* a series of seven essays on the philosophy of art written before he actually began to paint, Rudhyar demonstrates his thorough grounding in theosophical ideas. Speaking of "etheric vibrations," "All-Form," Jay Hambidge, and Goethe's color theories, Rudhyar's prose orients the reader to a wide variety of philosophic, musical, and visual postulations. At the same time, in essays such as "The New Sense of Space," he reveals an early involvement and understanding of current theories and problems in the plastic arts. Although he does not mention Kandinsky, Rudhyar's ideas clearly reflect an interest in problems to which Kandinsky's art offered acceptable solutions:

> A questioning of esthetical principles is in process. A vast reaction against romanticism, subjectivism and personal expression is taking place. But unfortunately only the shadow of the true objectivism is perceived; intellectual rules and traditions are worshipped where spiritual-vital *processes* ought to be understood; Form becomes the idol to which Life is sacrificed, instead of being recognized merely as the vehicle for all Life-manifestations.[156]

Stating that line, form, and mass are all elements of "the one reality," space, Rudhyar considers space the "most profound mystery," which must be understood to create true art. Rudhyar's belief in the primacy of space in any art of spiritual consequence led him, of course, to Hambidge's theory of dynamic symmetry—a theory he fully explores in his essay.[157]

Rudhyar is unique among the artists being studied here because he emerged fully as a painter in the style of Kandinsky almost immediately.[158] Philosophically and intellectually seasoned in the theories that underlay Kandinsky's art, his artistic development was not subject to the long search or evolutionary process that was the case for Harris and Jonson. Rudhyar discovered Kandinsky's vocabulary at the same time he discovered painting. As such, much of his oeuvre of the period, while often imbued with an almost heroic energy, quotes Kandinsky's formal language and reinterprets it in overtly theosophical or mystical terms. In works such as *Storm Gods* (1938; plate 39), Rudhyar uses motifs from a number of Kandinsky's works illustrated in the 1936 and 1938 catalogues of the Guggenheim collection. The lightning bolt and line punctuated with a large point can be seen in a 1924 watercolor by Kandinsky in the 1938 catalogue, for example. The triangular planes appear in any number of Kandinsky exemplars.[159]

Interestingly, Alfred Morang minimizes the influence of Kandinsky on Rudhyar, stating that

> the art of Rudhyar is built upon a non-objective pattern, but is not at all like the work of any other non-objective painter. . . . His placing of shapes upon an oblong is not dictated by any rules of, let us say, Kandinsky or Picasso. Rather the motive force that actuates Rudhyar is a desire to express the intangible something that he has learned to recognize through his music and his writing.[160]

While Rudhyar's work most certainly was inspired by his own desire to express certain universal concepts to which he alone had specific insight, there can be little question that it was Kandinsky to whom he turned in seeking his primary means of expression.

Agnes Pelton

In October 1938, just months after the TPG had been formed, Rudhyar wrote *The Transcendental Movement in Painting and the Creative Destiny of Twentieth Century America*.[161] In this manuscript Rudhyar pays particular attention to the work of Agnes Pelton, the "Honorary President" of the Transcendental Painting Group. In his discussion, Rudhyar contrasts Pelton and Kandinsky:

> This synthesizing character characterizes, perhaps most essentially the work of these American Painters [members of the Transcendental Painting Group] and their tran-

scendental approach. Kandinsky, at times, had produced such synthesis; but on the whole, his paintings tend toward the inchoate, the inorganic and subconscious, while in Agnes Pelton—the closest perhaps of all the painters of the Group to the Kandinsky type of creative movement, there is never anything which is not fully organized and self-contained in form or color. Her works are the projections of fully integrated experiences of an inner reality—not the results of inchoate, spiritual longings of an inorganic mysticism and confused "cosmic consciousness."[162]

Rudhyar's perception that Kandinsky leaned too far toward disorganization and rambling may, as we have seen above in Jonson and Harris, have been shared by other members of the Transcendental Painting Group. Even as they borrowed from his vocabulary, the complexity, intricacy, and subtlety of Kandinsky's Bauhaus compositions did not strike the same responsive chord in Jonson, Harris, Pelton, and Rudhyar as they did in some of the other artists of the American avant-garde.

Rudhyar's identification of Pelton as "the closest of all the painters to the Kandinsky type of creative movement" is significant given the fact that, of all the painters of the Transcendental Painting Group, Pelton's work bears the least visual resemblance to Kandinsky's. Grounded in a symbolic, largely nature-based artistic vocabulary, Pelton's work prior to the late 1930s displays little of Kandinsky's abstract vocabulary. Indeed, Pelton, who throughout her career carefully read and even transcribed notes from various theosophical and occultist books, fails to mention Kandinsky until 1946.[163] An examination of Pelton and Kandinsky reveals primarily a sharing of sources in Leadbeater and Blavatsky rather than a direct or early influence. As such, one must view any early connection with caution.

Pelton was born in 1881 to American parents in Stuttgart, Germany, and spent her early years in Europe. In 1890, after the death of her father, she and her pianist mother returned to Brooklyn, where her mother taught piano, French, and German. Hampered by ill health, which forced her to be educated at home, Pelton studied piano with her mother and Arthur Whiting and continued these studies along with her art courses at the Pratt Institute, which she began at age fourteen and completed five years later. After finishing the regular art course at Pratt, she took private art instruction with Arthur Wesley Dow and Hamilton Easter Field. In 1900, Pelton was Dow's assistant in Ipswich, Massachusetts. Dow, an early advocate of the decorative and expressive power of Oriental art as well as of late nineteenth-century French symbolism, was key in Pelton's development of an art based on interior, spiritual values. Dow believed strongly in the historical determinism of modern art but generally found that the Japanese and Chinese had long ago discovered and perfected that which modernism so vigorously sought:

> The brush strokes of the great Sesshu have more condensed power in them than Matisse ever dreamed of. . . . Two years ago I saw in Germany and France great numbers of prints of brush-work by modernists, mostly in big wide black lines. Only D'Espagnat and two or three others approached the expressiveness of the Japanese. Kandinsky does not equal Keisai Yeisen.[164]

A trip to Italy a year later "liberated the creative impulse," and Pelton began a series of imaginative paintings. These years were frequently filled with painting outdoors and making "many studies from memory of the natural effects and the significance of lights."[165] During this period Pelton also spent several summers on a farm in Connecticut, where she took an interest in the "abstract beauty of form and color mood" inspired by the effects of light and color on neighboring children.[166]

In 1911, 1912, and 1913 Pelton had a series of exhibitions at Field's Studio in Ogunquit, Maine. Walt Kuhn, who saw the 1912 show, invited her to exhibit two paintings, *Vine Wood* and *Stone Age,* in the Armory Show.[167] Pelton's mother, Florence, reflected on their visit to the exhibition on its closing day:

> Agnes and I took our last view of the show this afternoon. In spite of the pelting rain, the great Armory had been filled to suffocation all day. . . . Nothing in the art line has ever caused the sensation that has been this exhibit. . . . and although it has caused endless criticism from all sources, it remains the great event of events, and everyone regrets its closing. Agnes could not resist going to see the last of it and brought home a Matisse photograph as a final souvenir.[168]

Pelton's interest in Matisse is instructive here. For while Kandinsky exhibited only one painting at the Armory Show, compared to Matisse's seventeen, his work and writing were undoubtedly known to Pelton through Stieglitz's *Camera Work.*[169] One of the passages Stieglitz chose to translate and publish in July 1912 concerned the work of Matisse, of whom Kandinsky writes:

> Matisse lays the greatest stress and weight on color. Like Debussy, he is not always able to free himself from conventional ideas of beauty—impressionism runs in his blood. That is why we find in Matisse's work which is the expression of the larger, inward, living fact and which has been called forth as the necessary product of his point of view, other paintings which are chiefly the product of outward influences, outward stimuli . . . and chiefly or finally expressions of the outer world.[170]

Pelton would have responded to Kandinsky's emphasis on Matisse as colorist and conveyor of the "inward, living fact," for her own work was moving increasingly toward an inner orientation with color as a primary means of expression. Another bout of illness in 1914 caused Pelton to curtail her painting activities for a period. In 1917 she was part of a group exhibition at the Knoedler Gallery of some thirty American painters entitled Imaginative Paintings. In the catalogue for that exhibition, Pelton is quoted as saying:

> Painting is the art of Visualization; and color its essential means of expression. All its other elements, form, space, and those less tangible, are produced by illusion.
>
> Color may be considered the language of painting, by which it demonstrates itself to the world of the spectator. As color is a primary sense perception, it is apprehended emotionally—whether sombre or gay, serene or turbulent.
>
> Though aiming at obvious visible beauty, the art of painting should convey through its language of color, and by a harmonious relation of its other elements, the interpretation of the higher possibilities of vision—the without seen from the within. . . . It should convey to the beholder those aspects of beauty which have passed the more direct and elemental emotion of sound as music.[171]

While these words echo Kandinsky as they speak to the primacy of color as a means of expressing "higher possibilities" in the way sound does for music, Pelton's concept of space and form as illusionistic, rather than as equally expressive, elements demonstrates that she was as yet unconvinced of Kandinsky's theory that both form and color and their combined use were the means for expressing ideas. Pelton sought to imbue the outer world with inner meaning, which is distinct from Kandinsky's concept of form as the "outward expression of inner meaning."[172] Nonetheless, during this period Pelton was formulating ideas, some of which would not bear artistic fruit until much later, about the spiritual basis for art. In a notebook entry of 1917 Pelton states: "An abstraction rising from a material thought which recognizes the spiritual quality in matter itself will convey the thought of beauty and loveliness."[173] A year later these thoughts were still with her: "Art will develop as an expression of the perfect consciousness. The divine reality will reveal itself through the life above material—for here Reality is apparent, it needs no seeking."[174]

In the winter of 1919 Pelton visited Mabel Dodge Luhan in Taos and began to paint portraits and landscapes in a realist mode. These landscapes and portraits occupied her on occasion for years to come. As with Jonson, Pelton's art tended to lag behind her thinking. As Margaret Stainer has remarked: "In the 1920's and '30's of American Modernism, we find a painter ideating 'pure abstractions' while painting representational landscapes."[175] On her return from Taos, Pelton wintered in New York and summered in rural New England until 1923, the year she began painting her Symbolic Abstractions. From 1923 to 1931, when she settled permanently in Cathedral City, California, Pelton led a peripatetic existence, traveling to or living in Hawaii, New Hampshire, Beirut, Syria, Georgia, and Pasadena.

By 1929, Pelton's abstract/symbolic voice had found its way into her painting, and her words and work began to voice thoughts that reflect those of Kandinsky more thoroughly. On the occasion of her first major exhibit at the Montross Gallery in New York, Pelton wrote:

> These pictures are like little windows, opening to the view of a region not yet much visited consciously or by intention—an inner realm, rather than an outer landscape.
>
> Sometimes the view is peaceful, even complete calm, or it may be active, stirring; but there is no semblance of material things or substances visible here, except when a symbol materializes into the language of named things.
>
> Here color is like a voice, giving its message directly, without translation into the presentment of recognizable colored objects. Like music without an instrument, it acts on the perception which is sympathetically ready to receive it; but as the creative faculty acts in building forms, the colors are active, produce forms in space according to their nature and the quality of life and light which they represent. . . .
>
> As the fragrance of a flower fills the consciousness with the essence of its life without the necessity for seeing its material form, it seems that color will some day speak directly to us; not only as the expressive clothing of material forms, or the harmonious recipes of decorative design, but by its own vibratory nature, with a beauty not for the eye alone, but of a more comprehensive nature, carrying a more direct impact on our newly developing perception, as we learn to perceive and to use our colors with more clarity and power.[176]

A parallel for Pelton's interest in synesthesia, as evidenced in the statement above, can be found in Kandinsky's discussion of color in *The Art of Spiritual Harmony,* where he talks of "scented colors" and "the sound of colors."[177] But more important, Pelton's acknowledgment that colors produce forms in space "according to their nature" clearly reflects Kandinsky's ideas on the "mutual influence of form and colour."[178] In addition, Pelton's acknowledgment that the "vibratory" nature of color can impact a nascent, developing perception that transcends the purely visible is akin to Kandinsky's belief that to the "more sensitive soul the effect of colours is deeper and intensely moving," thus producing a *"psychic effect"* that produces a corresponding spiritual vibration in the soul.[179] While Pelton's ideas closely reflect her familiarity with Kandinsky's writings during this period, they were also informed by her close reading of esoteric texts by Blavatsky, Richard Ingalese, and A. S. Raleigh.

White Fire (c. 1930) and *The Ray* (1931) represent Pelton's full development toward spiritual/symbolic abstraction. Soft, rounded forms in deep colors surround central vertical shapes of highly intensified white—which for Kandinsky was the color of silence, pregnant with possibilities. These works may have their source in Kandinsky's essay in *Der Blaue Reiter* entitled "On the Question of Form." There Kandinsky writes:

> Consciously or unconsciously man tries, from this moment on, to find a material form for the spiritual form, for the new value that lives within him.
>
> This is the search by the spiritual value for materialization. Matter is a kind of larder from which the spirit chooses what is *necessary* for itself, much as a cook would.
>
> This is the positive, the creative. This is goodness. *The white, fertilizing ray.*
>
> This white ray leads to evolution, to elevation. Behind matter, within matter, the creative spirit is hidden.[180]

Pelton, with her knowledge of German, could well have read the almanac in the original. Again, however, the fact that Pelton shared theosophical sources with Kandinsky could account for the imagery in *The Ray* and *White Fire*.

Pelton's association with the Transcendental Painting Group resulted from her acquaintance with Raymond Jonson, who became aware of her work when she had an exhibition at the Delphic Studios in New York in April 1932. Jonson was extremely supportive of Pelton's work and often was a source of her painting supplies.

The late 1930s found Pelton at an artistic juncture that led inevitably toward a direct involvement with Kandinsky's art. Clear visual evidence of Pelton's interest in and experimentation with Kandinsky's improvisational style can be seen around 1938 in a drawing in her notebooks entitled *Morning Hymn* (fig. 4.11). There she combines Kandinsky's curving forms intersected by straight lines to create one of her few purely improvisational works. In *Future* (1941; plate 41) and *Challenge* (1940; plate 40) Kandinsky's influence, perhaps as an outgrowth of her increased contact with Rudhyar and Jonson, is also more direct. *Challenge* makes use of Kandinsky's improvisational linear effects and overlapping triangles and combines them with Pelton's own symbolist-based vocabulary. The evolution in Pelton's ideas toward Kandinsky's ideal of form as the outer expression of inner meaning is clearly evidenced in the following statement:

> Abstract paintings should be a new experience in seeing without reference to what has been familiar in the past. They communicate to us through color, as music does through sound.
>
> These paintings are seldom presentations of forms in Nature—except in a symbolic sense; they are impressions of inner visual experiences, bringing light out of darkness— serenity out of oppression, by the sensitive use of a wide range of color, and of forms which either in movement or at rest maintain their relationships in space.[181]

The floating squares and abstract linear sweeps of *Future* also reveal Pelton's use of Kandinsky's abstract geometry, not to formulate images of strict non-objectivity, but rather to transform "the external physical aspects of a thing into a self-sustaining spiritual reality."[182] Pelton's poetic "statements" on her paintings reveal further her dependence on an essentially symbolic language that, while resulting from "inner seeing," nonetheless remains referential. Of *Future,* she writes: "Through darkness and oppression across a stormy desert, and through a symbolic arch appears a mountain of vision. Above it, opening by degrees, windows of illumination."[183]

Pelton, unlike Jonson, did not make the leap from symbolic abstraction to pure non-objectivity. Even works such as *Departure* (1946–1952), done after her documented reading

Fig. 4.11 Agnes Pelton.
MORNING HYMN. c. 1938.
Pencil on paper.
Agnes Pelton Papers, Archives of American Art
Smithsonian Institution, Washington, D.C.

and consideration of Kandinsky and utilizing simple, iconic Kandinskyesque non-objective orbs, were rooted in spiritual yet concrete ideas.

Ed Garman

Ed Garman, one of the younger members of the Transcendental Painting Group, recalls that his first contact with Kandinsky occurred in 1935 at the Art Institute of Chicago, where he saw one of Kandinsky's Improvisations.[184] Further exposure came that same year when he read Arthur Jerome Eddy's *Cubists and Post-Impressionism* and then in 1938 when he read *The Art of Spiritual Harmony* for the first time. According to Garman, he found in Kandinsky "confirmation . . . that I had chosen the right direction for investigation and development of my statement of the Modern ideal in painting. The ideal of pure painting."[185] Garman had met Bill Lumpkins while working on the National Youth Administration Project near Jemez, New Mexico, in the late 1930s. Jonson came to know Garman's work after seeing Garman's first one-man show at the Santa Fe Museum. Shortly thereafter, he invited Garman to become a member of the Transcendental Painting Group.[186] A visit in the fall of 1940 by Garman to the Museum of Non-Objective Painting, where he saw a selection of the work of Kandinsky and Bauer, furthered his understanding of non-objectivity:

> This exhibit impressed me deeply. I went there not to look at something but to find something. A practicing artist who develops independently is looking for a broader use of the "tools" of art for his expression. By "tools" I mean the kind of forms, organizations and how space, shape and color is used. When I left the Guggenheim I came away with my art toolbox considerably more complete than before.[187]

Garman was particularly interested in Kandinsky's Bauhaus works because they offered new solutions for the use of space in abstract painting. The concept of cosmic, free-floating shapes in ambiguous space was of great importance to Garman. Like "cherubims and angels" defying the laws of gravity and perspective, Kandinsky's planar shapes intimated a realm of spirituality. As Garman explains it: "By grouping lines, colors, non-figurative shapes in an ambivalent space in varied relationships controlled by a specific order, [his] art evoked emotions, not unearthly, but something [Kandinsky] felt should be designated as 'spiritual.'"[188] Works from 1941 and 1942, such as *Untitled, Red Circle on Black (No. 297)* (plate 43), and *Untitled, Orange Triangle (No. 202)* (plate 42), demonstrate Garman's adoption of Kandinsky's "free space" to articulate an ideal of universality. Thus, through the means of pure painting alone, a higher, democratic ordering of elements could be expressed and discovered. Garman calls this "working from the void."[189]

Emil Bisttram and His Circle

Besides Jonson, the other major force behind the Transcendental Painting Group was Emil Bisttram. Bisttram was born in a small town on the Hungarian-Rumanian border, and in 1906, at the age of eleven, he immigrated with his parents to New York.[190] Taking a job with a commercial art firm in New York in 1912, the ambitious Bisttram had his own firm by 1915. In 1918, he began studying art at the National Academy under Ivan Olinsky, at the Parsons School of Art and Design with Jay Hambidge and Howard Giles, and at the Art Students League under Leon Kroll. By 1920 he was teaching at the Parsons School, a position he held until 1925. From 1922 to 1931 he organized and taught art classes at the new

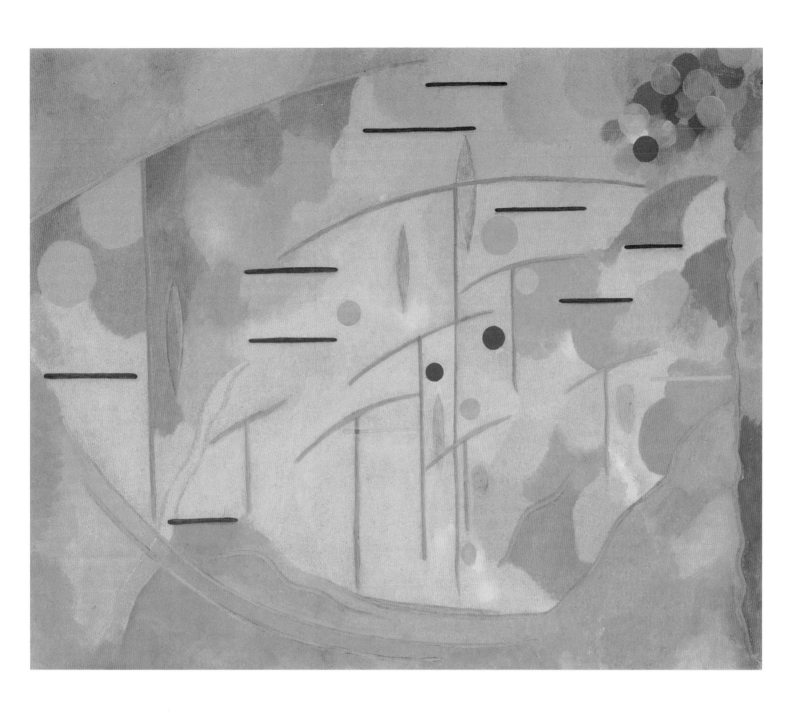

Plate 50
Oskar Fischinger
FAVORITE, 1944
Private collection

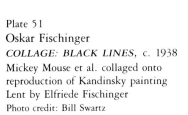

Plate 52
Osker Fischinger
COLLAGE: PAINTING WITH WHITE FORM, c. 1938
Mickey Mouse et al. collaged with reproduction of Kandinsky painting
Lent by Elfriede Fischinger
Photo credit: Bill Swartz

Plate 51
Oskar Fischinger
COLLAGE: BLACK LINES, c. 1938
Mickey Mouse et al. collaged onto reproduction of Kandinsky painting
Lent by Elfriede Fischinger
Photo credit: Bill Swartz

Plate 53
Knud Merrild
JAN. '37 NON-OBJECTIVE SPACE
PICTURE, 1937
Steve Turner, Steve Turner Gallery,
Los Angeles

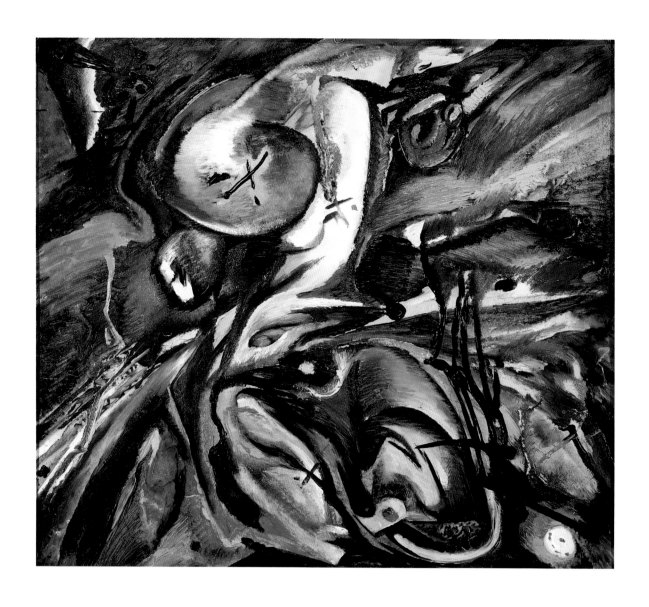

Plate 54
Hilla Rebay
COMPOSITION NO. 9, 1916
Portico Fine Art, New York

132

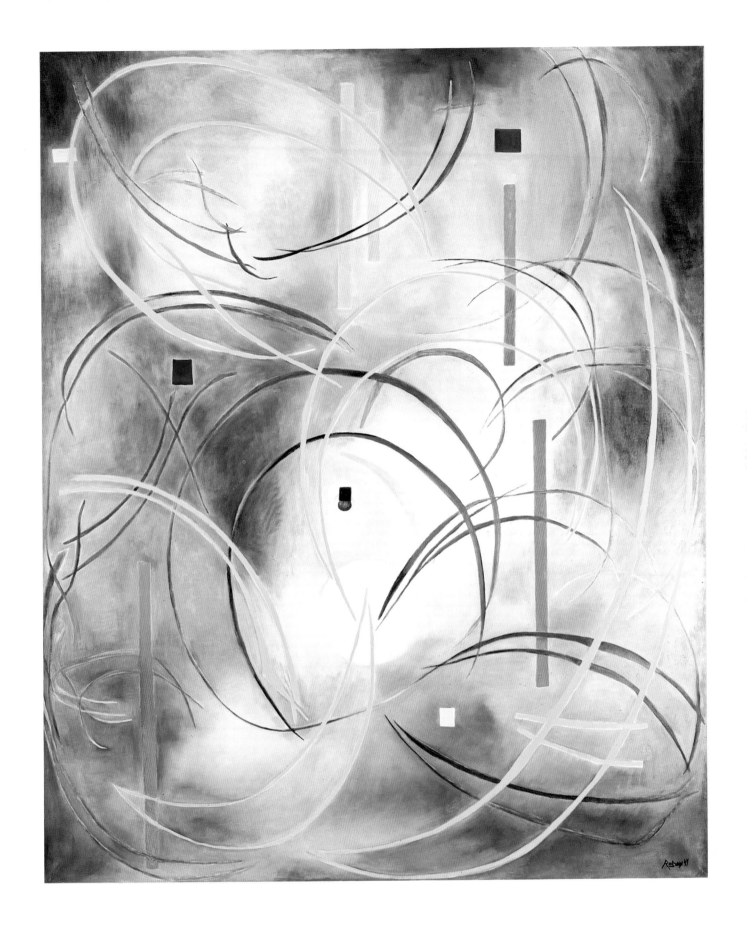

Plate 55
Hilla Rebay
UNTITLED, c. 1944
Portico Fine Art, New York

133

Plate 56
Dwinell Grant
WATERCOLOR NO. 66:
SOPHISTICATION, 1938
Dayton Art Institute
Photo credit: Bill Swartz

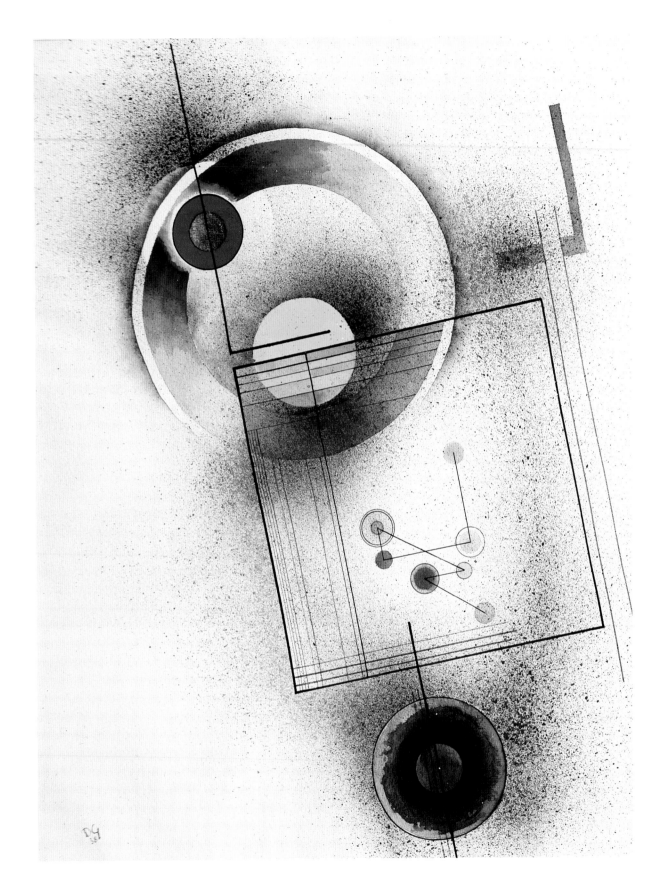

Plate 57
Dwinell Grant
WATERCOLOR NO. 67: YELLOW CIRCLE,
1938
Dayton Art Institute
Photo credit: Bill Swartz

Plate 60
Rolph Scarlett
UNTITLED ABSTRACTION, n.d.
Estate of the artist, courtesy Harriet Tannin
Photo credit: Ed Watkins, New York

Plate 61
Rolph Scarlett
UNTITLED ABSTRACTION, n.d.
Estate of the artist, courtesy Harriet Tannin
Photo credit: Ed Watkins, New York

138

Plate 62
John Sennhauser
BLACK LINES NO. 2, 1943
Courtesy Struve Gallery, Chicago

Plate 63
John Sennhauser
BLACK LINES NO. 4, 1943
Collection of Keith and Robin Struve, Chicago

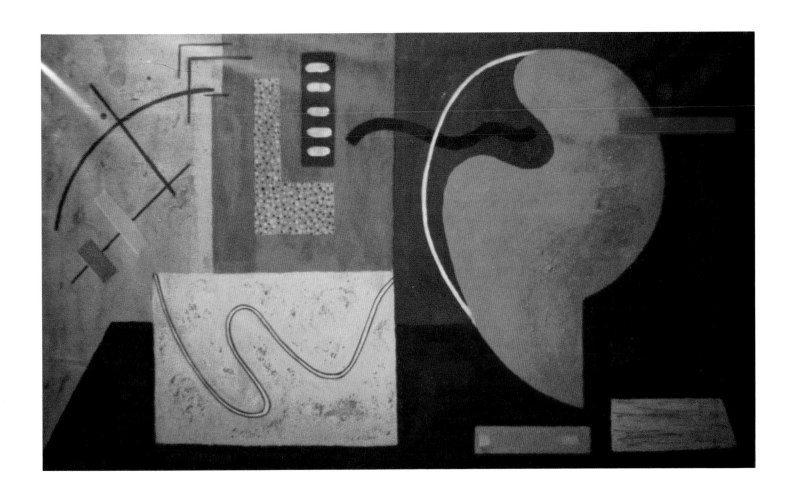

Plate 64
Burgoyne Diller
EARLY GEOMETRIC, 1933
Meredith Long & Company, Houston

Plate 65
Ilya Bolotowsky
*FIRST STUDY FOR THE WILLIAMSBURG
MURAL,* 1936
Courtesy Washburn Gallery, New York

Plate 66
Alice Trumbull Mason
SPRING, 1931
Courtesy Washburn Gallery, New York

Plate 67
George L. K. Morris
UNTITLED, c. 1936–1938
Collection of Jane and Ron Lerner

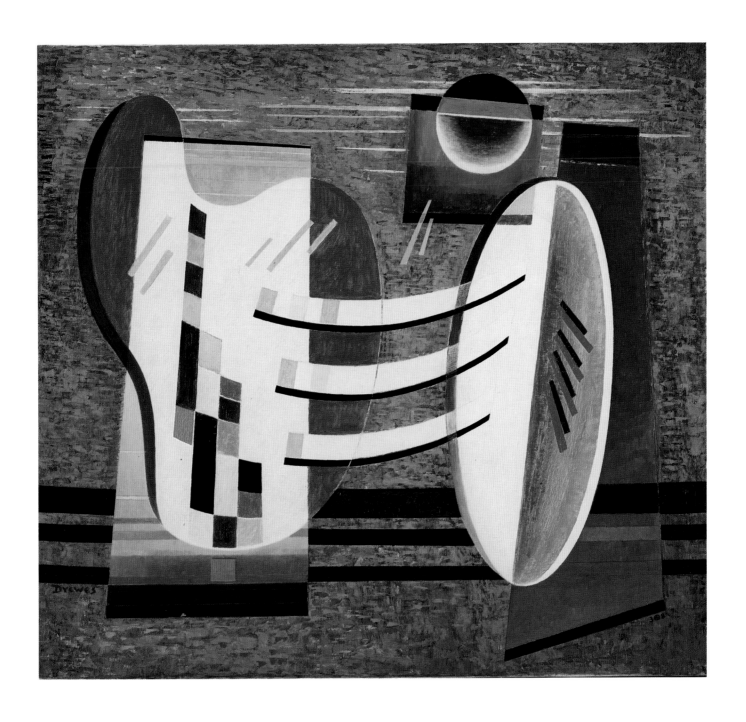

Plate 68
Werner Drewes
LOOSE CONTACT, 1938
Meredith Long & Company, Houston

Plate 69
Werner Drewes
DANCE IN THE DARK, 1949
Private collection

146

Plate 70
John von Wicht
VISTA, 1939
Lee Ehrenworth
Photo credit: Ed Watkins, New York

Plate 73
John Ferren
UNTITLED ABSTRACTION WITH
ORANGE, 1934
Nora Eccles Harrison Museum of Art, Utah
State University, Logan
Gift of Marie Eccles Caine Foundation
Photo credit: Gary J. Mamay

Plate 74
Benjamin Benno
UNTITLED ABSTRACTION, 1936
Michael Rosenfeld Gallery, New York

Plate 75
Benjamin Benno
UNTITLED, 1936
Michael Rosenfeld Gallery, New York

Plate 76
Benjamin Benno
UNTITLED, 1936
Michael Rosenfeld Gallery, New York

Roerich Museum in New York. His acquaintance with Nicholas Roerich and his art resulted in an ongoing interest in mysticism and theosophy, which he later passed on to his students.[191] In 1930 he visited Taos for the first time and ultimately settled there in 1932. Upon his arrival in Taos, he opened an art school and the Heptagon Gallery, one of the first commercial galleries in the town.

It was undoubtedly while Bisttram was associated with the Roerich Museum, where his interest in spiritual and theosophical ideas was piqued and developed, that he took his first steps toward an art based on spiritual, abstract values. Nicholas Roerich, a cultured and influential Russian artist and philosopher with an interest in theosophy and eastern religions, established a presence in the United States in 1920 when Dr. Robert Harshe, director of the Chicago Art Institute, invited him to tour America with an exhibition of his work. The exhibition traveled from the Kingore Gallery in New York to Boston, Buffalo, Chicago, Omaha, Denver, Santa Fe, and San Francisco. Noting America's lack of interest in the arts, Roerich was active in founding Cor Ardens in Chicago and the Master Institute of United Arts in New York in 1921. At the Master Institute the curriculum of music, painting, sculpture, architecture, ballet, and drama was infused with Roerich's idealistic spiritualism. The school's credo read:

> Art will unify all humanity. Art is one—indivisible. Art has its many branches, yet all are one. Art is the manifestation of the coming synthesis. Art is for all. Everyone will enjoy true art. The gates of the "sacred source" must be opened wide for everybody, and the light of art will ignite numerous hearts with a new love. At first this feeling will be unconscious, but after all it will purify human consciousness.[192]

Roerich was personally involved with the Master Institute until 1923, when he left for India.

Bisttram met Roerich in 1922 soon after he began teaching at the museum. Although Bisttram was inspired by Roerich's persona and his "ideas of culture and beauty, and peace,"[193] Roerich had little direct influence on Bisttram's painting style. Bisttram later noted that Roerich, after seeing an exhibit of Bisttram's work, gave him a handful of thick brushes in order to "broaden the whole thing, simple sky, simple mountain, simple form, direct . . ."[194] The exposure to Roerich's synthesis of the arts and his universal approach to philosophy, which included a belief in reincarnation, remained part of Bisttram's teaching and working credo throughout his life:

> He [Roerich] always insisted that it must have beauty. Everything that you create everything that you touch, must have quality. And this is what I feel personally from my 50 years of experience in teaching that when a student recognizes this, when they have studied philosophy and have accepted the idea of philosophy, they immediately begin to think in terms of order, rhythm, harmony and unity.[195]

A page of sketches from a 1931 folio containing Bisttram's New York address (fig. 4.12) indicates that Bisttram may have begun to experiment with Kandinsky's non-objective style before leaving New York. Bisttram's later recollections place his discovery of Kandinsky somewhat later, around 1933 or 1934:

> I became aware of Indian painting. . . . They were never permitted to paint anything realistic. They were painting ideas. Something to do with the spirit of man's inner nature. . . . When this began to change my whole life, I realized for the first time what the abstract artists were trying to do. . . . I didn't understand the abstract artists. I thought the Renaissance and Chinese and the Orient were the greatest things in the world. But what these abstractionists were doing didn't mean anything. I couldn't

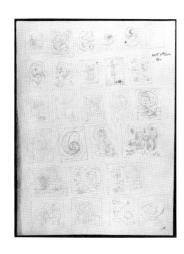

Fig. 4.12 Emil Bisttram. Page from folio of drawings, 1931. Pencil on paper. Harwood Foundation Archives The Foundation Museum, Taos, New Mexico

Fig. 4.13 Emil Bisttram.
MUSICAL NOTES, 1951.
Acrylic on canvas, 50 × 80''
(128.2 × 205 cm)
Collection of Mr. and Mrs. Walt
Wiggins, Santa Fe, New Mexico

figure it out. . . . I copied everything I could think of, the Picassos and the Cézannes, Kandinskys, Miros and all of them. I wanted to know what is it they're doing. Well, I learned something. But all of a sudden, I discovered a book by Kandinsky called *The Spiritual in Art.*[196]

In any case, the series of drawings makes ample use of Kandinsky's abstract vocabulary—points, lines, and planes combined in seemingly infinite ways. It is important to point out here that Bisttram obviously appreciated not only Kandinsky's work but also that of Rudolf Bauer.[197]

That Bisttram was also theoretically committed to non-objective art as early as 1931 can be detected in an article he wrote for *Art in America* that year. Remarking that America was living in a sort of artistic chaos, he asserted that "modernism is firmly entrenched in American art centers and is seeping into the provinces, among them the South and Southwest." Bisttram goes on to state that the new artist "will find that art is created on a foundation of geometry—the one unique and indispensable transformer by which chaos resolves itself into order."[198]

Bisttram found in Kandinsky, whom he called "a very religious man,"[199] the key to expressing a wide variety of spiritual and occult ideas that occupied him for a lifetime. In *Pulsation* (1938; plate 44), Kandinsky-like pulsating circles and undulating motion lines are combined with a series of transparent planes. Transparency was particularly important to Bisttram's work of the period and contributed to the otherworldly quality of paintings such as *Pulsation.*[200] Essential life forces, expressed in absolute terms, undulate in an indeterminate universe. *Cactus* (1938; plate 45) is a playful application of Kandinsky's Bauhaus vocabulary to landscape painting. While much of Bisttram's work of the 1930s and 1940s utilizes Kandinsky's Bauhaus vocabulary, he was also interested in Kandinsky's earlier work. *Musical Notes* (1951; fig. 4.13) can be compared to Kandinsky's *Blue Segment* (1921) (in the Guggenheim collection, shown in New York in 1923; Oakland, California, in 1926; and Chicago in 1932). Bisttram has chosen intense colors—blue, red, gold—to denote musical qualities in much the same way advocated by Kandinsky in *The Art of Spiritual Harmony.*[201]

Bisttram was an important factor in introducing his students Florence Pierce, Horace Towner Pierce, and Robert Gribbroek to the ideas of Kandinsky. As a vibrant and charismatic teacher, Bisttram had a profound influence on these younger members of the Transcendental Painting Group. Neither Florence nor Horace Pierce had painted abstractly prior to beginning their studies with Bisttram in 1936, and their first experiments with abstraction took place under what Florence Pierce recently recalled as the "indoctrination" of Bisttram's lectures on Kandinsky, Mme. Blavatsky, and Claude Bragdon. All of Bisttram's students read *The Art of Spiritual Harmony.*[202] Bisttram's belief that abstraction is "expressing ideas in simple symbolic fashion . . . in simple planes and colors, lines and so on"[203] assured that these young artists' early work would reflect Kandinsky's ideas.[204] A set of problems for a course in the fundamental principles of space relationships among the Bisttram papers reflects a strong orientation toward Kandinsky's principles as outlined in *Point and Line to Plane.*[205] There are exercises on "Points, Lines and Planes" and instructions to create designs to express "pointed and round" (Kandinsky did two works, *Pointed and Round*—shown at the Museum of Non-Objective Painting exhibition in Philadelphia in 1937—and *Pointed-Round,* in 1925), "light and heavy" (see Kandinsky's *Light in Heavy,* 1929, formerly in the Guggenheim collection), and "musical themes" (*Point and Line to Plane* represented the first measures of Beethoven's Fifth Symphony in points and lines).[206] There are also exercises in which the student was asked to produce works "suggested" by such words as "interlocking," "harsh and mild," "loud and soft," "war," "joy," and so on, all of which suggest Kandinsky's thinking. Also among Bisttram's notes, perhaps intended as a handout for students, is a paper entitled "The Art of Pure Design" by Dr. Denman W. Ross. To Ross's concepts of design, Bisttram added several pages of notes that strongly reflect Kandinsky's ideas as outlined in *Point and Line to Plane*. Without attribution, a number of the illustrations used by Kandinsky, including those that contrast "warm rest" to "cold rest" and "obstinacy with forbearance" to "obstinacy in stiff tension," are reproduced and discussed. Thus, students may have been exposed to Kandinsky without knowing it directly.[207]

Horace Towner Pierce, who had studied at the Maryland Art Institute up to the time he became Bisttram's student, was particularly interested in film. He began his major project of the period, which was referred to simply as the "Movie" but whose tentative title was *The Spiral Symphony*, in 1939. This work consisted of thirty small airbrushed watercolors and was originally inspired by Disney's *Fantasia*. Pierce planned to have Rudhyar write the score for the film. Pierce and his new wife, Florence, took the watercolors to New York in an effort to raise enough money to produce the film but had little success. The drawings were exhibited in April 1940 at the Museum of Modern Art in a show entitled American Design for Abstract Films, and six of the paintings for the Fourth Movement illustrated the Spring Bulletin of the Museum.[208] As the film was never made, we content ourselves with the drawings made in its preparation. *Key Drawing from Movement 1* (1939; plate 46) indicates the extent to which Pierce's film was to be based on Kandinsky's ideas of non-objectivity. (Florence Pierce has noted that Kandinsky was "an especially strong influence on Horace's movie.")[209] As with much of Bisttram's, Jonson's, and Harris's work of the period, the setting is cosmic. A spiraling ball of light moves across the plane of another swirling empyrean form. To the right are orbs of blue and violet echoing those Kandinsky used in *Several Circles* (1926). The combination of Kandinsky's non-objective language with Pierce's ethereal vision creates a feeling similar to that of Jonson's *Cycle of Science: Astronomy*.

Horace Pierce's commitment to making non-objective films corresponded with that of Dwinell Grant and Oskar Fischinger. Rebay's interest in these efforts helped support Fischinger's and Grant's films of the period, but Pierce was evidently not able to interest her in his work.[210]

Rebay's lack of interest must have increased the resentment the Transcendental Painting Group felt by 1941 toward one of the most important figures in bringing Kandinsky's work to America. The disappointment in not finding a greater place in her collection and activities must have been acute for the group, who generally agreed with the goals of the collection and thought that their works should logically be housed among those of Kandinsky and Bauer. That Rebay's indifference extended to Pierce's film efforts must have reinforced their sense of isolation.

When compared to Kandinsky's oeuvre, the works done by the Transcendental Painting Group generally demonstrate a high degree of simplification and contain, for the most part, an iconic quality missing from the majority of Kandinsky's Bauhaus works. This can be seen very clearly in the work of Florence Pierce, who prior to enrolling in Bisttram's School of Art attended the Duncan Phillips Collection "Studio School" in Washington D.C. In works such as *Rising Red* (1942; plate 47) her use of a single centralized sphere being intersected by a contrasting red ellipse reflects her assimilation of Kandinsky's geometric vocabulary via Bisttram, while the spare, unembellished directness of the image allies it to her New Mexican colleagues.

William Lumpkins came to know Kandinsky's work through Bisttram sometime in 1932 or 1933.[211] Lumpkins was born on a ranch near Clayton in what was then Territorial New Mexico. His youth was punctuated by studies in Oriental philosophy with an Orientologist, Dr. Eberhart, who was employed as a tutor for the Lumpkins children on one of the large ranches where their father worked as a cowhand. Lumpkins's early interest in art was fueled by informal outdoor sketching with the well-known representational painter Peter Hurd.

In 1929 Lumpkins enrolled in his first formal art class at the University of New Mexico in Albuquerque. There he met Robert Gribbroek and Stuart Walker. In 1931 Lumpkins was exposed to John Marin's watercolors of New Mexico and, through them, began to understand his own earlier experiments in abstraction, which were done while he was still in high school.[212] After graduating from UNM with a degree in art and architecture in 1934, Lumpkins began working for the WPA Architectural Division in New Mexico. His meeting with Jonson took place in 1935 when he purchased art supplies from the art supply store Jonson maintained in his garage.

Lumpkins's use of Kandinsky's non-objective language can be seen in an early watercolor, *Transparency* (1933; plate 48). His interest in Kandinsky's overlapping biomorphic planes of color and geometric grids is combined here with the ochres and browns of the native New Mexican landscape. By the late 1930s and early 1940s, Lumpkins's work had taken on a more abstract-expressionist quality—using large areas of bold, highly saturated watercolor, his work moved away from Kandinsky's language during the very period when other members of the Transcendental Painting Group were under his greatest influence.

Stuart Walker, who befriended Lumpkins in the early 1930s, was born in Kentucky and studied at the Herron Art Institute in Indianapolis. He moved to Albuquerque in 1925 and by 1930 was doing abstract compositions.[213] Lumpkins recalls that at the time they met, in 1930 or 1931, Walker was "certainly influenced by Kandinsky's work of 1908–15."[214] Like Kandinsky's early paintings, Walker's work of the early 1930s consisted of abstracted landscape motifs. Walker also had viewed Kandinsky's later work with interest. *Composition 65* (1939; plate 49) reflects Walker's appreciation of Kandinsky's geometric compositions from his Bauhaus period and combines them with the pinks, beiges, and ochres of the New Mexican landscape.

California

California was introduced to modernism through the Panama-Pacific International Exposition in 1915. In contrast to the vehement negative press that the Armory Show received, California critics chose to applaud what they liked (Monet, Pissarro, Puvis de Chavannes) and express wonderment at what appeared incomprehensible (Kokoschka and the futurists—Kandinsky was not included in the exposition): "Many of them defy explanation as to how the results have been obtained; some look as though they had been splotched with pigment in the hope that the splotches would assume a form of verity, and with a good imagination the onlooker can do his own interpreting."[215] The relatively mild response did not connote greater receptivity to modernism on the West Coast—in most cases it masked a benumbed indifference.

California received an early and substantial introduction to Kandinsky through the efforts of Galka Scheyer. After her 1924 arrival in New York from Germany, she traveled to the

West Coast and began lecturing, exhibiting, and selling the work of Kandinsky, Paul Klee, Lyonel Feininger, and Alexey Jawlensky, who comprised the Blue Four. Scheyer's activities in California commenced in 1925 when she sent out over a thousand inquiries to American colleges and museums regarding exhibitions and programs on the Blue Four. Only William H. Clapp, director of the Oakland Municipal Art Museum and a member of the Bay area art group the Society of Six, responded. The first Blue Four exhibition in California took place there in the fall of 1925.[216] Through Clapp, members of the Society of Six came to know the work of the Blue Four, and Louis Siegriest recalled that the group's work influenced Society of Six artists Seldon Gile and Bernard von Eichman: "They got rather bold with their work after seein' that. They used a bigger brush, I know, after that, and more powerful."[217] Siegriest's own reaction to Kandinsky's work, however, was probably characteristic: "I guess it didn't influence me a great deal because I thought they were kind of crazy at that time. I mean it was a little beyond me."[218]

In 1940 Scheyer stated that her purpose with the Blue Four had been "to arrange exhibitions and lectures of the works of these artists in America, trusting to interest the United States in the spiritual significance of their work with the hopes that through it might come an exchange of spirits between the artists of the two continents."[219] Writing in the context of World War II, Scheyer stressed mutual understanding between American artists and those in Europe. But Scheyer had from the beginning sought such understanding, and her tireless efforts on behalf of the group reflect a deep commitment to the spiritual and artistic values the group represented.

Despite her energy and enthusiasm, it was difficult for Scheyer to interest the public on the West Coast in the work of Kandinsky and his colleagues. In 1929 Scheyer sold, but was unable to collect the $8.00 price for, Kandinsky's 1923 lithograph *Orange.* Works that sold went for what now seem unbelievable prices: In 1927 Edward Weston purchased a Kandinsky lithograph for $3.00.[220] In 1931 Scheyer sold to Walter Arensberg *Circles in a Circle* (1923)— Kandinsky's first picture to use circles as the "main theme."[221] In San Francisco, collectors such as Mrs. Adolph Mack purchased a number of Kandinsky works on paper. But overall, the task was formidable. As early as 1924, Kandinsky had heard enough reports from others to realize the difficulties confronting Scheyer: "Muche [a fellow teacher at the Bauhaus from 1920 to 1927] is back, very impressed by America . . . but found art, in our sense of the word, is completely superfluous there and that a European can only accomplish things if he not only puts aside, but completely forgets our standpoints and mentality. Hopefully you will have a different experience there."[222]

In 1929, Scheyer gave Kandinsky a one-man show at the Oakland Municipal Art Museum. Criticism was mixed. For some, the work resembled "eye-test charts," "astronomical charts," and "kindergarten exercises."[223] Bay Area art figure Ray Boynton mounted a particularly vocal anti-Kandinsky campaign. In a letter to the editor of *The Argus,* a northern California art journal dedicated to modern art, Boynton stated that the Blue Four should be "debunked" in the same way that Merton Clivette (1868–1931), a minor artist who had recently been shown in Oakland, had been upon a showing of his work there. Boynton then goes on to decry Kandinsky's mysticism and his art:

> It is an astonishing experience to have one of the illuminati explain to you the significance of a Kandinsky, for instance. You are made to feel that you are being initiated into a cult whose symbolism is being carefully revealed to you, and that you are yet too low to understand its mysteries. Kandinsky's ideal would be a blank

him with the numerous publications from the Guggenheim Foundation, including Kandinsky's *Point and Line to Plane*. RJ to Hilla Rebay, February 27, 1950, AAA RJ 4:2700.

105. RJ to Arthur Jonson, October 23, 1940, AAA RJ 1:590.

106. RJ to Peter Larisey, November 14, 1973, in Jonson Gallery archives.

107. Jeremy Adamson, *Lawren S. Harris: Urban Scenes and Wilderness Landscapes 1906–1950* (Toronto: Art Gallery of Ontario, 1978), p. 22.

108. Ibid.

109. For background information on the Group of Seven, see J. A. Morris, *Group of Seven*, exhibition catalogue (Vancouver: Vancouver Art Gallery, 1954).

110. Harris to Sydney Key, May 9, 1948, quoted in Adamson, *Lawren S. Harris*, p. 51.

111. Harris, "The Story of The Group of Seven," in Morris, *Group of Seven*, pp. 10–11.

112. "The Group of Seven Exhibition," *The Canadian Bookman*, vol. 10, no. 2 (February 1928), p. 43.

113. "The Group of Seven Display Their Annual Symbolisms," *Toronto Star*, February 8, 1928.

114. *The Canadian Theosophist*, vol. 7, no. 10 (December 15, 1931) and vol. 8, no. 5 (July 15, 1926).

115. For a discussion of Kandinsky's sources, see Sixten Ringbom, *The Sounding Cosmos: A Study of the Spiritualism of Kandinsky and the Genesis of Abstract Painting*, Acta Academiae Aboensis, series A, XXVII (Abo, Finland: Abo Academi, 1970).

116. Adamson, *Lawren S. Harris*, pp. 190, 193.

117. Kandinsky, *Concerning the Spiritual in Art* (New York: 1972), as quoted in Adamson, *Lawren S. Harris*, p. 193.

118. For a complete discussion of the Brooklyn exhibition and its subsequent venues in Buffalo, Toronto, and the Anderson Gallery in New York, see Ruth Louise Bohan, "The Société Anonyme's Brooklyn Exhibition, 1926–1927: Katherine Sophie Dreier and the Promotion of Modern Art in America" (Ph.D. dissertation, University of Maryland, 1980). See also Sandra Shaul, *The Modern Image: Cubism and the Realist Tradition*, exhibition catalogue (Edmonton: The Edmonton Art Gallery, 1982).

119. Bohan, "Société Anonyme's Brooklyn Exhibition," pp. 1–84.

120. Lawren Harris to Katherine Dreier, [early December 1926], Katherine Dreier–Société Anonyme Collection, Collection of American Literature, Yale, as quoted in Bohan, "Société Anonyme's Brooklyn Exhibition," p. 141.

121. Lawren Harris, "Modern Art and Aesthetic Reactions," *Canadian Forum*, May 1927, p. 240.

122. Ibid.

123. Ibid., p. 241.

124. Bohan, "Société Anonyme's Brooklyn Exhibition," p. 195.

125. Lawren Harris, "Revelation of Art in Canada," *Canadian Theosophist*, vol. 7, no. 5 (July 15, 1926),

p. 85.

126. Adamson, *Lawren S. Harris*, p. 179.

127. See Sandra Shaul, *The Modern Image*, pp. 11–18, for a discussion of Harris's evolution toward abstraction. See also Dennis Reid, *Atma Buddi Manas: The Later Work of Lawren S. Harris* (Toronto: Art Gallery of Ontario, 1985), for a full discussion of Harris's later abstractions and a summary of the literature.

128. Harris, "Revelation of Art in Canada," *Canadian Theosophist*, vol. 7, no. 5 (July 15, 1926), pp. 85–88.

129. Harris, "Modern Art," pp. 240–241.

130. Lawren Harris, "Creative Art and Canada," *Yearbook of the Arts in Canada*, 1928–1929, pp. 184–185, as quoted in Shaul, *The Modern Image*, p. 18. Also of note here is the 1927 exhibition of abstractions by Harris's friend Bertram Brooker; see Dennis Reid, *Bertram Brooker* (Ottawa: National Gallery of Canada, n.d.), where Reid observes that Brooker's abstractions resulted from a close reading and viewing of Kandinsky after he had been introduced to the latter by Harris.

131. Harris to Emily Carr, June 1930, Emily Carr papers, British Columbia Province Archives, Victoria (on permanent loan from the Public Archives of Canada, Ottawa, as quoted by Reid, *Atma Buddi Manas*, p. 15).

132. Kandinsky, *Art of Spiritual Harmony*, p. 30.

133. Reid, *Atma Buddi Manas*, p. 19.

134. Harris to Carr, November 4, 1932, Emily Carr papers, as quoted in Reid, *Atma Buddi Manas*, pp. 20–21. See also Douglas Worts, "Lawren S. Harris: Transition to Abstraction, 1934–45" (final paper, Master of Museum Studies Programme, University of Toronto, 1982), for a discussion of this period in Harris's career.

135. Christopher Jackson, *North by Northwest: The Arctic and Rocky Mountain Paintings of Lawren Harris 1924–1931* (Calgary: Glenbow Museum, 1991), p. 76, states that "Harris met Kandinsky and discussed his theories with him first-hand while Harris was artist-in-residence at Dartmouth College, Hanover, New Hampshire in the 1930's." This would have been impossible, as Kandinsky never visited the United States.

136. Reid, *Atma Buddi Manas*, p. 24. According to Reid, Harris had a complete collection of this publication in his library at his death.

137. In Bess Harris and R. G. P. Colgrove, eds., *Lawren Harris* (Toronto: The Macmillan Company of Canada, 1969), p. 3.

138. Kandinsky, *Art of Spiritual Harmony*, p. 51.

139. Reid, *Atma Buddi Manas*, p. 24.

140. Kandinsky, *Art of Spiritual Harmony*, p. 30.

141. Reid and others have noted the continuing landscape allusions in the later work of Harris.

142. Harris to Carr, Emily Carr Papers, as quoted by Reid, *Atma Buddi Manas*, p. 26.

143. RJ to Larisey, November 14, 1973, Jonson Gallery archives.

144. Ibid.

145. See RJ to Lawren and Bess Harris, August 5, 1938, AAA RJ 3:1962, where Jonson writes: "I am working on a plan for it [the Foundation] right now, but do not want to do anything final without your word of O.K. Because I realize you started the idea going and as it is therefore a kind of child of yours I want you with me 100% if we are to continue with it. If you are in favor and I rather imagine you are I want you to be the President of said Foundation." Harris replied on August 19 (AAA RJ 3:1967) that he was "firstly a painter" and that the "Foundation is not basic, fundamental, primary. It can only become a success when the painters themselves produce works to justify it. And how many such works are there?—a good many of yours and damn little else as yet. . . . It may and perhaps should be a few years before most of the program will be justified. . . . As for me, I would rather be the humblest painter in the Transcendental Painting Group than ten thousand times president of any Foundation however excellent."

146. Lawren Harris, *Abstract Painting, A Disquisition* (Toronto: Rous and Mann Press, 1954), p. 8.

147. This work also displays Harris's interest in Jay Hambidge's theories of dynamic symmetry, which were being taught by Bisttram in Taos at the time. One can also detect the possible influence of Annie Besant and Charles W. Leadbeater's *Thought Forms* (1905); for instance, Plate G, *Gounod*, a thought-form produced by the performance of "Soldiers' Chorus" from *Faust*, illustrated in *Thought Forms*.

148. "Transcendental Painting Group Sends Exhibition to San Francisco to be Shown During World's Fair," *Santa Fe New Mexican*, January 17, 1939.

149. "I had visited the opening of the famous Guggenheim Foundation collection of non-objective or abstract pictures at Charleston, N.C. [sic], the largest collection of its kind in the world." Harris, in "Letters to the Editor," *Santa Fe New Mexican*, March 16, 1939.

150. Hilla Rebay, "Non-Objectivity is the Realm of the Spirit," in *Solomon R. Guggenheim Collection of Non-Objective Paintings*, exhibition catalogue for Gibbes Memorial Art Gallery show, Charleston, S.C. (New York: Solomon R. Guggenheim Foundation, 1938), p. 9.

151. "I knew Mr. McKinney [the organizer of the San Francisco exhibition] was having a fairly large representation from the Guggenheim collection for San Francisco and I was so deeply impressed by the local [New Mexico] works *in the same idiom* [emphasis mine] that I suggested to him that he see these pictures on his way west. . . . My suggestion was inspired by the fact that the Guggenheim collection is composed almost entirely of European works and that works of equal merit done by Americans with a somewhat new slant might prove a happy balance for the European canvases." Harris, "Letters to the Editor."

152. For a complete discussion of Rudhyar's life and career, see Robert C. Hay, "Dane Rudhyar and the Transcendental Painting Group of New Mexico" (master's thesis, Michigan State University, 1981), pp. 19–113; see also Alfred Morang, *Dane Rudhyar, Pioneer in Creative Synthesis* (New York: Lucis Publishing Co., 1939). Copy in Jonson Gallery archives.

153. Nicholai Fechin, the Taos landscape painter and father-in-law of Rudhyar, wrote in 1939: "It is to me a wonder how Rudhyar finds the vitality, interest, and energy at the same time to paint outstanding non-representational paintings." Quoted in "Dane Rudhyar Seedman," *Human Dimensions Quarterly*, vol. 3, no. 3 (Buffalo, N.Y.: Human Dimensions Institute, 1975), p. 7.

154. Dane Rudhyar, *Art As Release of Power* (Carmel, Calif.: Hamsa Publications, 1930). Copy in Jonson Gallery archives.

155. RJ to Larisey, November 14, 1973. In Jonson Gallery archives. In the same letter, Jonson remembers that Harris would frequently come to the Jonson house and "read about theosophy, Mme. Blavatsky, I think, followed by discussion."

156. Rudhyar, *Art As Release*, p. 9.

157. Ibid., p. 5.

158. In a July 23, 1938, letter to Pelton, Rudhyar wrote: "It may amuse you to know that I, too, am working on transcendental compositions. So far they have been only drawings, but I may indulge in paint before long. Curiously enough even the painters seem to appreciate very much my first efforts." (AAA 3426:189).

159. According to Hay, "Dane Rudhyar," p. 44, Rudhyar described his work as "an interplay among three figures under a bolt of lightning: one is feminine, one masculine, the third is an ironical kind of personage."

160. Morang, *Dane Rudhyar*, p. 17.

161. This unpublished manuscript was copyrighted by the American Foundation for Transcendental Painting, Inc., on October 14, 1938. The book was left unpublished due to the intervention of World War II. In Jonson Gallery archives.

162. As quoted by Hay, "Dane Rudhyar," p. 43.

163. Sketchbook notes, November 22, 1946, AAA 3427:82. Pelton made notes on Kandinsky's discussion of the color yellow and went on to discuss how the canvas can be "laced" over with linear movements "as an improvisation." Below these comments, Pelton drew a rough sketch with freely applied lines, echoing Kandinsky's Improvisations of circa 1911 to 1913. This cursory treatment can be compared with a full page of notes she made on reading a book on Paul Klee that noted specific works she admired.

164. See Arthur Wesley Dow, "Modernism in Art," a paper presented at the Annual Meeting of the College Art Association of America, Philadelphia, April 20–22, 1916, in *Art and Progress (American Magazine of Art)*, vol. 8 (January 1917), pp. 113–116.

165. Agnes Pelton, as quoted in a personality essay

by Annie Laurie Hopkins in the *Keyport Weekly,* November 1926. Typed manuscript in Jonson Gallery archives.

166. Ibid.

167. Margaret Stainer, *Agnes Pelton,* exhibition catalogue (Fremont, Calif.: Ohlone College Art Gallery, 1989). I would like to thank Ms. Stainer for her help in my research on Pelton.

168. Florence Pelton notebook entry, March 15, 1913, as quoted by Stainer, *Agnes Pelton,* p. 25.

169. Pelton was familiar with the Stieglitz group at the time of the Armory Show, as her October 6, 1933, letter to Raymond Jonson indicates: "I knew [Arthur Dove's] work some years ago when he was active with a group around Stieglitz about the time of the Armory Show in New York, 1913. They were fine small pictures rather romantically abstract or I had better say the reverse. If you feel drawn to them perhaps you will write him sometime." AAA RJ 4:2569.

170. Wassily Kandinsky, excerpt from *Concerning the Spiritual in Art,* in *Camera Work,* no. 39 (July 1912), p. 34.

171. Pelton, statement from *Imaginative Paintings* (New York: Knoedler Gallery, 1917). Typescript in Jonson Gallery archives.

172. Kandinsky, *Art of Spiritual Harmony,* p. 29.

173. Pelton, January 21, 1917. Typescript in Jonson Gallery archives.

174. Pelton, notebook entry, October 26, 1918. Typescript in Jonson Gallery archives.

175. Stainer, *Agnes Pelton,* p. 8.

176. Pelton, Montross Gallery exhibition catalogue, November 1929. Typescript in Jonson Gallery archives.

177. Kandinsky, *Art of Spiritual Harmony,* p. 25.

178. Ibid., p. 29.

179. Ibid., p. 24.

180. Wassily Kandinsky and Franz Marc, eds., *The Blue Rider Almanac,* new documentary edition, trans. Klaus Lankheit (New York: Da Capo Press, 1974), p. 147.

181. Pelton, undated manuscript, AAA 3427:180.

182. Pelton to Jonson, October 6, 1934, as quoted by Stainer, *Agnes Pelton,* p. 8.

183. Pelton produced a number of poetic statements to accompany her major paintings. AAA 3427:178.

184. Ed Garman, letter to the author, December 22, 1990. Garman notes that he did not retain a "strong impression" of Kandinsky's work at that time because he was completely absorbed and overwhelmed by the Vincent Van Gogh retrospective that was then on view.

185. Ibid.

186. Interview by Tiska Blankenship and Joe Traugott with Ed Garman, September 4, 1990. Transcript in Jonson Gallery archives.

187. Ed Garman, letter to author, December 22, 1990.

188. Ed Garman letter to author, January 24, 1991.

189. Ed Garman letter to author, December 22, 1990.

190. For Bisttram's biography and a general discussion of his artistic development, see Walt Wiggins, *The Transcendental Art of Emil Bisttram* (Ruidoso Downs, N.M.: Pintores Press, 1988), and Sharyn Rohlfsen Udall, *Modernist Painting,* pp. 196–198.

191. Rohlfsen Udall, *Modernist Painting,* p. 196.

192. As quoted in Jacqueline Decter, *Nicholas Roerich: The Life and Art of the Russian Master* (Rochester, Vt.: Park Street Press, 1989, p. 121). See also Shirley Meador, "Nicholas Roerich: Heroes, Myths, and Ageless Mountains," *American Artist,* December 1974, pp. 32–37, for a discussion of Roerich's life and work.

193. Typescript of Bisttram biographical interview, n.d., p. 6. Typescript courtesy Walt Wiggins.

194. Ibid.

195. Ibid., p. 9.

196. Bisttram, lecture at Smithville Flats, New York, October 15, 1971. Typescript courtesy of Walt Wiggins. I would like to thank Walt Wiggins for the information and documentation he made available to me in doing research on the Transcendental Painting Group.

197. Bauer's name does not appear in any of the extant Bisttram documentation. However, the visual evidence of Bisttram's interest in Bauer is overwhelming. Florence Pierce recalls Bisttram's discussing Bauer on many occasions, in particular Bauer's painting *Blue Balls,* about which various jokes were made. Interview with the author, March 28, 1991.

198. Emil Bisttram, "Art's Revolt in the Desert," *Art in America,* 1931, pp. 3–4.

199. Bisttram, lecture at Smithville Flats, New York, c. 1970. Recording courtesy of Walt Wiggins.

200. Bisttram later attributed the "discovery" of transparency to the scientists who gave us x-rays, thus allowing us to "look through one plane over another." Bisttram, lecture at Smithville Flats, New York, c. 1970. Recording courtesy of Walt Wiggins.

201. Kandinsky, *Art of Spiritual Harmony,* p. 25. It is important to point out that Bisttram's ideas about color, as well as other formal aspects of art, were not derived from Kandinsky alone. Many of his other sources, however, held beliefs similar to Kandinsky's or were informed by the same ideas that inspired Kandinsky. Thus, Bisttram's use of color can be traced not only to Dr. Denman W. Ross's theories, but also to such figures as Shri Vishwanath Keskar, who gave a studio talk at the Roerich Institute in February 1930 (reproduced in Wiggins, *Transcendental Art of Emil Bisttram,* pp. 85–91). That talk concentrated heavily on the spiritual aspects of color and drew heavily from Charles W. Leadbeater's "Key to the Meanings of Color" in his *Man Visible and Invisible* (London: Theosophical Publishing Society, 1902). Keskar's identification of yellow as the color of intellect and blue as the color of spirituality corresponds

with that of Leadbeater, for example. But while Kandinsky agreed with the theosophists that blue was a spiritual color, he saw yellow as a typically earthly color. Bisttram, like Kandinsky before him, assimilated numerous ideas into his own system of thought. For a discussion of Kandinsky's sources, see Sixten Ringbom, *The Sounding Cosmos.*

202. Florence Pierce, conversation with the author, March 28, 1991.

203. Lecture at Smithville Flats, New York, October 15, 1971. Typescript courtesy of Walt Wiggins.

204. Florence Pierce recently recalled that such indoctrination was not necessarily "liberating" but rather "formal" and "academic." Conversation with the author, March 28, 1991.

205. In Harwood Foundation files, Taos, N.M. Copy courtesy of Walt Wiggins.

206. Wassily Kandinsky, *Point and Line to Plane,* trans. Howard Dearstyne and Hilla Rebay (New York: Solomon R. Guggenheim Foundation for the Museum of Non-Objective Painting, 1947; reprint ed., New York: Dover, 1979), pp. 43–45. Florence Pierce recalls Bisttram's emphasis on Kandinsky's ideas on music and painting and remarks that Bisttram frequently required his students to do "Symphony in Blue" or "Symphony in Red." Interview with the author March 28, 1991.

207. The Kandinsky illustrations in question are pp. 130–131 and figures 89 and 90 in *Point and Line to Plane.* The exercises are in Harwood Foundation files, Taos, N.M., n.d. While these notes could easily date from later than the 1938–1941 period, they correspond substantially with Florence Pierce's recollections of the curriculum she and her fellow students were offered in the late 1930s.

208. Iris Barry of the film department at MOMA wrote to cartoonist Max Fleischer about the film. In June 1940 Fleischer wrote Pierce of the difficulties in finding an audience and funding for such projects. He did, however, recognize the serious, spiritual underpinnings for Pierce's film: "These things are way ahead of this time and unfortunately, one cannot take a canvas, brush, and paint and continue the effort. This letter is not intended to discourage such efforts, but in times like these, when civilization seems to be making desperate efforts to avoid its own destruction, the searcher for abstract art must find himself in a lonesome spot indeed. There may come a time . . . when our thoughts and efforts can be more logically directed towards the higher things in life, but the present trend of humanity is indeed discouraging, particularly for the higher arts." (Max Fleischer to Horace Towner Pierce, June 10, 1940, transcript in Jonson Gallery files)

209. Interview with Florence Pierce on April 29, 1986; in Jonson Gallery files.

210. In 1941 Rudhyar was present at the viewing of Fischinger's work at the Museum of Non-Objective Painting. By this time the resentment toward Rebay and all those associated with her was obvious: "I saw the Guggenheim place and heard the Baroness gush

out. Whooo!—it would make anyone with sense hate abstract art and the word 'spiritual.' There were also abstract films, very unimaginative, by the man who did parts of 'Fantasia.' People are so damned literal! When music goes with staccatos [sic] eighth-notes, the film goes . . . <ooo at full speed 'til your eyes get completely whoozy. What a pity Pierce did not do his film. It would have been so immensely greater." Rudhyar to RJ, June 5, 1941, AAA RJ 5:2731.

211. William Lumpkins, letter to author, October 12, 1990. Walt Wiggins, *William Lumpkins, Pioneer Abstract Expressionist* (Ruidoso Downs, N.M.: Pintores Press, 1990), p. 73, places the date of Lumpkins's meeting with Bisttram in 1937.

212. Lumpkins to author, October 12, 1990.

213. Wiggins, *Lumpkins,* p. 13.

214. Lumpkins to author, October 12, 1990.

215. Anna Cora Winchell, *San Francisco Chronicle,* March 17, 1915, p. 24, as quoted in Joseph Armstrong Baird, Jr., ed., *From Exposition to Exposition: Progressive and Conservative Northern California Painting, 1915–1939* (Sacramento: Crocker Art Museum, 1981), p. 11.

216. Further exhibitions of the Blue Four were held in 1925 at the Stanford University Gallery and Mills College Gallery; in 1926 at the California School of Fine Arts (San Francisco), the San Francisco Conservatory of Music, the Los Angeles Museum, UCLA, the Denny and Watrius Studios (Carmel), and the University of Washington (Seattle); in 1927 at the Spokane Art Association, the Fine Arts Building (San Diego), the Oakland Museum, and the Portland Museum (Portland, Oregon); in 1928 at the Los Angeles Museum and the Withorne and Swan Department Store (Oakland); in 1930 at the Braxton Gallery (Hollywood) and Hale Brothers (San Francisco); in 1931 at the Biblioteca Nacional de Mexico (Mexico City) and the California Palace of the Legion of Honor (San Francisco); in 1932 at the Faulkner Memorial Art Gallery (Santa Barbara), the Arts Club (Chicago), the Renaissance Society (University of Chicago); in 1933 at the Oakland Art Gallery and the Los Angeles Museum; in 1936 at the Stendahl Art Gallery (Los Angeles), the Cornish School (Seattle), and the Henri Art Gallery, University of Washington (Seattle); in 1937 at the San Francisco Museum of Art, the Los Angeles Museum, and UCLA.

217. Louis Siegriest interview with Corinne Gilb, December 22, 1933. AAA 3978:417.

218. Ibid., 418.

219. Galka Scheyer, application form for a John Simon Guggenheim Memorial Foundation Fellowship, 1940. The fellowship Scheyer sought would have supported a teaching project, Free Imaginative and Creative Art, for underprivileged children and adolescents. Courtesy the Fischinger Archive.

220. Edward Weston, *The Daybooks of Edward Weston,* ed. Nancy Newhall, vol. 2 (California), (New York: Horizon Press in collaboration with the George Eastman House, Rochester, N.Y., 1966), p. 30. Weston wrote that Kandinsky is "one of the few

moderns whose work will live: he has something very personal, genuine—he has both intellectual and emotional ecstasy. This print will bring me much joy." Diary entry from July 21, 1927.

221. Kandinsky to Galka Scheyer, May 9, 1931, as quoted in Robert Haas, "The Blue Four," *du,* June 1975, n.p. My translation from the German.

222. Kandinsky to Scheyer, May 2, 1924, as quoted in Haas, "Blue Four." My translation.

223. As quoted by C.D., "Views on Kandinsky by a Member of the Younger Generation," *The Carmelite,* April 24, 1929, p. 9.

224. *The Argus,* vol. 4, no. 6, March 1929.

225. Ibid., vol. 5, no. 1, April 1929.

226. Ibid.

227. As quoted by C.D., "Views on Kandinsky," p. 9.

228. Scheyer to Kandinsky, March 11, 1936, as quoted in Amy Baker Sandback, "Galka Scheyer: Print Emissary," *Print Collector's Newsletter,* vol. 21, no. 2 (1990), p. 49.

229. Kandinsky to Scheyer, as quoted in Amy Baker Sandback, "Blue Heights Drive," *Artforum,* March 1990, p. 124.

230. Scheyer to the Blue Four, October 15, 1926, AAA:1858.

231. "Art Reviews Briefly Told," unidentified newspaper clipping. Courtesy Fischinger Archive, Los Angeles.

232. Merle Armitage, untitled review, *Topics of the Town,* no. 6, March 10, 1930.

233. Elise Armitage was born in 1900 in Philadelphia and studied art at the Pennsylvania Academy of Fine Arts. For the Armitage biography, see *Elise,* exhibition brochure (Los Angeles: Turner Dailey Gallery, n.d.).

234. Conversation with Elfriede Fischinger and William Moritz, October 14, 1991. I would like to thank Mrs. Fischinger and Mr. Moritz for their invaluable help in my research on Fischinger.

235. Ibid.

236. Undated (c. 1939?) letter from Karl Nierendorf to Oscar Fischinger. Courtesy Fischinger archives.

237. Galka Scheyer to Kandinsky, October 3, 1937. Original in Norton Simon/Galka Scheyer archives.

238. William Moritz, "The Films of Oscar Fischinger," *Film Culture,* nos. 58–60 (New York: H. Gant, 1974), p. 44.

239. William Moritz, "Abstract Film and Color Music," in *The Spiritual in Art, Abstract Painting 1890–1985,* exhibition catalogue (New York: Los Angeles County Museum of Art and Abbeville Press, 1986), p. 301.

240. William Moritz, "You Can't Get Then from Now," *Journal: Southern California Art Magazine,* no. 29 (Summer 1981), pp. 27–33, 70–72.

241. Moritz ("You Can't Get Then," p. 30) has noted that "while Oskar found Bauer pompous and definitely preferred the paintings of Klee, Mondrian, Kandinsky, and Feininger, something of Bauer's serial compositions of the late twenties through the mid-thirties (the triptychs and tetra-ptychons with musical titles that Rebay used as illustrations in most of her publications), a sense of lightness and geometrical substitution, may have influenced Oskar's serial designs in films like *Allegretto* and *Radio Dynamics,* or in Oskar's serial paintings."

242. Walt Disney, transcript of a story meeting on *Fantasia,* February 28, 1939, as cited by Moritz in "Fischinger at Disney (Or, Oskar in the Mousetrap)," *Millimeter,* vol. 5, no. 2 (February 1977), p. 66.

243. Moritz, "Films of Oskar Fischinger," p. 65.

244. Ibid., p. 67. In "You Can't Get Then," p. 2, Moritz has also speculated that these works are a satirical comment on his stormy dealings with Hilla Rebay at MNOP.

245. For Merrild biography and artistic development, see Victoria Dailey, *Knud Merrild,* exhibition catalogue, (Los Angeles: Steve Turner Gallery, September–November 1991), and Susan Ehrlich, "Knud Merrild," in Ehrlich and Barry M. Heisler, *Turning the Tide: Early Los Angeles Modernists, 1920–1956,* exhibition catalogue (Santa Barbara: Santa Barbara Museum of Art, 1990), pp. 138–142. I would like to thank Victoria Dailey and Steve Turner for their help in my research on Merrild.

246. Knud Merrild, as quoted in *Knud Merrild,* exhibition brochure (New York: Boyer Galleries, February 1939).

247. Henrietta Shore (1880–1963) was very interested and knowledgeable about Kandinsky, but her work remained almost exclusively nature-based and did not display any significant influence of Kandinsky. See Susan Ehrlich, *Turning the Tide,* pp. 150–152.

248. Susan Ehrlich, *Turning the Tide: Early Los Angeles Modernists, 1920–1956,* exhibition brochure (reprinted from *Art of California Magazine*) (Laguna Beach, Calif.: Laguna Art Museum, July–September 1990, n.p.), has discussed the growth of postsurrealism in the context of Hollywood culture.

249. Louise Arensberg to John Davis Hatch, April 24, (1934?), John Davis Hatch papers, Archives of American Art, as quoted by Barry M. Heisler, "Modernism in Southern California, 1920–1956: Reflections on the Art and the Times," in Susan Ehrlich and Heisler, *Turning the Tide: Early Los Angeles Modernists, 1920–1956,* exhibition catalogue (Santa Barbara: Santa Barbara Museum of Art, 1990), p. 14.

Kandinsky and American Abstraction: New York and Europe in the 1930s and 1940s

Marianne Lorenz

Kandinsky's dramatic debut in America in the teens and the rapid assimilation of his work by a limited number of important American artists in the 1920s was followed in the 1930s by a more widespread dissemination that permitted a growing number of American artists to become involved in his art and ideas. An increasingly sophisticated, well-educated, and committed artistic community grew in its understanding of Kandinsky's non-objective art through international travel and education, the efforts of Hilla Rebay and the Museum of Non-Objective Painting, and major exhibitions at the Valentine and Nierendorf galleries in New York. Kandinsky's prominence in the abstract art establishment was evidenced in invitations for him to teach at the Art Students League in 1931 and to serve as artist-in-residence at Black Mountain College in 1935 (he declined both offers). Alfred Barr's 1936 exhibition and catalogue, *Cubism and Abstract Art,* expanded on Sheldon Cheney's and Arthur J. Eddy's books and demonstrated to a new generation of artists the potential of Kandinsky's ideas. Thus, the 1930s saw Kandinsky take his place with Picasso, Mondrian, and Marcel Duchamp as one of the most influential artists in America.[1]

Museum of Non-Objective Painting

If it were possible to single out one person whose reach exceeded all others in the story of Kandinsky and America during this period, it would be Hilla Rebay. Born in Strassburg, Alsace, to a noble family, Rebay began taking classes in theosophy from Rudolf Steiner at the age of fourteen. In Freiburg, where the family moved one year after her birth, Rebay studied painting, drawing, and music. During a year at the Académie Julian in Paris (1909–1910), Rebay decided to commit her life to art. Her interest in theosophy deepened at this time as well: "The deeper I delve into it [theosophy], the happier it makes me; everything becomes clear, especially that spiritual sensitivity necessary for an artist to experience nature and to feel one with it."[2] In the ensuing years Rebay continued her art studies in Munich and Paris, steeping herself in the work of Ferdinand Hodler, Eugène Delacroix, the impressionists, the neo-impressionists, and other modernists.

Rebay's identification with modernism evidenced itself very early in her friendships with Hans Arp, Hans Richter, and Wilhelm Lehmbruck. Arp was of particular significance to Rebay as it was he who supplied her with Kandinsky's *Über das Geistige in der Kunst* in 1916. Further exposure to Kandinsky came in the fall of the same year, when Rebay became associated with Herwarth Walden's Berlin gallery, Der Sturm. Through Walden, Rebay was able to study in depth the work of Kandinsky, Marc, Klee, and other German avant-garde painters.[3] At Der Sturm, Rebay also met and fell in love with Walden's gallery assistant, Rudolf Bauer. Bauer, who became a lifelong obsession for Rebay, was already a fervent advocate of Kandinsky, considering him "the strongest and most advanced of all—theoretically and practically, synthetically and analytically."[4] Bauer's work, at the time considered by many to be overly and poorly derivative of Kandinsky, never received the universal acclaim that accrued to

173

Fig. 5.1 (Left to right): Irene Guggenheim, Vassily Kandinsky, Hilla Rebay, and Solomon R. Guggenheim at the Bauhaus, Dessau, 1930. Courtesy Solomon R. Guggenheim Museum Archives, New York

Kandinsky's oeuvre. Rebay's own inherent interest and belief in Kandinsky's art and ideas were, however, reinforced and deepened at their earliest stages by an artist whom Rebay admired and respected highly.

In 1927 Rebay moved to the United States and immediately began to make important contacts in New York art circles. She arranged to have exhibitions of her own work in galleries and museums in New York and Massachusetts, and in 1928 Solomon R. Guggenheim commissioned her to do his portrait. By this time, her belief in the power and greatness of the art of Kandinsky and Bauer had taken on a messianic quality, and she used the portrait sittings to introduce Guggenheim to non-objective art. Hoping to create a market and audience for the work of Kandinsky, Bauer, Klee, and other non-objective artists, she began to fill her studio with works by those painters.[5] Guggenheim was interested enough to purchase a work by Kandinsky,[6] and Rebay arranged a meeting between the artist and his new patron in Europe in the spring of 1929. At that time, Guggenheim purchased Kandinsky's *Composition 8* (1923). Thus began America's largest and most influential collection of Kandinsky's work.

Initially, Guggenheim appeared to be as interested in the work of Bauer as he was in Kandinsky's paintings. In the summer of 1929 he began paying Bauer a monthly stipend in return for his paintings. Guggenheim's interest in Bauer may have been the result of Rebay's influence, as she was anxious to have Bauer's work be a major part of the Guggenheim collection, but Guggenheim's reported preference for "geometric" or "constructivist" works may also have played a role.[7]

By 1931 the Guggenheims' growing collection of non-objective painting was installed in a suite at the Plaza Hotel, as no permanent display space had been decided on. The collection was not available for general public viewing until later in the decade. The late thirties saw major exhibitions of the collection at the Gibbes Memorial Art Gallery in Charleston, South Carolina (1936 and 1938), the Philadelphia Art Alliance (1937), and the Baltimore Museum of Art (1939). Response to these shows was mixed. Charleston received them with grace and interest (see page 86). In Baltimore, the headlines read "Paintings That Have No Sense." Kandinsky's *Painting with White Form* (1913) was illustrated (incorrectly, right side down) with the caption "You have to send your spirit into space to understand this." The reviewer, who had obviously read Rebay's catalogue, took Rebay's high-minded prose and used it mockingly to poke fun at non-objectivity:

> And now see what the New Year has brought to Baltimore—Non-Objective Paintings. You look at them and instantly your Intuition is supposed to begin working. This in turn develops your Highest Intelligence. Then comes beauty through space relationship. After that you get Balance. Not like the man on the flying trapeze, but Balance in life which develops refinement and spiritual faculties. DO YOU GRASP IT? YES? NO?[8]

Rebay's lecture on the night of the opening was covered in less facetious terms. Rebay characterized surrealism as a "crazysm [sic], the result of inferiority complex or criminal foolishness," and stated that intuition, upon which non-objective art is based, would "lead and rule human races" and would help nations to live together "harmoniously."[9]

Luxurious catalogues of the exhibitions were produced, and Rebay was careful to distribute them to her extensive network of artists throughout America. Rebay's introductory essays focused on the spiritual, intuitive qualities of non-objectivity and did not discuss the artists in great detail. Her words, clearly addressed to the nonspecialist, encouraged the audience

to enjoy the color and form combinations and to discard preconceived ideas about meaning and representation. Kandinsky, of course, was completely behind these exhibitions and saw them as "strong propaganda"[10] for non-objective art that could compete with the efforts the surrealists were making to bring their art before a larger public. Despite a few factual errors in his biography and a dispute with Rebay over whether his work should be termed "abstract" or "non-objective," Kandinsky was heartened by the exposure and educational function he thought the catalogue to the Charleston exhibition would have.[11] In the catalogue accompanying the Philadelphia exhibition, Rebay credited Kandinsky as "the first painter with such intuitive and spiritual freedom as to eliminate entirely the unnecessary hindrance of intellect for the art of vision." At the same time, however, Bauer was acclaimed as "the greatest master of non-objectivity," whose "perfection of composition" had "never been reached by anyone before."[12] The catalogues, while not necessarily complete and accurate accounts of non-objective art, did provide the American public and artists with an in-depth exposure to Kandinsky's work and the basic ideas that underlay the non-objective ideal in painting.

The catalogues and exhibitions of the collection outside New York created a national awareness of non-objective art. Thus, when in late May 1939 the collection was placed on permanent display in a rented space on East 54th Street, it found an immediate and large audience. Joan M. Lukach reports that it was the work of Kandinsky that impressed those who recalled their visits to the Museum of Non-Objective Painting. Emily Genauer's review of the museum's opening singled out Kandinsky's works for particular praise, calling them "complex, full of action, invested with a subtle, sensitively balanced counterpoint, variations in tone, shape and texture which are endlessly fascinating."[13]

Rebay's own abstract painting began to show the influence of her encounter with Kandinsky quite early, as *Composition No. 9* (1916; plate 54) demonstrates. The improvisational, freely painted, but densely composed organization reflects her initial experiments with Kandinsky's work from about 1913 to 1917. *Untitled* (c. 1944; plate 55) represents Rebay's full assimilation of Kandinsky's Bauhaus works. Rebay's ongoing personal interest in Kandinsky's work and ideas and the incorporation of these into her painting made her an insightful mentor to artists working non-objectively.

Rebay's goal of encouraging artists interested in non-objectivity made her a well-known, if not always universally popular, figure among young painters. Artists were encouraged to submit their works to the museum for criticism and possible exhibition. In addition, the Guggenheim Foundation provided funds for deserving artists (stipends varied from $50 to $150 a month). The dispersal of these funds was determined by Rebay. The presence of the museum in the heart of Manhattan combined with the potential for financial support through Guggenheim's (via Rebay's) largesse made the Museum of Non-Objective Painting very visible to New York artists. Reproductions of Kandinsky's work were sold to the public, as were the catalogues of the collection and various exhibitions. Rebay also employed young artists at the museum as guards, janitors, lecturers, and assistants. Thus, for someone interested in working in a non-objective style, Rebay and the museum provided financial, career, and artistic opportunities.

Given Rebay's strong personality and by this time somewhat dogmatic ideas about what constituted genuine non-objective art, it is not surprising that a good many artists who became associated with the museum produced what could be called "cookie cutter" non-objective painting. Under Rebay's (and later Bauer's) tutelage, artists eager for support and exhibition opportunities often painted openly in the style of Kandinsky or Bauer.[14] These derivative works were frequently supplemented (away from Rebay's watchful eye) or followed by works that incorporated Kandinsky's lessons while at the same time revealing the artists' own visions.

Rebay's reach extended as far as Seattle, where she supported the work of Maude Kerns, but she also had an influence in the Midwest. Lucia Stern in Milwaukee was able, through her contact with Rebay, to incorporate non-objective ideas into her textiles (fig. 5.3). Stern and her husband, in turn, arranged for the exhibition of Kandinsky's work in Milwaukee.[15] In Dayton, Ohio, Dwinell Grant, a student at the Dayton Art Institute and later an art instructor at Wittenberg University, was in contact with Rebay by 1937. By 1941, Grant's work had been purchased by Guggenheim, and he had been hired as Rebay's assistant in New York. Two watercolors, *Sophistication No. 66* (1938) and *Yellow Circle* (1938; plates 56, 57), demonstrate that before leaving Ohio to work for Rebay, Grant had assimilated Kandinsky's geometric style. His paintings of the period carried titles, such as *Improvisation, Light and Heavy,* and *Scherzo,* reminiscent of Kandinsky and indicative of his familiarity with *The Art of Spiritual Harmony.* For Grant, non-objectivity afforded the opportunity to "produce a color art that is as dynamic and as moving as music and an art that is rid of the confining, restricting bonds of race or nationality."[16]

At the time, Grant was also an aspiring filmmaker and was anxious to go to New York to produce a non-objective film. In 1939 Rebay had begun plans for a film center to be housed in the proposed Guggenheim museum. Although the center never materialized, Rebay supported non-objective filmmakers such as Norman McLaren, Hans Richter, John and James

Fig. 5.3 Lucia Stern.
COMPOSITION XXI, 1948.
Ink, watercolor, metallic paints, and netting paper, 13½ × 9″ (34.6 × 23 cm)
Milwaukee Art Museum, Anonymous Gift
(Photograph by Efraim Lev-er)

Whitney, and Oskar Fischinger, and non-objective films were nonetheless made an integral part of the museum's program, often being screened after a gallery talk or lecture by Rebay. Learning of Grant's film aspirations, Rebay sent him a copy of one of Oskar Fischinger's films and offered to loan him film equipment. *Contrathemis,* Grant's 1941 non-objective film, capitalizes on Kandinsky's lines, circles, and planes to approximate visually what had always been possible in music. The drawings for this film (plate 58) demonstrate Grant's reliance on Kandinsky's Bauhaus vocabulary in his conception. Grant wanted to extend the possibilities of "musical painting" to the realm of film in an effort to expand and broaden the audience: "The innate relationship of music and painting, especially the non-objective form of the latter, is an accepted fact with the art critics of today. Through a collaboration of painter, musician, and technical staff in the making of animated sound, color movies, this fact may be demonstrated to the general public."[17]

Rolph Scarlett

Rolph Scarlett, a Canadian by birth, was associated with the Museum of Non-Objective Painting from 1938 to 1951. Scarlett's uncle was in the jewelry business, and Scarlett apprenticed himself to him in order to have a useful trade. At the age of eighteen Scarlett moved to New York. Scarlett, who had little formal art training, gained firsthand exposure to modernism in 1913, when he visited the Armory Show, and again in 1923, when he met Paul Klee during a business trip to Switzerland. By 1924, he was working abstractly, experimenting with cubist shapes and freely applied areas of pure color. Scarlett was in Hollywood from the late 1920s to the early 1930s, designing sets for Pathé Studios and for the production *Man and Superman* at the Pasadena Playhouse. Although there were opportunities during this period for him to view the work of Kandinsky through the Blue Four exhibitions, Scarlett recalled having seen only black-and-white reproductions of Kandinsky's work until he visited Rebay at the Museum of Non-Objective Painting in 1936.[18] *Untitled* (c. 1936; plate 59) demonstrates Scarlett's response to first seeing Kandinsky's early improvisations such as *Fugue* and *Painting with White Border,* both of 1913. Scarlett recalled his first impressions:

> The experience was overwhelming to me, for I was seeing them in full size and color. The wonder of them. The freshness, the beauty. This took the blinders off my eyes and I saw in them the wonder of his creativity. These paintings intimately exposed the human soul. They talked to me. They had a sort of cosmic order that made me feel at peace and at home for perhaps the first time in my life. The effect was hypnotizing.[19]

These words, which speak to an almost transcendent power that Kandinsky's work held for Scarlett and other Americans, do not mean, however, that Scarlett subscribed to the theosophical underpinnings of Kandinsky's early writings. And like Dwinell Grant and many other artists of the 1930s who were influenced by Kandinsky's Bauhaus work, Scarlett did not find a spiritual interpretation of the Russian's work particularly compelling:

> Rebay had a very emotional temperament and she fancied herself a spiritualist. She would look into Bauer's work or Kandinsky's work and find something spiritualistic that could be read into it. Kandinsky did that too. It was a mistake. The main thing is not spiritualism or metaphysical phenomena, it's esthetics, order, form, color and rhythm.[20]

Thus, Scarlett, Grant, and other American abstract artists sought during the 1930s and 1940s to ground their works in clearly defined aesthetic terms and refrained from theories of divine intervention in the creation of the work of art. This more practical approach to the creative process did not prevent them from attempting to create works of art that in some way were expressive of "mysticism, inner order, and intrigue."[21] Scarlett's drawings and paintings of the period clearly reveal his interest in creating, like Kandinsky, a "cosmic order" through the juxtaposition and ordering of color and shape against a picture plane which Kandinsky had shown to be elastic in nature.[22] Scarlett's description of non-objective painting reflects to a great degree his interest in the purely artistic or visual aspects of Kandinsky's work: "Let him [the beholder of non-objective painting] trace for himself the rhythm pattern of the lines and other elements. Study the juxtaposition of mass against mass, feel the receding and advancing of the colors in spiritual space."[23]

Scarlett was hired as a lecturer at the museum and became one of Rebay's prized artists; much of his work of the period was acquired by Guggenheim for the collection. Of all the artists associated with the museum, Scarlett had perhaps the most contact with Bauer, who was brought by Guggenheim to New York in 1939. Rebay encouraged artists associated with the museum to study Bauer's work carefully, and Scarlett spent many hours speaking to him personally and having him critique his work. In much of Scarlett's painting of the period, then, the influence of Kandinsky is to be detected only through the more rigid veil of Bauer's geometric style.

John Sennhauser

John Sennhauser joined the Museum of Non-Objective Painting staff in 1943. Sennhauser, who immigrated to the United States from Switzerland in 1928, began experimenting with abstraction while studying at Cooper Union in the early 1930s. The rigid interlocking areas of geometric color in his early abstractions gave way in 1943 to a more improvisational, freely conceived style based on Kandinsky's non-objective paintings. His series of Black Lines paintings, done shortly after he began working at the museum, pay homage in their title to Kandinsky's 1913 work of the same name but go beyond that work to explore in a more general way Kandinsky's pictorial discoveries. In *Black Lines No. 2* (1943; plate 62), Sennhauser explores Kandinsky's combination of large color areas with an overlay of black linear elements, but Sennhauser has set the pictorial drama against a gray-green background. The palette of blue, yellow, red, green, and orange echoes that of Kandinsky's *Black Lines I* (see fig. 3.2), but Sennhauser himself had long worked with similar colors. Sennhauser's overall statement is bolder and contains fewer lyrical passages than Kandinsky's, but the opening up of his pictorial space combined with the improvisational linear techniques shows his debt to his mentor. *Black Lines No. 2* demonstrates Sennhauser's interest in the expressive quality of certain motifs Kandinsky employed in paintings such as *Blue Circle* (1922). With *Black Lines No. 4* (1943; plate 63), Sennhauser has further opened up the space of the picture and has juxtaposed straight linear accents with curvilinear ones. The combination of such elements with "points" of red, blue, and brown and advancing planes of color indicates that Sennhauser may have read *Point and Line to Plane* during this period.

As Virginia Mecklenburg has pointed out, Sennhauser's aims for his painting during the period coincided with those Rebay espoused, namely the mystical:

Lines, planes, forms, colors, rhythmically moving . . . intuitively conceived . . . intuitively born of life eternal. Plastic integration of form and space of body and spirit. . . . The everlasting negative in all its positive manifestations, pure as immortality, free as the infinite. . . . The essence of all that is and is not . . . The Mythical . . . Timeless . . . Mystical . . .[24]

While most artists did not have the daily exposure to Kandinsky's work that Grant, Scarlett, and Sennhauser did, the reach of the Museum of Non-Objective Painting penetrated to virtually every corner of artistic activity in New York during the period. The importance and influence of the museum and Rebay can be seen in the extent to which some abstract artists protested Rebay's ideas. In 1937 *Art Front* published a letter signed by Hananiah Harari, Jan Matulka, Byron Browne, and other abstract artists who disagreed with Rebay's espousal of the spiritual foundations of abstract art:

> We wish it understood that with the works of art themselves and with the artists who created the works in Mr. Guggenheim's collection, we will not disagree. But we cannot accept with approbation the opinions which Baroness Rebay seems to have that abstract art has "no meaning and represents nothing," that it is the "prophet of spiritual life," something "unearthly"; that abstractions are "worlds of their own" achieved as their creators "turned away from contemplation of earth." The meaning implied in these phrases is that abstract artists preclude from their works, and lives too (for after all, an artist must live some super-worldly existence in order to create super-worldly works of art), worldly realities and devote themselves to making spiritual squares, and "triangles, perhaps, less spiritual," which will exalt a certain few souls who have managed, or can afford, to put aside "materialism."
>
> We abstract artists are, of course, first to recognize that any good work of art has its own justification, that it has the effect of bringing joyful ecstasy to a sensitive spectator, that there is such a thing as an esthetic emotion, which is a particular emotion, caused by a particular created harmony of lines, colors and forms. But the forms may not be so ghostly-pure-spirit-suspended as Baroness Rebay would wish. Who knows whether the divorce of cosmic atmosphere and earthly air is so absolute?[25]

This letter makes clear that the argument here is not with Kandinsky and Bauer (with whom the collection was equated) but rather with Rebay's interpretation of their work. American artists of the period, who were struggling on various fronts (artistic, political, economic, and social), were anxious to couple art with life, not isolate it in esoteric realms of mysticism where it could be ridiculed by the press and public, as happened in Baltimore. Two years later, in 1939, Stuart Davis carried the argument one step further, indicting Bauer and Rebay for being "reactionary":

> In abstract art it [reactionary art] would be the "non-objectivism" of the Baroness Rebay and the "non-objective" art king, Bauer. The Baroness Rebay's pronouncement that art "is like music: it means nothing" and it is "not for the masses, but for the elite of humanity" is the essence of reaction, striking at the objective truth of the democratic social origin and meaning of art.[26]

But while some may have disagreed with the spin Rebay placed on Kandinsky's ideas, this did not prevent many American abstract artists from experimenting with Kandinsky's visual language at some point in their careers. The dubious social/philosophical connotations of Kandinsky's non-objectivity as expressed through Rebay clearly touched a nerve with American

Fig. 5.4 Third floor, Solomon R. Guggenheim Foundation Museum of Non-Objective Painting, New York. Paintings, left to right: Rudolf Bauer, *INTERMEZZO* (oil on canvas); Bauer, *COLORED SWINGING* (oil on canvas); Bauer, *TOP POINT EFFICIENCY*; Kandinsky, *COMPOSITION NO. 8* (oil on canvas); Kandinsky, *WHITE EDGE* (oil on canvas). Courtesy Solomon R. Guggenheim Museum Archives

abstractionists who saw their work in more utilitarian terms, but his significant contributions to the development of modernism made him indispensable to artists of the period. As Mecklenburg has noted, artistic theories and practices during this period were often difficult to "disentangle," as the avant-garde "blended sources, drawing formal devices from one group, theoretical concerns from others."[27]

Burgoyne Diller

Fig. 5.5 Burgoyne Diller.
UNTITLED, 1933.
Watercolor and ink on paper,
12 × 9'' (30.76 × 23 cm)
Location unknown
(Photograph courtesy Meredith
Long & Company)

One of those to flirt briefly with Kandinsky before developing a fully mature abstract style associated with Mondrian was Burgoyne Diller. By the time he enrolled in the Art Students League in 1929, Diller was absorbing the lessons of Cézanne's late work. While at the league, Diller experimented with cubism under the tutelage of Jan Matulka, who introduced his students to a variety of modernist currents. In 1932 Hans Hofmann came to teach at the league. Diller joined his class despite the fact that Diller's penchant for the lucid was at odds with Hofmann's expressionist style.[28] Diller was known among his peers for his knowledge of and interest in European modernism. He had copies of *Cahiers d'Art* in his home and was aware of major developments in Europe. His position was such that in 1934 Katherine Dreier asked him to organize a group of artists to explore exhibition and publication possibilities for American abstract artists.[29]

In November 1932, Kandinsky was given a one-man exhibition at the Valentine Gallery in New York. The reviewer for the *New York Times,* Elisabeth Luther Cary, relied heavily on *The Art of Spiritual Harmony* to explain the genesis and meaning of the works, which dated roughly between 1925 and 1932. Cary praised Kandinsky for his "liberality of mind," which allowed him to "invent combinations and gradations of color, red, yellow, blue, violet, with a sense of harmony that has grown to impressive proportions since his beginnings in this form of art. Free to limit these colors with a framework of line describing circles, triangles, other geometrical forms, linear arabesques, complications of lattice and scroll."[30]

The transformation in Diller's work the following year is a testament to the impact the Valentine Gallery exhibition likely had on his work. *Early Geometric* (1933; plate 64) interjects a number of independent linear and geometric elements characteristic of Kandinsky's Bauhaus work into an architectural, stagelike space. The band of color containing a row of five contrasting splotches of paint, the large biomorphic shapes, and whiplash lines are all to be found in *Secure Position* (1932) and *Light* (1930) and other works shown at Kandinsky's Valentine Gallery exhibition. In another untitled work from 1933 (fig. 5.5), Diller eliminates the stage space to create an open field in which the geometric elements can float freely. The intersecting triangles, floating circles, and semicircles anchored by a thin line are to be seen in Kandinsky's *Angular Swing* (1929) and *Round and Pointed* (1930; see fig. 4.3), also in the Valentine exhibition.[31]

If the Valentine Gallery exhibition showed Kandinsky to be a master of Bauhaus geometry, Christian Zervos's article in *Cahiers d'Art* in 1934 proved that Kandinsky was also a purveyor of exuberant biomorphism. The influence of *Cahiers d'Art* on American abstract artists is well documented, with Diller being a major source of the publication for his peers.[32] Zervos's article reproduces a number of Kandinsky's works from 1934, including *Each for Itself, Black Forms on White, In Between* (fig. 5.6), *Blue World,* and *Dominant Violet.*[33] These paintings were a strong counterpoint to the geometry of Kandinsky's earlier work and stimulated a number

Fig. 5.6 Vassily Kandinsky. *IN BETWEEN*, 1934. (Photograph of page from *Cahiers d'art*)

of experiments by American artists interested in fusing surrealist biomorphism with geometric abstraction. Kandinsky took his place alongside Miró, then, in introducing Americans to the expressive potential of the curvilinear and amorphous shapes associated with surrealism.

Alfred Barr recognized that Kandinsky's later work represented a departure from the strict geometry of his Bauhaus period: "In the last few years [Kandinsky] has turned to more organic forms, perhaps under the influence of the younger Parisians, Miró and Arp, to whom he pointed the way twenty years before."[34]

Diller was the director of the WPA mural program, and his commitment to abstraction made itself felt in the murals produced under his direction. His own 1934 designs for the project (now lost) attest to his continuing interest in geometric shapes poised in an ambiguous space. One of the largest and most important mural sites was the Williamsburg (Brooklyn) Housing Project, which Diller conceived as an experiment in wedding non-objective art with proletarian ideals:

> The decision to place abstract murals in these rooms was made because these areas were intended to provide a place of relaxation and entertainment for the tenants. The more arbitrary color, possible when not determined by the description of objects, enables the artist to place an emphasis on its psychological potential to stimulate relaxation. The arbitrary use of shapes provides an opportunity to create colorful patterns clearly related to the interior architecture and complementing the architect's intentions.[35]

Diller's description of the psychological working of color, of course, is a theory that Kandinsky discussed at length in *The Art of Spiritual Harmony*, with which Diller, as well as most abstract artists of the period, was undoubtedly familiar.

Ilya Bolotowsky

One of the artists who worked with Diller on the Williamsburg Project was Ilya Bolotowsky, a Russian who immigrated to New York in 1923. After studying at the National Academy of Design between 1924 and 1930, he spent ten months in Europe. His first experiments with abstraction in 1934 ultimately developed into a mature style based on the Neo-Plastic principles of Mondrian. During this period Bolotowsky explored, fleetingly, Kandinsky's ideas. *First Study for the Williamsburg Mural* (1936; plate 65), produced during a period of extensive experimentation by Bolotowsky, demonstrates the artist's interest in Kandinsky's Bauhaus vocabulary—a vocabulary he later claimed not to have understood and ultimately rejected.[36] Bolotowsky filled the picture plane with a densely packed configuration of geometric forms in this first study. His adoption of the intersecting circles and triangles and parallel lines of Kandinsky's Bauhaus work was at odds, however, with the overall density of the composition, and Bolotowsky's incorporation of geometric motifs proved more successful in later studies in which he voided the picture plane, thus allowing the motifs to float freely. The organic-geometric combinations are consistent with the work by Kandinsky, which Bolotowsky would have seen in *Cahiers d'Art,* the Museum of Non-Objective Painting, and the Valentine Gallery exhibition.

Bolotowsky, a founding member of the American Abstract Artists, was included in a number of group shows at the Museum of Non-Objective Painting. His comments on Rebay and her program typify the thoughts of his colleagues and reveal once again that Kandinsky was not cast in the same negative light that frequently shone on Rebay and Bauer:

> The Museum of Non-Objective Art developed a bit later than the Modern Museum. It started first as a small collection at the Plaza Hotel. They had weekly tea receptions the Baroness used to hold there. They had a nice collection—they had some horrors too—Rudolf Bauer and her own stuff, but many things were nice. . . . She was rather a difficult personality, like an opera prima donna. She was often impossible and overwhelming . . . and yet generous and impulsive.[37]

The "horrors" alluded to by Bolotowsky were considered by Edward Alden Jewell to be a new form of academicism:

> Let tempests threaten and break in full fury, the Museum of Nonobjective Painting goes its way unperturbed. Indeed, it has even announced plans that will involve departure from the present leased quarters in East Fifty-fourth Street, when a projected palace has been brought to completion on Fifth Avenue, almost adjoining the National Academy. Such neighborliness isn't as incongruous as it may first appear, for with the exception of Kandinsky's, the art sponsored by the Museum of Nonobjective Painting, or a very great deal of it, is purely academic too.[38]

For Jewell and others, then, the specter of an abstract academy threatened not from Kandinsky, whose work and words attested to a lively open-mindedness, but from the rigid attitudes of Bauer, who gave weekly criticism at the MNOP, and Rebay, who had control over purse and exhibition strings.

Alice Trumbull Mason

Like Bolotowsky, Alice Trumbull Mason was a founding member of the American Abstract Artists. From 1927 to 1931, Mason studied with Arshile Gorky, who introduced her to Kandinsky's work and may have made her aware of Kandinsky's "spiritual approach."[39] It seems unlikely, however, that Mason would have responded to Kandinsky's spiritual ideas, as she apparently rejected mysticism and theosophy early in life.[40] Adopting a completely abstract style in 1929, Mason was a favorite of Rebay, who bought her work for the Guggenheim collection and sent her a monthly stipend. Mason responded particularly well to Kandinsky's improvisational linear effects used in combination with fields of rich color. *Spring* (1931; plate 66) epitomizes Mason's adaptation of Kandinsky's whiplash lines and indeterminate color fields to create a fully non-objective expression of landscape. Her ongoing appreciation of Kandinsky's work is revealed in a letter she wrote to Rebay concerning the Kandinsky Memorial Exhibition. In her letter Mason notes that "it will be an outstanding event, reflecting . . . the consideration Kandinsky's work deserves."[41]

George L. K. Morris

The echo of Kandinsky's voice is heard briefly and unexpectedly in the work of another founder of American Abstract Artists, George L. K. Morris. Morris, whose family wealth allowed him to travel and work freely, had firsthand knowledge and exposure to the European tradition of Léger and Ozenfant (with whom he studied in 1930), as well as Hélion, Picasso, Braque, and Brancusi (whom he met during later European travels). Morris adopted the cubist framework of his mentors and friends and became an active proponent of advanced European and American art. *Untitled* (c. 1936–1938; plate 67) was done during the period when Morris was active in the publication of *Plastique,* with A. E. Gallatin of the Gallery of Living Art, Sophie Taeuber-Arp, and Cesar Domela. *Plastique,* according to its opening statement, was "devoted to the study and appreciation of concrete art."[42] *Concrete* was the term that Kandinsky preferred during this period in describing his own work:

> No, you must not believe that *Abstract* painting (which I prefer to call *concrete*) is a sort of music in painting. Each art has its own means of expression (form) and an exact *translation* from one art into another is—fortunately—impossible. What I would like understood is that the method of listening to a work of "pure" music is identical to that of seeing a work of "concrete" painting.[43]

Untitled shows clearly Morris's knowledge of Kandinsky works such as *In Between*—it will be recalled that this work was prominently reproduced in the 1934 *Cahiers d'Art* article devoted to Kandinsky—where an amoeba-shaped form with circular "eye" is topped with a geometric headdress. The remainder of the canvas is peppered with the intersecting triangles, arched triangles, and curvilinear lines that predominated in the 1937 exhibition of Kandinsky's work at the Nierendorf Gallery. In 1938 Nierendorf presented Three Masters of the Bauhaus: Kandinsky, Klee, Feininger, a show that contained other Paris-period biomorphic works, such as *The Good Contact* (1938), which Morris may have known. In *Untitled,* the presence of such biomorphic and geometric motifs against the broad areas of rich, amorphous colors creates a feeling that is reminiscent not of Arp or Miró, but of Kandinsky.[44]

Werner Drewes

Werner Drewes shares with Konrad Cramer exposure to Kandinsky in his native Germany. On a visit to Herwarth Walden's Der Sturm gallery in 1919, Drewes saw Kandinsky's work for the first time. Two years later he stayed one year at the Staatliches Bauhaus Weimar, where he studied with Johannes Itten, Paul Klee, and Oskar Schlemmer. From 1923 to 1927, Drewes undertook several extensive trips throughout Europe, the Orient, South America, and the United States. On his return to Germany, Drewes enrolled again at the Bauhaus, which by this time had moved to Dessau, and he began to attend Kandinsky's creative painting classes. When he graduated in 1928, his diploma was signed by Kandinsky and Mies van der Rohe. In 1930, Drewes left for New York, where he settled permanently and became an important figure in New York art circles.[45]

In early 1931, Drewes and Kandinsky began a correspondence that was to last until shortly before Kandinsky's death. These letters reveal Kandinsky to be a dedicated and supportive mentor who not only took an active interest in his former pupil but was highly inquisitive about the American art scene. Kandinsky frequently engaged the younger artist to help him in his dealings with collectors and exhibitions in America. He provided Drewes with an introduction to Katherine Dreier so that the young artist could see Kandinsky's recent work; this important contact led to Drewes being included in Société Anonyme exhibitions.[46] Kandinsky also made Drewes known to Myfanwy Evans, the editor of the English journal *Axis* who had demonstrated her interest in non-objective art by publishing an article on Kandinsky in the magazine's first issue.[47] For his part, Drewes kept Kandinsky up to date on Rebay's activities at the Museum of Non-Objective Painting, acting as a source of independent information when Kandinsky and Rebay's relationship was strained.

Kandinsky's letters also touched on his own philosophy of art and provided Drewes with important insights into his teacher's Bauhaus vocabulary:

> Painting is not a simple thing, but the completely concise, when the few means really harmonize, requires such a great concentration and inner tension, that the outwardly opulent, almost seems easier to achieve. When I place ten lines on the paper, it is not so crucial that *each one* be perfectly correct. The predominant correctness outweighs the small irregularities. When, however only one line out of three is wrong, then the whole thing is worthless. . . . Thus I explain my longstanding love of the circle—it is the most concise form of all the planes while at the same time containing an inexhaustible opulence. No other plane has this union of the precise and imprecise, of stable and unstable, etc, etc, in it, as the circle.[48]

Drewes began developing his non-objective style based on Kandinsky's art and teaching after 1932. In 1933 Drewes sent Kandinsky a number of black-and-white photographs of his work, and Kandinsky commented on the "progress" Drewes was making with his painting: "I think that you are making good progress with abstraction which pleases me. Have you also done simpler abstract paintings, for example pictures with only very simple forms? Or ones where 'something happens' only in the middle of the picture and around the middle and the rim of the picture everything remains open?"[49] He also encouraged Drewes to do paintings that were very "light" without using "any heavy forms" or perhaps utilizing only very thin lines without any planes at all.[50] Suggestions for further exploration alternated with warm encouragement and genuine appreciation of Drewes's development as a painter: "Your drawings gave me real pleasure. You are really moving forward! Stability combined with freedom. Your 'wrist' has become looser, which is naturally the result of your developing inner freedom. . . . You had some inner shackles, which held you back. Now that is over!"[51]

Most revealing, however, are Kandinsky's thoughts about the risks of the student emulating too closely his teacher:

> I have occasionally shown your portfolio to people here and hear *every* time the same opinion, which I do not wish to keep from you. Your talent, seriousness, sensitive and accomplished technique are always praised. It is always stressed, however, that the pieces result from the influence of my work. Personally, I do not see it so much. In response, I always say that a certain influence is understandable as your work is still evolving and that this influence should not be considered superficially or outwardly but rather as a well digested one through which your own "note" can easily be detected. . . . Once I was made aware of this "negative" aspect of your work, I saw that I had been the stimulus in several of your pieces. Because I always want to be straightforward with you, I did not want to keep silent about this criticism.[52]

We do not know Drewes's response to these words, but in a letter written several months after the one above, Kandinsky responds to Drewes's comments:

> What you say about a "school" is quite right. A school is not an outward imitation of form, but rather a common root in the spirit. I have observed all my life the following: a new artist comes forward and the critics and general public say:
>
> 1. Ah, he's similar to artist x or y, so he's not original and therefore not strong and
> 2. Ah, he's not similar to anyone, he wants to be completely independent, so he's a fraud and therefore not strong.
>
> Find a way out please.
>
> Or:

1. He is not bad, but can't build a school (or influence the future), thus he's an isolated case and without great meaning, or

2. He is not bad, but has too many imitators (here it is not called "school" but imitation), thus his formal language is easily copied and without great meaning. Again, "please"![53]

Kandinsky had placed his concerns about Drewes's adaptation of his style into a larger context and found that evaluations of artistic originality cannot be resolved favorably for either the "teacher" or the "student." In Drewes's case, the similar imagery reflected not a slavish imitation of form but rather the presence of "a common root in the spirit," for Drewes shared Kandinsky's belief that the laws of art should be used to express the mysteries of the universe:

What are the laws which create the pattern of the frost which forms on our windows? . . . But art is also a world with its own laws, whether they underlie a painting of realistic or abstract forms. . . . To create new universes within these laws and to fill them with the experiences of our life is our task. . . . When they convincingly reflect the wisdom or struggle of the soul, a work of art is born.[54]

A year before writing this statement, Drewes had queried Kandinsky regarding the role that the rules of art should play in creating a successful work of art. Kandinsky replied that art, like nature, had laws but that such laws and principles, while important, could unnecessarily hamper a gifted artist possessed by inner strength. The talented artist would find it impossible to conform to rigid dicta; indeed he or she would find it necessary to break the rules at will: "There was a time when I thought that these secret laws would be known and that the artist could then come to his work *consciously*. I did not notice at the time the error of this hope . . . for [in the hands of an ungifted artist] knowledge of the rules would always replace feelings or 'intuition.' When I speak of the 'artist,' I always give free rein to the emotional correction of the 'law.' "[55]

Thus, Kandinsky himself, while acknowledging the existence of laws and rules, came down firmly in favor of breaking those laws for expressive purposes. He would have been in complete agreement, then, with those in America who feared that the seemingly boundless possibilities suggested by his discoveries would be limited by an orthodox view of non-objectivity.

Drewes did a number of paintings in the late 1930s where he magnified and dramatized the lines and biomorphic and geometric shapes that characterize his debt to Kandinsky. *Loose Contact* (1938; plate 68) a study in pictorial tension, sets two primary elements in opposition to one another, each attracted toward the other while at the same time gravitating outward toward the edge. The connecting bands that loosely link the forms emphasize the hovering quality of the forms. Drewes's firsthand knowledge not only of Kandinsky's art, but also of his theories as taught at the Bauhaus and discussed in *Point and Line to Plane,* make him, along with John von Wicht, one of Kandinsky's closest followers.

John von Wicht

John von Wicht, like Drewes, was a German immigrant; he arrived in the United States in 1923. Exposed to the work of Kandinsky in the early 1910s while studying at the Royal School for Fine and Applied Arts in Berlin, von Wicht quickly assimilated the lessons of

Kandinsky's emerging abstractions. Von Wicht's interest in discovering the essentials of the language of painting was such that he had Poussin's *Eliezer and Rebecca* blown up to enormous size in order to analyze its internal structure of lines, circular movements, and directional forces. Such inquiries could not help but lead him even more closely to Kandinsky, who had already sought to codify the governing factors of painting in *Point and Line to Plane.* Beginning in the 1920s, then, he adopted Kandinsky's geometric Bauhaus vocabulary, and much of his subsequent work openly emulated Kandinsky. Von Wicht worked on the WPA murals for the New York radio station WNYC with Byron Browne, Stuart Davis, and Louis Shanker in 1938. His mural displayed a Baueresque geometrical order. The year before, von Wicht had produced the first in what was to become the Force series of paintings. These works, reminiscent of Hartley's Kandinsky-inspired paintings, make ample use of triangular force lines combined with—and intersecting—circles against a tightly ordered, almost solid background of color. *Vista* (1939; plate 70) shares with the Force paintings an interest in Kandinsky's Bauhaus vocabulary against an animated ground. In other works, such as *Abstraction* (c. 1940; plate 71), von Wicht employs a more open structure, allowing his geometric forms to float freely in space in direct emulation of Kandinsky.

John Ferren

Given the complexity and diversity of the paths that led American artists to Kandinsky, it should come as no surprise that certain Americans discovered Kandinsky's work while studying or residing in Europe. Such was the case with John Ferren and Benjamin Benno. Born in Oregon, Ferren was raised in California, coming of age as a sculptor in the mid-1920s. It is entirely possible that he was aware of exhibitions organized by Galka Scheyer (which included Kandinsky) in San Francisco and Los Angeles during this period, although there is no record of his seeing these shows. Ferren did develop an interest in Zen Buddhism and Taoism during these early years, ultimately formulating an animistic view of the universe:

> I placed my hand on a tree trunk. I instantaneously felt that every element of the landscape was alive, the light, air, ground and trees. All were interrelated, living the same life, and (this is important to my art) their forms were all interchangeable. The forms of things were only the particular expression of an energy, or substance, which they all shared in common.[56]

In 1929, at the age of twenty-four, Ferren traveled to France, where he met Hans Hofmann and studied informally at the Académie Ranson and the Académie de la Grande Chaumière. A visit with Hofmann to a Matisse exhibition prompted Ferren to begin painting.[57] After a brief return to California, Ferren went back to Paris in 1931, where he was to remain for the next seven years. There, he befriended Hélion and met Picasso, Miró, Breton, and other European modernists. Within a year of his arrival, Ferren wrote in his diary:

> Reading recent Cahiers d'Art—the upholder of abstract art. *Kandinsky*—and the Director of the Musée de Hanover, A. Doerner. The two of them expressing perfectly my hitherto original opinion. . . . Voilà—Je ne suis pas seul!—I am reconvinced that my vague gropings are correct.[58]

Ferren and Kandinsky shared a variety of ideas concerning painting, including the conviction that the separation of color from the description of objects releases its power to affect the viewer psychologically. Ferren was also an avid believer in the power of abstract form to communicate more effectively: "The advantage of the circle over the apple is, that being a purer form, it permits a more accurate delineation of the creative emotion."[59] Ferren also subscribed to an essentially spiritual view of art. Believing in the concept of "creative necessity," Ferren did not mind, as did some of his American Abstract Artists colleagues, locating the meaning and power of artistic activity in the spiritual: " 'New' art is clearly after the reality behind appearances. Call it what you will, but inevitably the word 'spiritual' must be used, no matter how shopworn it may be."[60] Ferren's careful reading of *The Art of Spiritual Harmony* stayed with him and continued to figure in his interpretation of abstract painting until well into the 1950s. Thus, his description of the craft of painting owes much to Kandinsky's ideas:

> A horizontal line does not necessarily denote the horizon, it denotes calm. Blue is not only the color of the Virgin's dress or a flower or a symbol of purity, it is first a color which denotes calm and contraction. Prolonged exposure to it will lower the blood pressure. Red does the opposite and so on through all the elements. The forms, colors, planes, and spaces of the artist's craft have basic psychological and physiological realities beneath and beyond their use for descriptive purposes.[61]

These ideas fit Kandinsky's description of blue as "the typically heavenly color" that creates a feeling of "rest."

Ferren became acquainted enough with Kandinsky during his tenure in Paris to have Kandinsky help him with his 1936 Guggenheim Foundation application. Kandinsky offered to attest to Ferren's *"valeur artistique"* and even suggested that he could also get a "highly respected" American musician to do a recommendation as well.[62] (For his part, Ferren wrote in his grant application that his concept and manner of painting was centered in the work of Cézanne, but that Van Gogh, Kandinsky, Bauer, Léger, Matisse, and Picasso also played a vital role in his current orientation.)[63]

Ferren's involvement in Kandinsky's work during this period can be seen in two untitled paintings done in Paris in 1933–34. Working with a voided background, Ferren created a lyrical geometry of expressive shapes, lines, and colors. Subsequently, Ferren evolved a style that concentrated on complex relationships between swinging, spiraling, or rotating planes of color. Ferren's active involvement with Kandinsky's art was relatively brief, lasting only a year or two, but as we have seen, Kandinsky's ideas remained intellectually compelling for years to come.

Benjamin Benno

Like Arshile Gorky, Benjamin Benno sought to find his personal voice by working his way through the history of modernism. Benno was born in America of Russian-Jewish heritage and on the death of his mother in 1905 was sent to Russia. He was raised there by his maternal grandparents until his father brought him to New York in 1912. Benno's father was an anarchist and promptly placed his already recalcitrant son in the Ferrer School, which was run by Emma Goldman and affiliated with the anarchist movement in New York. There Benno had the opportunity to study art with Robert Henri and George Bellows and to become immersed in the art community that flourished around the Ferrer Center. That community included such members of the Stieglitz Circle as Abraham Walkowitz and Man Ray. Henri's philosophy of nonjuried exhibitions, which offered equal access to all artists, deeply impressed

Plate 78
Hans Hofmann
UNTITLED (LANDSCAPE), 1941
Dr. and Mrs. T. H. Kirschbaum

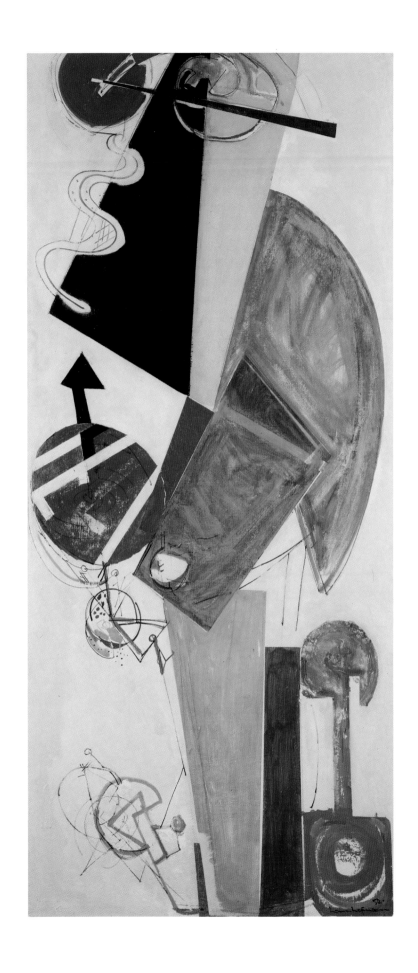

Plate 79
Hans Hofmann
CHIMBOTE MURAL, 1950
Courtesy Andre Emmerich Gallery, New York

203

Plate 80
Arshile Gorky
WATERFALL, 1943
Hirshhorn Museum and Sculpture Garden
Smithsonian Institution, Washington, D.C.
Gift of Joseph H. Hirshhorn, 1966
Photo credit: Lee Stalsworth

Plate 81
Jackson Pollock
UNTITLED, c. 1942
Collection of John C. L. and
Sarah V. C. Van Doren

Plate 82
Charles Seliger
PRIMAL MARKINGS 1, 1943
Michael Rosenfeld Gallery, New York

Plate 83
Charles Seliger
PRIMAL MARKINGS III, 1943
Michael Rosenfeld Gallery, New York

Plate 84
Norman Lewis
PHANTASY II, 1946
Collection of Mrs. Ouida Lewis
Photo credit: D. James Dee

Fig. 6.4 Arshile Gorky.
THE WATERFALL, 1943.
Oil on canvas, 6 × 4⅖″
(15.37 × 11.3 cm)
Courtesy Tate Gallery, London
(Photograph © 1992 Agnes
Fielding/ARS, New York)

periods, but a personal internalization of the essence of Kandinsky's color and fluid forms. Like Kandinsky's Improvisations, Gorky's works in the early 1940s relate to nature.

In the summer of 1943, Gorky and his wife, Agnes, went to live at her parents' new home, Crooked Run Farm, in Hamilton, Virginia. Feeling at home on the farm, Gorky responded to nature with renewed inspiration. Around this time he painted a number of canvases relating to waterfalls with appropriately wet-looking fluid shapes. One of these canvases, *Waterfall* of about 1943 (fig. 6.4), has been repeatedly linked to Gorky's interest in Kandinsky's art in general.[74] However, Kandinsky also painted waterfalls, such as *The Waterfall* of 1909, purchased by Katherine Dreier in 1924 and shown in various exhibitions of the Société Anonyme from 1932. In an exhibition, Some New Forms of Beauty, 1909–1936, shown in Springfield, Massachusetts, in 1939 and in Hartford in 1940, Kandinsky's *Waterfall* was on view with Gorky's own work, providing Gorky with an opportunity to know this picture. Thus, Gorky's *Waterfall* (as well as its variants, such as plate 80) probably reflects his knowledge of this particular painting by Kandinsky.[75] Gorky's forms in *Waterfall*, particularly the concentric "circle" motif in the top center, as well as the loose blots of color and the black linear drawing amid the thinly applied color, are also reminiscent of many of Kandinsky's Improvisations and other works, for example, his so-called *First Abstract Watercolor*, with which Gorky probably was familiar through reproductions. Although William Rubin has made a convincing visual comparison in his juxtaposition of Gorky's *Waterfall* to Kandinsky's *Sunday* of 1911, Gorky could not have known this work, which was then hidden away in the basement storeroom of Gabriele Münter (and was not exhibited until after her gift of several hundred paintings by Kandinsky to the Städtische Galerie in Munich during the fall of 1956).[76] Gorky's language of painterly forms, which seems so inspired by Kandinsky, must, then, be attributed to his admiration of many of Kandinsky's early works, both in exhibitions he saw and in reproductions in the books he studied.

For the next year, 1944, Gorky's paintings continued to demonstrate a relationship to Kandinsky's Improvisations both in form and color, as well as his growing interest in surrealist automatism. One may compare, for example, Gorky's *Water of the Flowery Mill* of 1944 to Kandinsky's *Impressions III* of 1911. Gorky has captured both Kandinsky's flowing, momentary shapes and his brilliant warm colors. Gorky, managing to use black and white in the midst of a dynamic color scheme in the same way that Kandinsky had before him, created an equally dramatic effect. Gorky has actually achieved the overall unity at which Kandinsky merely hinted through the use of dripping paint.

Gorky's major canvases usually were not, in fact, very spontaneously painted, for he usually worked out very specific studies on paper. Such is the case with one of Gorky's major works, *The Liver Is the Cock's Comb* (fig. 6.5), also of 1944, for which a study of 1943 exists in pencil, ink, and wax crayon. While his *Water of the Flowery Mill* of the same year is quite close in feeling to landscape, *The Liver Is the Cock's Comb* departs from this natural gentle aura to include fantastic-looking creatures with "tooth-like" claws and skeletal-looking forms. In this aspect, Gorky's work seems closer to that of some of the surrealist painters then living in New York, such as Yves Tanguy and Matta Echaurren, with whom Gorky became friendly around 1944. Gorky's lively use of color, however, and his floating forms with fluid edges would seem to indicate that in *The Liver Is the Cock's Comb* Gorky is still involved with the example set by Kandinsky. As Rubin has suggested: "The great plumes of color, probably inspired by Kandinsky's, on the order of *Black Lines* (1913; see fig. 3.2), are potently seductive even though as a group their registration does not finally cohere."[77] Indeed, Gorky could

Fig. 6.5 Arshile Gorky.
*THE LIVER IS THE COCK'S
COMB,* 1944.
Oil on canvas, 73¼ × 98''
(187.8 × 251.3 cm)
Albright-Knox Art Gallery,
Buffalo, New York, Gift of
Seymour H. Knox, 1956

easily have seen Kandinsky's painting *Black Lines* on exhibit at the Museum of Non-Objective Painting. The painting had been given to the museum in 1937 by Solomon R. Guggenheim and was later included in the Kandinsky memorial retrospective exhibition in 1945, as well as reproduced as the frontispiece to the museum's publication *In Memory of Wassily Kandinsky.*[78]

The Art of Spiritual Harmony would also have been appealing to Gorky, particularly for such ideas as the parallels that Kandinsky saw between emotions and colors. For Kandinsky, feelings such as joy or grief were "only material expressions of the soul," and shades of color "awaken in the soul emotions too fine to be expressed in prose."[79] This thinking may well have appealed to Gorky, who as an art instructor at the Grand Central Art School (circa 1925 to 1931) "stressed getting emotion into a drawing and underlined the point by bringing a Hungarian violinist to fiddle for the class."[80] Gorky appears to have agreed with Kandinsky's statement that "music is found to be the best teacher. . . . Music has been the art which has devoted itself not to the reproduction of natural phenomena, but to the expression of the artist's soul."[81] In Gorky's canvases in the 1940s, he came to understand Kandinsky's art and then progressed beyond these ideas to create an art that is both totally personal and powerful.

Initially critical of Gorky's interest in Kandinsky's work, Clement Greenberg did not immediately share the general enthusiasm for Kandinsky demonstrated by his contemporaries in the avant-garde. At the time of Gorky's first one-man show at the Julien Levy Gallery in 1945, Greenberg noted that the artist "broke his allegiance to Picasso and Miró and replaced them with the earlier Kandinsky," maintaining that this influence made "his work less serious and less powerful."[82] At the same time, Greenberg denounced Kandinsky's painting, in which he claimed that "the picture plane became pocked with 'holes.' "[83] Dore Ashton has suggested that Gorky's outright homage to Kandinsky irked Greenberg.[84] A decade later, Greenberg revised the opinion he had held in 1945 and expressed an appreciation of the importance of Kandinsky for Gorky's development:

> To break away from an overpowering precedent, the young artist looks for an alter-
> native one. The late Arshile Gorky submitted himself to Miró in order to break free

of Picasso, and in the process, did a number of pictures we now see have independent virtues, although at the time—the late '30s—they seemed too derivative. But the 1910–1918 Kandinsky was even more of a liberator and during the first war years stimulated Gorky to a greater originality.[85]

Around 1933, Gorky met Willem de Kooning, who became his close friend and with whom he shared a studio for a number of years during the late 1930s. De Kooning, who had arrived in New York from the Netherlands in 1926 at the age of twenty-two, also became friendly with John Graham, whom he met as early as 1927 in an art gallery. According to Dore Ashton: "De Kooning remembers that Pollock, who probably met Graham in 1937, once lent him an article by Graham and uncharacteristically insisted on getting it back."[86] This article must have been "Primitive Art and Picasso," where Graham distinguished between the "Greco-African culture" and the "Perso-Indo-Chinese culture": "The Perso-Indo-Chinese tradition . . . found in the paintings of van Gogh, Renoir, Kandinsky, Soutine, Chagal [sic]; the Greco-African is exemplified by Ingres, Picasso, Mondrian."[87] De Kooning has recalled that it was Graham who first discovered the unknown Jackson Pollock.[88]

De Kooning was cognizant of Kandinsky as early as 1928; he probably learned about Kandinsky from John Graham. Thomas Hess wrote of De Kooning's early work: "Some small pictures of around 1928 indicate that he was experimenting with abstraction at this time, some of it symbolic, some influenced by the flat colored geometries of Kandinsky."[89] In an interview with Harold Rosenberg in 1972, De Kooning claimed: "I am an eclectic painter by chance. I can open almost any book of reproductions and find a painting I could be influenced by."[90] As late as 1951, in a symposium held at the Museum of Modern Art, De Kooning stated: "I admire some of Kandinsky's painting very much," but he also explained what he considered the limitations inherent in Kandinsky:

> Kandinsky understood "Form" as a form, like an object in the real world; and an object, he said, was a narrative—and so of course, he disapproved of it. He wanted his "music without words." He wanted to be "simple as a child." He intended, with his "inner-self," to rid himself of "philosophical barricades" (he sat down and wrote about all this). But in turn his own writing has become a barricade full of holes. It offers a kind of Middle-European idea of Buddhism or, anyhow, something too theosophic for me.[91]

In his native Holland, De Kooning may have known of followers of theosophy, including Piet Mondrian.

Clearly De Kooning has indicated that he is familiar with Kandinsky's *The Art of Spiritual Harmony* and the Russian artist's ideas about music, "the principle of internal necessity," and theosophy. De Kooning may have read Kandinsky's treatise in its first English translation during the late 1920s or 1930s or at some time during the late 1940s, after two further English translations were published in 1946 and 1947.

De Kooning was much less influenced by Kandinsky than was Gorky, although he certainly knew Kandinsky's early Improvisations from their exhibition at the Museum of Non-Objective Painting, particularly in the major memorial retrospective exhibition held there in 1945. Indeed, De Kooning's gestural style of painting relates in its spontaneity and fluidity of surface to Kandinsky's early Improvisations. Kandinsky's Improvisations, however, still maintain an illusionistic space and relate to landscape, while De Kooning created canvases composed of purely abstract shapes and lines floating on the surface plane without a discernible figure–ground relationship. In this achievement, De Kooning credited Jackson Pollock's own break with cubist space, asserting that Jackson had broken the ice. De Kooning also learned from Gorky, who, like Pollock, found in Kandinsky's art much more inspiration than he did.

Close examination of Jackson Pollock's early works suggests that the young artist was just as much an eclectic as Gorky before him; Pollock's eclecticism, however, is less obvious, for he always translated the borrowed vocabulary into his own very personal idiom. Pollock's early style is consistently rough; rather than attempting a more exacting copy relationship to the art he emulated, Pollock merely borrowed forms and radically reassembled them in a new manner.

In answering a questionnaire published in the February 1944 issue of *Arts & Architecture*, Jackson Pollock stated that "the two artists I admire most, Picasso and Miró, are still abroad."[92] A careful study of Pollock's work from 1944 to 1946 suggests that a year or so later he might have added the name of the recently deceased Wassily Kandinsky to his list of most admired artists.

Pollock would have been sympathetic to Kandinsky's spiritual concerns such as theosophy, which captivated John Graham, his friend and mentor. Marcia Epstein Allentuck has pointed out that "Kandinsky's felicitous phrase 'the purposive vocation of the human soul,' by which he meant its quest for formal embodiment and affective expression in a work of art, could serve as an epigraph for [Graham's] *System and Dialectics of Art*."[93] Pollock owned a copy of Graham's book, which was inscribed to him by the author. Graham first recognized Pollock's talent and included him along with Lee Krasner, Willem de Kooning, and other American and French painters in a group show that he organized for the McMillen Gallery in New York, which ran from January 20 to February 6, 1942. Graham was an important early influence on Pollock, who may have picked up Kandinsky-like ideas from him.

In *The Art of Spiritual Harmony* Kandinsky wrote: "That is beautiful which is produced by the inner need, which springs from the soul."[94] Pollock, who executed a series of drawings for a Jungian analyst in 1941, was well aware of the relationship of his inner needs to his art. Alfonso Ossorio described this aspect of Pollock: "He was also extremely intrigued with the inner world—what is it all about? He had a sense of mystery. His religiousness was in those terms—a sense of rhythm of the universe, of the big order—like the Oriental philosophies."[95] While still in high school, Pollock listened to lectures by the Hindu poet and mystic Krishnamurti, in Ojai, California. Anthony Smith recalled that "Pollock mused aloud about esoteric ideas, Oriental Philosophy, things I knew nothing about."[96]

Whenever Pollock borrowed forms and occasionally compositional arrangements from Picasso, Miró, or Kandinsky, he translated the borrowed material into the context of his own developing style. Thus, it is more difficult to identify and to adequately understand examples of specific influences on Pollock. This is particularly true of Kandinsky's impact on Pollock, which writers have usually underplayed, ignored, or denied outright.[97] More recently, Ellen Landau has acknowledged Kandinsky's role in Pollock's development.[98]

Significantly, some of Pollock's early critics recognized the artist's debt to Kandinsky. Ironically, their initial insights were later either denied or forgotten. In the April 1945 issue of *Art News*, an anonymous reviewer of Pollock's one-man show at Art of This Century wrote that Pollock "derives his style from that of Kandinsky though he lacks the airy freedom and imaginative color of the earlier master."[99] Pollock had not yet found his own very personal style. Two years later Clement Greenberg wrote: "The most powerful painter in contemporary America and the only one who promises to be a major one is a Gothic, morbid and extreme disciple of Picasso's Cubism and Miró's post-Cubism, tinctured also with Kandinsky and

Fig. 6.6 Jackson Pollock.
THE KEY, 1946.
Oil on canvas, 58½ ×
84⅕″ (149.9 × 215.9 cm)
The Art Institute of Chicago,
through Prior Gift of Mr. and
Mrs. Edward Morris, 1987.261
(Photograph © 1992 The Art
Institute of Chicago. All rights
reserved.)

Surrealist inspiration. His name is Jackson Pollock."[100]

Pollock's most intensive encounter with Kandinsky's art came in 1943 when he managed to get a custodial job at the Museum of Non-Objective Painting. His employment on the WPA Art Program was terminated on January 29, 1943. Having attended an interview with Hilla Rebay, Pollock wrote to her the next day, on April 15, 1943, thanking her and telling her "how stimulating and vitally alive" he found her criticism; he also claimed to have "been very interested in the work you have been doing, and the Museum of Non-objective Art, for some time."[101] Having had a second interview on April 30, Pollock received a check from Rebay for art supplies. In the brief "biography" he submitted to Rebay, Pollock identified his current artistic development as "non-objective spatial intensity."[102]

On May 8, after being forced to decorate ties and lipsticks for a living, Pollock began working at the museum, where he remained until midsummer. Then, however, Peggy Guggenheim gave him a year's contract, scheduled a one-man show at Art of This Century, and commissioned a mural for her entrance hall, so he resigned his position. Pollock's duties at the museum had included running the elevator and working on frames.[103] Pollock saw numerous paintings by Kandinsky since Rebay featured his work along with her own and that of Rudolf Bauer during her administration of the museum (1937–1952).

Pollock's next formal encounter with Kandinsky's work was from April 11 until May 6, 1944, in a small group show selected by a jury at Art of This Century. Called First Exhibition in America, it consisted of only twenty paintings, all being shown in the United States for the first time and including one work each by Pollock and Kandinsky, along with works by Braque, Dali, Ernst, Léger, Masson, Matta, Miró, Motherwell, Picasso, Rothko, and Tanguy.

The earliest indication that Pollock had been studying Kandinsky's art was probably his 1944 *Untitled Drawing* in gouache, brush, pen and ink, and wash. Comparing Pollock's drawing to Kandinsky's so-called *First Abstract Watercolor* of 1910 reveals how Pollock used the same tiny black blots, short skinny lines of black, and thicker, longer lines of orange-red, yellow, and blue, all of which attempt to avoid the definition of shapes. Yet in both Kandinsky's abstract works of the early period and in Pollock's drawings of the early 1940s, non-representational but figurative shapes are still in evidence. Pollock painted shapes very similar to those in Kandinsky's most famous compositions. For example, one can compare this 1944 Pollock drawing to Kandinsky's *Light Picture* or *Black Lines,* both dated 1913 and owned by the Museum of Non-Objective Painting since its inception in 1939. In these, a preponderance of skinny black lines and of V-shapes at various angles compares to Pollock's drawing. In this drawing, Pollock utilized the technique of wash and dissolving color that Kandinsky used in works such as *Light Picture.*

Pollock, who regularly visited museums and galleries before moving to East Hampton on Long Island in October 1945, undoubtedly saw the Kandinsky memorial exhibition at the Museum of Non-Objective Painting the previous spring. The catalogue of this exhibition remained at East Hampton among the books that Pollock accumulated over the years. Pollock may also have picked up an interest in Kandinsky's ideas from Stanley William Hayter, whose article "The Language of Kandinsky" appeared in *Magazine of Art* in the issue of May 1945.[104] Pollock worked on experimental graphics at Hayter's Atelier 17 during the fall of 1944 and into the next year.

During 1945, Kandinsky was in the air in New York, and Pollock, like other young artists, could hardly escape his liberating influence. His friends Gorky and De Kooning had already felt his influence. Gorky's interest, unlike Pollock's, was basically limited to Kandin-

Fig. 6.7 Vassily Kandinsky.
DEEP BROWN, 1924.
Oil on canvas, 32⅖ ×
28⅖″ (83.1 × 72.7 cm)
Solomon R. Guggenheim
Museum, New York

sky's earliest abstract paintings. This may partially explain critics' failure to see Kandinsky's significance for Pollock, since these early paintings account for only one aspect of the influence Kandinsky's oeuvre had on Pollock.

Pollock definitely had ample opportunity to study Kandinsky's art in depth and, like Gorky, he may have read some of Kandinsky's theories.[105] When Pollock had a one-man show at Art of This Century, from March 17 through April 14, 1945, it coincided with the Kandinsky retrospective, where he saw more than two hundred examples of Kandinsky's work. Certain of Pollock's works in the next year and a half clearly reveal the powerful impact of Kandinsky.

After the Kandinsky memorial exhibition, Pollock experimented with forms from Kandinsky's Bauhaus years. *The Key* (fig. 6.6), one of Pollock's paintings from a series of 1946, relates visually to several Kandinsky works dating from 1924 to 1926, during this geometric period: *Deep Brown* (fig. 6.7), *Lighter,* and *Green Connection,* all of which were in the 1945 retrospective. In *The Key,* one notices that Pollock pushes his forms very close to the picture plane; the forms, although similar in shape to those in Kandinsky's early Bauhaus paintings, seem to have been smashed to flatness in Pollock. Although his surface, unlike Kandinsky's, is characteristically rough, the arrangement of his forms appears to be closely related to Kandinsky. This similarity is not that of a direct copy of any one of Kandinsky's paintings, but a very personal and powerful assimilation by Pollock.

In *The Key,* Pollock utilizes Kandinsky's vocabulary of forms, albeit in an extremely personal manner. Yet the repetition of motif indicates Pollock's intense study of Kandinsky. His *Deep Brown* of 1924 has on the lower right side a blue jagged mountain-like form (with a white crescent with a yellow spot just below it) similar to that in Pollock's *The Key;* likewise, both forms are just above a hill-like formation, blue in Kandinsky and green in Pollock. Both compositions contain red semicircles and varicolored arched lines around a circle.

Kandinsky's *Lighter* of 1924 is very close to *The Key* in color; in both, a rust orange, dark blue, yellow, and dark green predominate. Both works have a central dark green triangle and heavy black lines (each has a black X) superimposed throughout each composition. While Pollock's large green triangle lies flat, he adopts Kandinsky's use of translucent overlapping shapes, where one shape overlaps another and their two colors blend into a third.

Kandinsky's *Green Connection* of 1926 has a large dark green triangle and also the horizontal hill-like form of *The Key.* There are many mandorla-like shapes in this Kandinsky and crude approximations of them in *The Key.* Most interesting is a crescent form in each—lying on a diagonal, half pink and half white. Many of Pollock's forms, then, are common to Kandinsky's works, and their appearance in *The Key* cannot be called a coincidence. One finds similar instances of Kandinsky's influence in yet other paintings of 1946 by Pollock.

Even the titles that Pollock chose for some of his paintings in 1946 recall those among Kandinsky's oeuvre: Pollock's *Yellow Triangle, Magic Light,* and *Shimmering Substance* can be compared to Kandinsky's *Yellow Circle* (1926), *Green Wedge* (1925), and *Self-Illuminating* (1924), all in the Museum of Non-Objective Painting at that time. One suspects that Pollock was reading *The Art of Spiritual Harmony* when he painted *Yellow Triangle,* for Kandinsky had written:

> The mutual influence of form and color now becomes clear. A yellow triangle, a blue circle, a green square, or a green triangle, a yellow circle, a blue square—all these are different spiritual values. It is evident that many colors are hampered and even nullified in effect by many forms. On the whole, keen colors are well suited by sharp

forms (e.g. a yellow triangle), and soft, deep colors by round forms (e.g. a blue circle). But it must be remembered that an unsuitable combination of form and color is not necessarily discordant, but may, with manipulation, show the way to fresh possibilities of harmony.[106]

Pollock had some other ideas in common with Kandinsky. In Kandinsky's *Point and Line to Plane*, prints of photomicrographs from botanical and biological texts were included to demonstrate the use of line in nature. It may be only coincidence that one of Pollock's favorite books, D'Arcy Wentworth Thompson's *On Growth and Form* (1942), investigated forms of nature. Pollock's love of American Indian art also corresponded to Kandinsky's choice of illustrations for the almanac *Der Blaue Reiter*.

Other drawings by Pollock from this period also indicate relationships to the art of Kandinsky. An *Untitled Drawing*, datable approximately 1946, is linked to at least two Kandinsky paintings of 1923 shown in the 1945 memorial exhibition. *Emphasized Corners* by Kandinsky contains the same pastel red, yellow, and blue bands and squiggled lines found in the Pollock drawing. In Pollock's composition, lines radiate from a dark black ink blob, which corresponds to a dark circle in the center of Kandinsky's *Without Support*. As in *Emphasized Corners*, Pollock's lines radiate outward toward the four corners, which remain nearly blank. *Without Support* also has the pastel bands and wavy lines in red, yellow, and blue found in the Pollock drawing and in still other Kandinsky paintings.

Another Pollock *Untitled Drawing* of 1946 is related to a Kandinsky woodcut, *Kleine Welten VIII* (1922; fig. 6.9). Pollock's drawing, with its clearly designated focal point at dead center, about which the rest of the composition revolves, is similar to Kandinsky's abstract woodcut. A fundamental difference, however, is that Pollock's design approaches the edges in a way that predicts his "all-over" pattern of the "drip" paintings to come. Yet these two compositions have many similar configurations; for example, the nearly triangular shape pierced by a line that appears on the lower left edge of Kandinsky's work appears reversed on the upper left edge of Pollock's drawing. Heavy black lines that cross to create an X-shape appear at the

Fig. 6.9 Vassily Kandinsky.
PLATE VIII FROM PORTFOLIO,
KLEINE WELTEN, 1922.
Woodcut, 10¾ × 9⅛″
(27.6 × 23.4 cm)
Courtesy Milwaukee Art Center,
Schuchardt Fund Purchase from
Suggested Additions Show

top center of both compositions. Pollock probably adopted the furry or spiky black lines of this drawing from other works by Kandinsky such as *Black Lines* or *Light Picture.* In the upper left of the Pollock drawing is a horizontal V-shaped configuration consisting of red color over black lines similar to the green and purple horizontal V-shapes in *Black Lines.* In both these works of 1913, Kandinsky experimented with using line in a nonfigurative way with only a very few shapes. Pollock began where Kandinsky left off.

Thus, Kandinsky's art influenced Pollock's developing style in a crucial time, the period from 1944 to 1946, punctuated by the 1945 Kandinsky memorial exhibition. And to understand Pollock's most original artistic endeavors, one must first grasp the genesis of his paintings of 1946; for it is from these works that the great "poured" paintings emerged in the winter of 1946–47.

The Museum of Non-Objective Painting offered inspiration to others among the Abstract Expressionists, including Charles Seliger. He remembered seeing Kandinsky's paintings there during 1942 and 1943, when he was still a teenager. He recalled: "I was instantly attracted to the early Kandinsky. I was impressed by his early improvisational approach and the images of elemental organic forces. There were no recognizable images and they were not as geometric as his later work."[107]

Seliger later showed at Art of This Century, where he met Pollock, Breton, Rothko, and others. He remembered the gallery as "exciting," noting that he saw later work by Kandinsky there, which he described as having "shapes that resembled life under a microscope. They were more controlled and deliberate than the earlier paintings but still had the organic quality that I felt in the earlier works." Seliger noted: "At that time, I read the Art of Spiritual Harmony, but must confess that its effect on me was far less than the paintings. It was the physical qualities of the actual paintings and the imagery in his work that stayed with me." Seliger utilized similar organic forms in a series of small paintings in 1943, including *Festival* and a group called *Primal Markings* (plates 82 and 83).

A few years after Seliger, but about the same time as Pollock, Norman Lewis developed an interest in Kandinsky's work. Like Pollock and so many other New York artists, Lewis saw the Kandinsky memorial exhibition at the MNOP in the spring of 1945. He bought both the catalogue and *Kandinsky,* a second, more lavish book on the artist published by the museum on this occasion. In 1947, Lewis purchased the new translation of Kandinsky's treatise as *Concerning the Spiritual in Art.* He kept all these books for the rest of his life.

Lewis's development parallels that of some of the other Abstract Expressionists who experimented with Kandinsky's work. During the 1930s, Lewis painted in a representational figurative style, at times reminiscent of Social Realists like Raphael Soyer or the Mexican muralist Diego Rivera. Like many of the Abstract Expressionists, he worked in the art program of the WPA, and he taught at various schools.[108] From 1944 to 1949, Lewis taught art with Ad Reinhardt at the Thomas Jefferson School of Social Science, an alternative school in New York City. In 1946, Lewis wrote of wanting to create an art that "breaks away from its stagnation in too much tradition and establishes new traditions to be broken away from by coming generations of artists."[109]

Lewis's move to non-objective painting was in 1945, just after the Kandinsky retrospective. He gradually abandoned the more "cubist" structure of *Composition #1* (1945) to work in an increasingly organic abstraction. *Phantasy II* of 1946 (plate 84) reveals floating triangles and squiggly lines that recall Kandinsky's paintings. In Lewis's *Phantasy I* (fig. 6.11), painted in 1946, the artist confidently produced an abstraction in which the lessons of Kandinsky's early Improvisations were absorbed. Both the areas of fluid color and the delicate overlay of black lines recall Kandinsky's work.

Lewis was also attracted to ideas in *Concerning the Spiritual in Art*. For him, Kandinsky's emphasis on musical analogy in abstract painting was appealing. Lewis's friend, jazz musician Julian Euell, has stressed Lewis's deep interest in many kinds of music, his use of musical analogies in his speech, and his love of jazz in particular.[110] It is, then, in the context of both Lewis's love of music and his understanding of Kandinsky's emphasis on musical analogy that we can view such abstract paintings by Lewis as *Musicians* (1945), *Twilight Sounds* (1947), and *Jazz Musicians* (1948).

Lewis saved part of an article, "ABC (or XYZ) of Abstract Art," from the *New York Times Magazine* of July 11, 1948, which he tucked into his catalogue of the Kandinsky retrospective. Beneath a reproduction of Kandinsky's *Black Lines* is the following passage:

> Such designs, with their freely meandering or scratchy lines and blurred areas of tone, all floating lightly over the surface, seem to be made up of growing, or organic forms. Kandinsky called such paintings "improvisations," explaining that they were "intuitive, for the greater part spontaneous expressions of incidents of an inner character or impressions of the inner nature." They are intended to suggest mood and emotion, and the artist compared his work to music.[111]

Lewis's marks and notes indicate how seriously he digested this article.

Lewis, and a number of the Abstract Expressionists, might have agreed with this article's assertion that "Kandinsky is the father of what has come to be known as 'automatic' painting, which, in the case of the layman waiting for a long-distance telephone number, is known as 'doodling.' " As the idea of these spontaneously recorded scribbles interacted with many other catalysts, from primitive art to Nietzsche to anarchism, they were transformed into the gestural strokes and color fields of Abstract Expressionism. Kandinsky's art and theory played a significant role in the creation of this new art.

Fig. 6.10 Installation view: "In Memory of Wassily Kandinsky" exhibition, Museum of Non-Objective Painting, 24 East 54th Street, New York, 1945. Courtesy Solomon R. Guggenheim Museum Archives

Fig. 6.11 Norman Lewis. *PHANTASY I*, 1946. Oil on canvas, 32 × 46″ (82 × 117.9 cm) Collection of Reginald F. Lewis, New York (Photograph courtesy Ouida B. Lewis, New York)

1. The scope of this study does not include interest in Native American Art by Jackson Pollock, Barnett Newman, Adolph Gottlieb, and others; interest in folk art and culture by Arshile Gorky and others; or interest in African art by John Graham, David Smith, and others. See William Jackson Rushing, "Native American Art and Culture and the New York Avant-garde, 1910–1950," doctoral dissertation, University of Texas at Austin, 1989; Gail Levin, "American Art"; Donald Gordon, "German Expressionism," and Kirk Varnedoe, "Abstract Expressionism," in William Rubin, ed., *"Primitivism" in 20th Century Art: Affinity of the Tribal and the Modern* (New York: Museum of Modern Art, 1984).

2. Wassily Kandinsky, *The Art of Spiritual Harmony,* trans. Michael T. H. Sadler (Boston: Houghton Mifflin, 1914), p. 1.

3. Kandinsky again referred to his interest in philosophical anarchism in 1920 after his return to Russia. In his article "The 'Great Utopia,' " published in the journal *Khudozhestvannaia Zhizn'* [Artistic Life], Kandinsky remarked: "Barely a decade ago, I unwittingly called forth an outburst of indignation among groups of radical artists and aestheticians, still young men at that time, with my assertion that there would soon be 'no more frontiers between countries.' This was in Germany, and those artists and intellectuals who were outraged by this 'anarchistic idea' were Germans. At that time there was a partly natural, partly artificial cultivation of the spirit of German nationalism in general, and in art in particular." Reprinted in Kenneth C. Lindsay and Peter Vergo, eds., *Kandinsky: Complete Writings on Art,* trans. Peter Vergo, vol. 1 (Boston: G. K. Hall, 1982), p. 445.

4. Kandinsky, *The Art of Spiritual Harmony,* p. 10.

5. Thomas Craven, *Modern Art: The Men, The Movements, The Meaning* (New York: Simon & Schuster, 1934), p. 227. Perhaps Craven read Michael Sadler, "After Gauguin," in *Rhythm, Art, Music, Literature* 1 (Spring 1912), which incorrectly identified Kandinsky as Polish. See chapter 2, p. xx.

6. See " 'The True Revolution Is Anarchist!': Foreword to Memoirs of a Revolutionist by Peter Kropotkin," in John P. O'Neill, ed., *Barnett Newman: Selected Writings and Interviews* (New York: Knopf, 1990), pp. 44–52. A few examples of Newman's works of the 1940s, characterized by fluid forms and lyrical colors, such as *The Song of Orpheus* (1944–45), suggest his interest in Kandinsky's Improvisations.

7. Quoted in John Fischer, "The Easy Chair/Mark Rothko: Portrait of the Artist as an Angry Man," *Harper's,* no. 241 (July 1970), p. 17. Although Rothko denied Kandinsky's influence, Anna C. Chave, in *Mark Rothko Subjects in Abstraction* (New Haven: Yale University Press, 1989), p. 207, note 17, for example, discusses parallels in Rothko and Kandinsky.

8. Serge Guilbaut, *How New York Stole the Idea of Modern Art* (Chicago: University of Chicago Press, 1983), p. 199.

9. For example, this led to the eventual disintegration of the American Artists' Congress in 1942. See Matthew Baigell and Julia Williams, *Artists Against War and Fascism: Papers of the First American Artists' Congress* (New Brunswick, N.J.: Rutgers University Press, 1986). See also Guilbaut, *How New York Stole the Idea of Modern Art.* Ignoring Kandinsky's political philosophy and its close link with his aesthetics, Guilbaut arbitrarily ruled out any impact of Kandinsky on Abstract Expressionism. Instead of recognizing how the American artists' individualist or "anarchist" desires for aesthetic freedom were satisfied by both theory and art in Kandinsky, Guilbaut reduces everything to Cold War propaganda, failing to acknowledge Kandinsky's expressed hostility to socialism.

10. Kandinsky, *The Art of Spiritual Harmony,* p. 10.

11. See Dore Ashton, *The New York School: A Cultural Reckoning* (New York: Viking, 1972), pp. 124 and 187–188; Stephen Polcari, *Abstract Expressionism and the Modern Experience* (New York: Cambridge University Press, 1991), p. 33; Ann Gibson, "Theory Undeclared: Avant-Garde Magazines as a Guide to Abstract Expressionist Images and Ideas" (Ph.D. dissertation, University of Delaware, 1984), pp. 228–230.

12. Polcari, *Abstract Expressionism,* p. 34.

13. Kandinsky, *The Art of Spiritual Harmony,* p. 10. Walter Kaufmann, ed., *The Portable Nietzsche* (New York: Viking, 1954), Prologue 2, p. 124: "This old saint in the forest has not yet heard anything of this, that *God is dead!*"

14. Kandinsky, *The Art of Spiritual Harmony,* p. 14.

15. Louis Danz, *Zarathustra Jr Speaks of Art* (New York: Brentano's, 1934).

16. Danz, *Zarathustra Jr,* p. 25.

17. Alfred H. Barr, Jr., *Cubism and Abstract Art* (New York: Museum of Modern Art, 1936), p. 84.

18. Meyer Schapiro, "The Nature of Abstract Art," *Marxist Quarterly,* 1937, reprinted in Meyer Schapiro, *Modern Art 19th & 20th Centuries: Selected Papers* (New York: Braziller, 1978), p. 205.

19. Alfred H. Barr, Jr., "Introduction," *The New American Painting: As Shown in Eight European Countries 1958–1959* (New York: Museum of Modern Art, 1959), p. 16.

20. Robert Coates, "The Art Galleries," *The New Yorker* XXII (March 30, 1946). Barr, "Introduction," p. 16.

21. Harold Rosenberg, "The American Action Painters," *Art News,* December 1952, reprinted in Harold Rosenberg, *The Tradition of the New* (London: Paladin, 1970), pp. 35–36.

22. For an example of a newspaper review that gives a detailed account of both Kandinsky's art and his treatise *The Art of Spiritual Harmony,* see also Elizabeth Luther Cary, "Kandinsky's Abstract Painting," *New York Times,* November 13, 1932.

23. John Graham, *System and Dialectics of Art* (New York, 1937). Reprinted in Marcia Epstein Allentuck,

ed., *John Graham's System and Dialectics of Art* (Baltimore: Johns Hopkins University Press, 1971).

24. John Graham, "Primitive Art and Picasso," *Magazine of Art,* April 30, 1937, pp. 236–239, 260.

25. Allentuck, *Graham's System,* p. 116.

26. Allentuck, *Graham's System,* "Introduction," p. 8.

27. Philip Pavia, "The New York School and the Jungian Ideal," *The Journal of Art,* 1, October 1991, p. 70.

28. Emily Genauer, "Capsule Reviews," *Art News,* 44, January 15, 1945, p. 29; quotation cited here is from a longer review originally published in the *New York World Telegram.*

29. Reproduced in *Ad Reinhardt: Art Comics and Satires* (New York: Truman Gallery, 1976).

30. Joan M. Lukach, *Hilla Rebay: In Search of the Spirit in Art* (New York: Braziller, 1983), p. 152.

31. See Hans K. Roethel and Jean K. Benjamin, *Kandinsky Catalogue Raisonné of the Oil Paintings* (Ithaca, N.Y.: Cornell University Press, 1982), numbers 407, *Angel of the Last Judgment* (1911?); 498, *Study for Panel for Edwin R. Campbell No. 4* (1914); 502, *Untitled Improvisation III* (1914); and a watercolor relating to 445, *With Pince-Nez* (1912).

32. Clement Greenberg, *Hofmann* (Paris: Editions George Gall, 1961), p. 15.

33. Lee Krasner, interview with the author, August 1971.

34. Greenberg, *Hofmann,* p. 12.

35. William C. Seitz, *Hans Hofmann* (New York: Museum of Modern Art, 1963), p. 7.

36. "Prospectus of the Hofmann School of Fine Arts," reprinted in Seitz, *Hans Hofmann,* p. 56.

37. Quoted in Seitz, *Hans Hofmann,* p. 14.

38. Greenberg, *Hofmann,* p. 12, states: "He has been called a 'German Expressionist,' yet little in what is known as Expressionism, aside from Kandinsky's swirl, predicts him." He also suggests (p. 14) that Hofmann had to "get over" Kandinsky and other artists.

39. Ibid., p. 16.

40. Kandinsky's iconography and imagery veiled by abstraction are well documented by Rose-Carol Washton Long in *Kandinsky: The Development of an Abstract Style* (Oxford: Oxford University Press, 1980). No one, however, has adequately explored Hofmann's iconography. Polcari, in *Abstract Expressionism and the Modern Experience,* p. 328, comes closest to decoding Hofmann when he sees works such as *Cataclysm* and *Resurrection* as "the classical themes of anthropological ritual" and relates these works to the war. Yet Polcari, who states of Hofmann in the 1940s that "the work as a whole resembles an automatist Kandinsky," missed making the iconographic connection to Kandinsky's themes.

41. *Improvisation No. 27* was number 48 in the MoMA show Alfred Stieglitz: "291" and After, June–August 1947. For an analysis of this theme, see Rose-Carol Washton Long, "Kandinsky's Vision of Utopia as a Garden of Love," *Art Journal* 43 (Spring 1983), pp. 50–55.

42. Reproduced on p. 39 in Greenberg, *Hofmann.*

43. See Long, *Kandinsky.* Plate 63 is a nineteenth-century example of a Bavarian *Hinterglasmalerei* with St. Michael holding scales.

44. Hans Hofmann, *The Search for the Real and Other Essays,* eds. Sara T. Weeks and Bartlett H. Hayes, Jr. (Cambridge, Mass.: MIT Press, 1967). Reprints earlier publication of 1948.

45. Hofmann, *Search,* p. 41. Wassily Kandinsky, *On the Spiritual in Art,* in Lindsay and Vergo, eds., *Kandinsky: Complete Writings on Art,* p. 219.

46. Hofmann, *Search,* p. 45.

47. Kandinsky, *On the Spiritual in Art,* p. 189.

48. Ibid., p. 187.

49. Hofmann quoted in Ashton, *The New York School,* pp. 82–83.

50. My discussion of Paalen has been enriched by the work of Amy Winter, whose forthcoming dissertation, "Wolfgang Paalen, *Dyn,* and the American Avant-garde of the 1940s" (Graduate School of the City University of New York) will enhance our understanding of his significance.

51. Wolfgang Paalen, *Form and Sense* (New York: Wittenborn, 1945). This volume was part of a series in "Problems of Contemporary Art," edited by Robert Motherwell.

52. Leonor Morales, *Wolfgang Paalen: Introductor de la Pintura Surrealista en México* (Mexico City: Universidad Nacional Autónoma de México, 1984), p. 20, note 170.

53. Among these publications was Will Grohmann, *Kandinsky* (Paris: Cahiers d'Art, 1930).

54. Harold Rosenberg, *Arshile Gorky: The Man, the Time, the Idea* (New York: Horizon Press, 1962), pp. 123–126, reprints "Fetish of Antique Stifles Art Here," from the *New York Evening Post,* September 5, 1926.

55. Robert Frank Reiff, "A Stylistic Analysis of Arshile Gorky's Art from 1943 to 1948" (Ph.D. dissertation, Columbia University, 1961), pp. 120–121.

56. Meyer Schapiro, "Introduction," in Ethel K. Schwabacher, *Arshile Gorky* (New York: Macmillan, 1957), p. 11.

57. Schapiro, in Schwabacher, *Gorky,* p. 11.

58. Julien Levy, "Foreword," in William C. Seitz, *Arshile Gorky: Paintings, Drawings, Studies* (New York: Abrams, 1962), p. 7.

59. Rosenberg, *Gorky,* reprints Arshile Gorky, "Stuart Davis," *Creative Art* 9 (September 1931), pp. 213–217.

60. Reiff, "Gorky's Art," p. 226.

61. Ibid.

62. Agnes Gorky Phillips to Robert Reiff, letter of December 1, 1958, quoted in Reiff, "Gorky's Art," p. 228.

63. André Breton, "Foreword," in *Arshile Gorky* (New York: Julien Levy Gallery, 1945), reprinted in André Breton, *Surrealism and Painting* (New York: Harper & Row, 1972), pp. 199–201.

64. Schwabacher, *Gorky*, p. 27.

65. Robert Motherwell in an interview with Sidney Simon, "Concerning the Beginnings of the New York School: 1939–1943," *Art International* 11, Summer 1967, p. 23.

66. Wassily Kandinsky, *Concerning the Spiritual in Art* (New York: Wittenborn, 1947).

67. David Smith, "Notes on My Work," *Arts Magazine* 34, February 1960, p. 44.

68. Allentuck, ed., *Graham's System*, pp. 128 and 154.

69. Smith, "Notes," p. 44.

70. Quoted in Allentuck, ed., *Graham's System*, p. 17.

71. Schwabacher, *Gorky*, p. 104.

72. Irving Sandler, *The Triumph of American Painting: A History of Abstract Expressionism* (New York: Praeger, 1970), p. 52.

73. Breton, *Surrealism and Painting*, p. 286.

74. Reiff, in "Gorky's Art," pp. 226–229, compares Gorky's *Waterfall* to Kandinsky. Rosenberg, *Gorky*, pp. 113–114, writes: "The relation to Kandinsky is very clear in paintings of '43–'44 such as *The Waterfall* and *The Liver Is the Cock's Comb*, with flowing edges of its forms. . . ." This same comparison of *Waterfall* to Kandinsky's work has also been made by William Rubin, in "Arshile Gorky, Surrealism, and the New American Painting," *Art International*, vol. 7 (February 1963). Reprinted in Henry Geldzahler, ed., *New York Painting and Sculpture, 1940–1970* (New York: Dutton, 1969), pp. 372–402.

75. Reiff, in "Gorky's Art," p. 226, argues that it is not likely that Gorky knew this work by Kandinsky. For information on Gorky's involvement with Dreier and the Société Anonyme, see Robert L. Herbert, et al., eds., *The Société Anonyme and the Dreier Bequest at Yale University* (New Haven: Yale University Press, 1984), pp. 305–307. For earlier examples of Kandinsky's waterfalls, see Roethel and Benjamin, *Kandinsky Catalogue Raisonné*, numbers 3 (1900) and 55 (1902).

76. Rubin, "Gorky," p. 391.

77. Ibid.

78. Hilla Rebay, *In Memory of Wassily Kandinsky* (New York: Museum of Non-Objective Painting, 1945).

79. Kandinsky, *The Art of Spiritual Harmony*, p. 41.

80. Rosenberg, *Gorky*, p. 45.

81. Kandinsky, *The Art of Spiritual Harmony*, p. 19.

82. Clement Greenberg, *The Nation*, March 24, 1945, reprinted in John O'Brian, ed., *Clement Greenberg: Arrogant Purpose, 1945–49* (Chicago: University of Chicago Press, 1986), p. 5.

83. O'Brian, *Arrogant Purpose*, p. 5.

84. Ashton, *New York School*, p. 159.

85. Clement Greenberg, "American-Type Painting," *Partisan Review*, no. 2 (Spring 1955), p. 182.

86. Ashton, *New York School*, p. 68.

87. Graham, "Primitive Art and Picasso," pp. 236–237.

88. Willem de Kooning, "De Kooning on Pollock: An Interview with James T. Valliere," *Partisan Review*, Fall 1967, p. 603.

89. Thomas B. Hess, *Willem de Kooning*, (New York: Braziller, 1959), p. 114.

90. Harold Rosenberg, *Willem de Kooning* (New York: Abrams, 1974), p. 38, reprints this interview.

91. Willem de Kooning, "What Abstract Art Means to Me," written for a symposium held at the Museum of Modern Art on February 5, 1951, and reprinted from *Museum of Modern Art Bulletin*, vol. 18, no. 3 (Spring 1951), in Thomas B. Hess, *Willem de Kooning* (New York: Museum of Modern Art, 1968), p. 145.

92. Jackson Pollock, "Answers to a Questionnaire," *Arts & Architecture* 61 (February 1944), p. 14. Reprinted in F. V. O'Connor, *Jackson Pollock* (New York: Museum of Modern Art, 1967), pp. 31–33.

93. Allentuck, ed., *Graham's System*, p. 8.

94. Kandinsky, *The Art of Spiritual Harmony*, p. 55.

95. Francine du Plessix and Cleve Gray, in "Who Was Jackson Pollock?" Interview with Lee Krasner, Alfonso Ossorio, and Anthony Smith, *Art in America* 55, May 1967, p. 55.

96. du Plessix and Gray, in "Who Was Jackson Pollock?," p. 58.

97. William Rubin, in "Jackson Pollock and the Modern Tradition: Part I," *Artforum* 5 (February 1967), p. 15, stated that "Expressionism—derived not from the German Expressionists but from the Expressionist Picasso—is manifest in Pollock's painting only up to 1946, that is, before the great drip pictures (and to a lesser extent, after them)." See Rubin's note 15, p. 22. John I. H. Baur, *Revolution and Tradition in Modern American Art* (Cambridge, Mass.: Harvard University Press, 1951), p. 74, stated incorrectly that Pollock had studied with Hans Hofmann: "A more easily traceable influence, though not on the whole a very large one, has been exerted by Central European expressionism, particularly the early style of Kandinsky, whose work became better known here in the 1930's than it had been before. This has been augmented by the example and the teaching of the German-born Hans Hofmann, who came to America in 1930. Among Hofmann's pupils, the young Jackson Pollock stands out for his impetuous use of the expressionist vocabulary in such pictures as 'The She-Wolf,' painted in 1943 before he turned to his linear, mazelike abstractions." Pollock never studied with Hofmann, but was introduced to him in 1942 by Lee Krasner, who had attended Hofmann's school.

98. Ellen G. Landau, *Jackson Pollock* (New York: Abrams, 1989), p. 153.

99. "The Passing Shows," *Art News,* April 1–14, 1945, p. 6.

100. Clement Greenberg, "The Present Prospects of American Painting and Sculpture," *Horizon,* October 1947, reprinted in O'Connor, *Jackson Pollock,* p. 41.

101. Quoted in Lukach, *Rebay,* p. 154.

102. Reproduced in Lukach, *Rebay,* fig. 50.

103. Author's interview with Lee Krasner, February 2, 1971.

104. Stanley William Hayter, "The Language of Kandinsky," *Magazine of Art* 28 (May 1945), pp. 176–179.

105. Pollock owned *In Memory of Wassily Kandinsky: The Solomon R. Guggenheim Foundation Presents A Survey of the Artist's Paintings and Writings* (New York: Solomon R. Guggenheim Foundation, 1945), edited by Rebay.

106. Kandinsky, *The Art of Spiritual Harmony,* p. 29.

107. Charles Seliger to Marianne Lorenz, letter of November 9, 1990. The following quotations are also from this letter.

108. See *Norman Lewis: From the Harlem Renaissance to Abstraction* with a chronology of the artist by Kellie Jones and documents and essays, including "Norman Lewis in the Forties," by Ann Gibson (New York: Kenkeleba Gallery, 1989).

109. Norman Lewis, "Thesis," reproduced in *Norman Lewis.*

110. Julian Euell, "Thoughts About Norman Lewis," in *Norman Lewis,* pp. 52 and 54.

111. Aline B. Loucheim, "ABC (or XYZ) of Abstract Art," *New York Times Magazine,* July 11, 1948, p. 17. The following quotation is also from this page.

Lenders to the Exhibition

Richard Blacher and Donald Bradley

Blue Spiral 1

Brooklyn Museum

The Buck Collection

Dayton Art Institute

Sid Deutsch Gallery

Nora Eccles, Harrison Museum of Art,
 Utah State University

Lee Ehrenworth

Andre Emmerich Gallery

Lucile and Donald Graham

Solomon R. Guggenheim Museum

Alfred and Ingrid Lenz Harrison Collection

Georgia de Havenon

Leyla Rudhyar Hill

Hirshhorn Museum and Sculpture Garden,
 Smithsonian Institution

University of Iowa Museum of Art

Jonson Gallery, University of New Mexico

Dr. and Mrs. T. H. Kirschbaum

Krannert Art Museum and Kinkead Pavilion,
 University of Illinois

Jane and Ron Lerner

Mrs. Ouida Lewis

Long Beach Museum of Art

Meredith Long & Company

Milwaukee Art Museum

University Art Museum,
 University of Minnesota

Modern Art Museum of Fort Worth

Museum of Fine Arts, Boston

Museum of Modern Art, New York

The Newark Museum

The Georgia O'Keeffe Foundation

Katharina Rich Perlow Gallery

Philadelphia Museum of Art

The Phillips Collection

Pinnacle West Capital Corporation

Portico Fine Art

Private Texas collection

Rose Art Museum,
 Brandeis University

Michael Rosenfeld Gallery

The Snite Museum of Art,
 University of Notre Dame

Hal Sonderegger

Struve Gallery

Keith and Robin Struve

Harriet Tannin

Steve Turner, Steve Turner Gallery

John C. L. and Sarah V. C. Van Doren

Walker Art Center

Washburn Gallery

Yale University Art Gallery

Richard York Gallery

Zabriskie Gallery

Checklist of Works of Art

1. Benjamin Benno
UNTITLED ABSTRACTION, 1936
Crayon and ink on paper
9 × 10 ⅝"
Michael Rosenfeld Gallery, New York
(Plate 74)

2. Benjamin Benno
UNTITLED, 1936
Ink and crayon on paper
9 ½ × 12 ½"
Michael Rosenfeld Gallery, New York
(Plate 75)

3. Benjamin Benno
UNTITLED, 1936
Ink and crayon on paper
8 ⅛ × 11 ¹¹/₁₆"
Michael Rosenfeld Gallery, New York
(Plate 76)

4. Emil Bisttram
PULSATION, 1938
Oil on canvas
60 × 45"
Lee Ehrenworth
Photo credit: Ed Watkins,
New York
(Plate 44)

5. Emil Bisttram
CACTUS, 1938
Oil on canvas
31 × 35 ½"
Lee Ehrenworth
Photo credit: Ed Watkins,
New York
(Plate 45)

6. Albert Bloch
LIED I, November 1913–April 1914
Oil on canvas
42 ½ × 39"
The Snite Museum of Art, University of Notre
Dame, Notre Dame, IN
Gift of Mr. Robert Shapiro
(Plate 28)

7. Albert Bloch
DIE HÖHEN, 1914
Oil on canvas
54 ½ × 40 ⅜"
Krannert Art Museum and Kinkead Pavilion
University of Illinois, Champaign-Urbana
(Plate 29)

8. Albert Bloch
HARLEQUINADE, 1911
Oil on canvas
36 × 46 ½"
Collection, The Museum of Modern Art,
New York
Given anonymously
(Plate 26)

9. Albert Bloch
*WORKING DRAWING FOR THE
    HARLEQUIN WITH 3 PIERROTS*, 1913
Ink and wash on paper
10 × 13 ½"
Courtesy Sid Deutsch Gallery, New York
Photo credit: Jim Enyeart
(Plate 27)

10. Ilya Bolotowsky
*FIRST STUDY FOR THE WILLIAMSBURG
    MURAL*, 1936
Oil on canvas
19 ½ × 34 ½"
Courtesy Washburn Gallery, New York
(Plate 65)

11. Konrad Cramer
STRIFE, 1913
Oil on canvas
28 × 24"
Hirshhorn Museum and Sculpture Garden
Smithsonian Institution, Washington, D.C.
The Joseph H. Hirshhorn Bequest, 1981
Photo credit: Lee Stalsworth
(Plate 20)

12. Konrad Cramer
IMPROVISATION, c. 1913
Oil on canvas
26 × 30"
Pinnacle West Capital Corporation
(Plate 21)

13. Burgoyne Diller
EARLY GEOMETRIC, 1933
Oil on canvas
41 × 25"
Meredith Long & Company, Houston
(Plate 64)

14. Arthur Dove
IMPROVISION, 1927
Oil on pressed board
15 ½ × 14 ½"
Lucile and Donald Graham Collection, Denver
(The Phillips Collection and Dayton Art
    Institute only)
(Plate 15)

15. Arthur Dove
*I'LL BUILD A STAIRWAY TO
    PARADISE—GEORGE GERSHWIN*,
    1927
Oil and metallic paint on artist's board
20 × 15"
Museum of Fine Arts, Boston,
    The Lane Collection
(Plate 14)

16. Arthur Dove
ABSTRACTION, 1929
Oil on copper
28 × 26"
Lee Ehrenworth
Photo credit: Ed Watkins,
    New York
(Plate 16)

17. Katherine S. Dreier
THE GARDEN, 1918
Oil on canvas
25 × 30"
Collection of The Newark Museum,
    Newark, NJ
Gift of Mrs. Charmion Von Wiegand, 1958
Photo credit: Sarah Wells
(Plate 22)

18. Katherine S. Dreier
UNKNOWN FORCES, before 1934
Oil on canvas
24 × 40"
Brooklyn Museum
John B. Woodward Memorial Fund
(Plate 23)

19. Werner Drewes
LOOSE CONTACT, 1938
Oil on canvas
42 × 38"
Meredith Long & Company, Houston
(Plate 68)

20. Werner Drewes
DANCE IN THE DARK, 1949
Oil on canvas
21 × 28"
Private collection
(Plate 69)

21. John Ferren
GREEN ABSTRACTION, 1933
Oil on canvas
25 ½ × 35 ½"
Lent by Katharina Rich Perlow Gallery,
    New York
Photo credit: Gary J. Mamay
(Plate 72)

22. John Ferren
*UNTITLED ABSTRACTION WITH
    ORANGE*, 1934
Oil on canvas
22 × 36 ½"
Nora Eccles Harrison Museum of Art,
    Utah State University, Logan
Gift of Marie Eccles Foundation
Photo credit: Gary J. Mamay
(Plate 73)

23. Oskar Fischinger
5 COLLAGES, c. 1938
Mickey Mouse et al. collaged onto
    reproductions of Kandinsky paintings:
        a) Pointed and Round

b) Black Lines (Plate 51)
c) Above and Left
d) A Center
e) Painting with White Form
(Plate 52)
Mixed media
11 × 8″ each
Lent by Elfriede Fischinger
Photo credit: Bill Swartz

24. Oskar Fischinger
FAVORITE, 1944
Oil on celotex
31 × 38″
Private collection
(Plate 50)

25. Ed Garman
UNTITLED, ORANGE TRIANGLE (NO. 220), 1941
Oil on board
23 ½ × 23 ¾″
Michael Rosenfeld Gallery, New York
(Plate 42)

26. Ed Garman
UNTITLED, RED CIRCLE ON BLACK (NO. 297), 1942
Oil on board
23 ¾ × 23 ¾″
Michael Rosenfeld Gallery, New York
(Plate 43)

27. Arshile Gorky
WATERFALL, 1943
Oil on canvas
38 ⅛ × 25 ⅛″
Hirshhorn Museum and Sculpture Garden
Smithsonian Institution, Washington, D.C.
Gift of Joseph H. Hirshhorn, 1966
Photo credit: Lee Stalsworth
(Plate 80)

28. Dwinell Grant
WATERCOLOR NO. 66: SOPHISTICATION, 1938
Watercolor on paper
18 ¼ × 13 ⅞″
Dayton Art Institute
Photo credit: Bill Swartz
(Plate 56)

29. Dwinell Grant
WATERCOLOR NO. 67: YELLOW CIRCLE, 1938
Watercolor on paper
18 ¼ × 13 ⅞″
Dayton Art Institute
Photo credit: Bill Swartz
(Plate 57)

30. Dwinell Grant
CONTRATHEMIS NO. 3240, 1941
Colored pencil and collage on paper
8 ½ × 11″
Michael Rosenfeld Gallery, New York

Photo credit: Roberta and Stuart Friedman,
Photography
(Plate 58)

31. Dwinell Grant
CONTRATHEMIS NO. 772, 1941
Colored pencil and collage on paper
8 ½ × 11″
Michael Rosenfeld Gallery, New York
Photo credit: Roberta and Stuart Friedman,
Photography

32. Dwinell Grant
CONTRATHEMIS NO. 2412, 1941
Colored pencil on paper
8 ½ × 11″
Michael Rosenfeld Gallery, New York
Photo credit: Roberta and Stuart Friedman,
Photography

33. Lawren Harris
UNTITLED, 1939
Oil on canvas
56 × 46″
Collection of Georgia de Havenon
(Plate 38)

34. Lawren Harris
ABSTRACT, c. 1939
Oil on masonite
21 ¾ × 23 ½″
Private collection
(Plate 37)

35. Marsden Hartley
MUSICAL THEME (ORIENTAL SYMPHONY), 1912–13
Oil on canvas
39 ⅜ × 31 ¾″
Rose Art Museum, Brandeis University,
Waltham, MA
Gift of Samuel Lustgarten
(Plate 24)

36. Marsden Hartley
ABSTRACTION WITH FLOWERS, 1913
Oil on canvas
39 ¼ × 31 ½″
Collection University Art Museum, University
of Minnesota, Minneapolis
Bequest of Hudson Walker from the Ione and
Hudson Walker Collection
(Plate 25)

37. Hans Hofmann
UNTITLED (LANDSCAPE), 1941
Oil on board
24 × 30″
Dr. and Mrs. T. H. Kirschbaum
(Plate 78)

38. Hans Hofmann
CHIMBOTE MURAL, 1950
Oil on board
84 × 36 ¼″
Courtesy Andre Emmerich Gallery, New York
(Plate 79)

39. Hans Hofmann
UNTITLED, c. 1914
Watercolor on paper
8 × 10 ½″
Courtesy Andre Emmerich Gallery, New York
(Plate 77)

40. Raymond Jonson
INTERLOCKED FORMS—ERUPTED, 1936
Watercolor on paper
23 × 33″
Jonson Gallery of the University Art Museum
University of New Mexico, Albuquerque
(Plate 35)

41. Raymond Jonson
WATERCOLOR NO. 9, 1938
Watercolor on paper
34 ¾ × 24 ½″
Jonson Gallery of the University Art Museum
University of New Mexico, Albuquerque
(Plate 36)

42. Raymond Jonson
CYCLE OF SCIENCE: MATHEMATICS,
1934
Oil on canvas
35 × 45″
Jonson Gallery of the University Art Museum
University of New Mexico, Albuquerque
Photo credit: Damian Andrus
(Plate 34)

43. Raymond Jonson
VARIATIONS ON A RHYTHM-B, 1931
Oil on canvas
32 ⅛ × 28 ¼″
Lee Ehrenworth
Photo credit: Ed Watkins, New York
(Plate 33)

44. Vassily Kandinsky
STUDY FOR IMPROVISATION 7, 1910
Oil on composition board
27 ³⁄₁₆ × 18 ⅞″
Yale University Art Gallery, New Haven, CT
Gift of Collection Société Anonyme, New
York
Photo credit: Joseph Szaszfai

Provenance
Katherine S. Dreier, New York

Exhibitions
Memorial Exhibition, Museum of Non-Objective
Painting, New York, 1945
(Plate 1)

45. Vassily Kandinsky
AUTUMN II, 1912
Oil and oil washes on canvas
24 × 32 ½″
The Phillips Collection, Washington, D.C.

Provenance
Nierendorf Gallery, New York

Exhibitions
Memorial Exhibition, Museum of Non-Objective
Painting, New York, 1945
(Plate 2)

46. Vassily Kandinsky
SKETCH FOR PAINTING WITH WHITE BORDER (MOSCOW), 1913
Oil on canvas
39 ⅜ × 30 ⅞"
The Phillips Collection, Washington, D.C.
Bequest of Katherine S. Dreier, 1953
(The Phillips Collection only)

Provenance
Katherine S. Dreier, New York

Exhibitions
Société Anonyme, New York, 1923
(Plate 4)

47. Vassily Kandinsky
FRAGMENT 1 FOR COMPOSITION 7
(Center), 1913
Oil on canvas
34 ¹⁵⁄₁₆ × 39 ⁷⁄₁₇"
Milwaukee Art Museum

Exhibitions
Memorial Exhibition, Museum of Non-Objective Painting, New York, 1945
(Plate 3)

48. Vassily Kandinsky
LITTLE PAINTING WITH YELLOW, 1914
30 ¾ x 39 ⅜"
Oil on canvas
Philadelphia Museum of Art, The Louise and Walter Arensberg Collection
(The Phillips Collection and Dayton Art Institute only)

Provenance
Arthur Jerome Eddy, Chicago
Louise and Walter Arensberg, Hollywood

Exhibitions
Stendahl Gallery, Los Angeles, 1936
Memorial Exhibition, Museum of Non-Objective Painting, New York, 1945
Arensberg Collection, Art Institute of Chicago, 1949
(Plate 5)

49. Vassily Kandinsky
BLUE LITHOGRAPH, 1922
Three-color lithograph on paper
12 ¹¹⁄₁₆ × 10 ⅞"
Long Beach Museum of Art, Long Beach, CA
(Plate 6)

50. Vassily Kandinsky
BLACK LINES, 1924
Lithograph on paper
13 ⁷⁄₁₆ × 10 ⅝"
Long Beach Museum of Art, Long Beach, CA
(Plate 7)

51. Vassily Kandinsky
BLUE PAINTING, 1924
Oil on canvas mounted on board
19 ⅞ × 19 ½"
Solomon R. Guggenheim Museum, New York
Gift of Fuller Foundation, Inc., 1976

Provenance
Galka Scheyer

Exhibitions
Oakland, *The Blue Four*, May 1926
(Plate 8)

52. Vassily Kandinsky
ABOVE AND LEFT, 1925
Oil on cardboard
27 ⁷⁄₁₆ × 19 ⅝"
Collection of the Modern Art Museum of Fort Worth, TX, made possible by a donation from Mr. and Mrs. J. Lee Johnson III

Provenance
Solomon R. Guggenheim, New York
The Solomon R. Guggenheim Foundation, New York

Exhibitions
Memorial Exhibition, Museum of Non-Objective Painting, New York, 1945
Memorial Exhibition, Carnegie Institute, Pittsburgh, 1946
(Plate 9)

53. Vassily Kandinsky
CONDENSATION, 1929
Oil on canvas
39 ½ × 31 ½"
The University of Iowa Museum of Art, Iowa City
Gift of Owen and Leone Elliott
Photo credit: Randall Tosh

Provenance
Galka Scheyer, Los Angeles

Exhibitions
Valentine Gallery, New York, 1932
Stendahl Gallery, Los Angeles, 1936
(Plate 10)

54. Vassily Kandinsky
SOFT PRESSURE, 1931
Oil on plywood
39 ¼ × 39"
Collection, The Museum of Modern Art, New York
The Riklis Collection of McCrory Corporation (fractional gift)

Exhibitions
Memorial Exhibition, Museum of Non-Objective Painting, New York, 1945
Memorial Exhibition, The Arts Club, Chicago, 1945
Memorial Exhibition, Carnegie Institute, Pittsburgh, 1946
(Plate 11)

55. Vassily Kandinsky
SUCCESSION, 1935
Oil on canvas
31 × 39"
The Phillips Collection, Washington, D.C.

Provenance
Nierendorf Gallery, New York

Exhibitions
Nierendorf Gallery, 1941
Nierendorf Gallery, 1943
Memorial Exhibition, Museum of Non-Objective Painting, New York, 1945
(Plate 12)

56. Vassily Kandinsky
POINTS, 1935
Oil and lacquer on canvas
32 × 39 ⅜"
Long Beach Museum of Art, Long Beach, CA

Provenance
Galka Scheyer, Los Angeles
Nierendorf Gallery, New York

Exhibitions
Nierendorf Gallery, New York, 1941
(Plate 13)

57. Norman Lewis
PHANTASY II, 1946
Oil on canvas
29 × 36"
Collection of Mrs. Ouida Lewis
Photo credit: D. James Dee
(Plate 84)

58. William Lumpkins
TRANSPARENCY, 1933
Watercolor
14 ¾ × 20 ½"
Hal Sonderegger Collection
(Plate 48)

59. Alice Trumbull Mason
SPRING, 1931
Oil on canvas
20 × 26 ⅛"
Courtesy Washburn Gallery, New York
(Plate 66)

60. Knud Merrild
JAN. '37 (NON-OBJECTIVE SPACE PICTURE), 1937
Painted wood construction with corrugated cardboard, abrasive paper, and wire screen
23 × 17 ½"
Steve Turner, Steve Turner Gallery, Los Angeles
(Plate 53)

61. George L. K. Morris
UNTITLED, c. 1936–1938
Oil on canvas
30 × 22"
Collection of Jane and Ron Lerner
(Plate 67)

62. Georgia O'Keeffe
SPECIAL 21, 1916
Oil on board
13 ⅜ × 16 ⅛"
The Georgia O'Keeffe Foundation
Photo credit: Malcolm Varon, New York
(Plate 19)

63. Agnes Pelton
CHALLENGE, 1940
Oil on canvas
32 × 26"
The Buck Collection, Laguna Hills, CA
Photo credit: Cristalen
(Plate 40)

64. Agnes Pelton
FUTURE, 1941
Oil on canvas
30 × 26"
The Buck Collection, Laguna Hills, CA
Photo credit: Cristalen
(Plate 41)

65. Florence Pierce
RISING RED, 1942
Oil on canvas
36 × 36"
Collection of Jane and Ron Lerner
(Plate 47)

66. Horace Pierce
KEY DRAWING FROM MOVEMENT 1,
1939
Watercolor on paper
25 ⅝ × 20 ⅛"
Collection of Georgia de Havenon
(Plate 46)

67. Jackson Pollock
UNTITLED, c. 1942
Gouache on cardboard
6 ⅞ × 8 ¼"
Collection of John C. L. and
Sarah V. C. Van Doren
(Plate 81)

68. Hilla Rebay
COMPOSITION NO. 9, 1916
Oil on panel
24 × 27 ½"
Portico Fine Art, New York
(Plate 54)

69. Hilla Rebay
UNTITLED, c. 1944
Oil on canvas
94 × 78"
Portico Fine Art, New York
(Plate 55)

70. Dane Rudhyar
STORM GODS, 1938
Ink and color
17 × 11"
Courtesy of Leyla Rudhyar Hill
(Plate 39)

71. Rolph Scarlett
UNTITLED, c. 1936
Oil on canvas
22 × 29"
Collection of Alfred and Ingrid Lenz Harrison,
Wayzata, MN
(Plate 59)

72. Rolph Scarlett
UNTITLED ABSTRACTION, n.d.
Watercolor on paper
8 ¼ × 13 ¼"
Estate of the artist, courtesy Harriet Tannin
Photo credit: Ed Watkins,
New York
(Plate 60)

73. Rolph Scarlett
UNTITLED ABSTRACTION, n.d.
Watercolor on paper
8 ¼ × 13 ¼"
Estate of the artist, courtesy Harriet Tannin
Photo credit: Ed Watkins, New York
(Plate 61)

74. William Schwartz
SYMPHONIC FORMS NO. 18, c. 1935
Oil on canvas
40 × 36 ½"
Courtesy private Texas collection
(Plate 30)

75. Charles Seliger
PRIMAL MARKINGS I, 1943
Oil on canvas
25 × 18"
Michael Rosenfeld Gallery, New York
(Plate 82)

76. Charles Seliger
PRIMAL MARKINGS III, 1943
Oil on canvas
16 ⅛ × 12 ¼"
Michael Rosenfeld Gallery, New York
(Plate 83)

77. John Sennhauser
BLACK LINES NO. 2, 1943
Oil on canvas
24 × 24"
Courtesy Struve Gallery, Chicago
(Plate 62)

78. John Sennhauser
BLACK LINES NO. 4, 1943
Oil on canvas
26 × 36"
Collection of Keith and Robin Struve, Chicago
(Plate 64)

79. Will Henry Stevens
SPATIAL ABSTRACTION, 1943
Pastel on paper
15 ⅞ × 19"
Richard York Gallery, New York
(Plate 31)

80. Will Henry Stevens
UNTITLED ABSTRACTION, 1945
Oil on board
22 × 30"
Blue Spiral 1 Gallery, Asheville,
North Carolina
(Plate 32)

81. John von Wicht
VISTA, 1939
Tempera
25 ⅛ × 33 ½"
Lee Ehrenworth
Photo credit: Ed Watkins, New York
(Plate 70)

82. John von Wicht
ABSTRACTION, c. 1940
Black ink on paper
24 × 18"
Richard Blacher and Donald Bradley
Courtesy of Michael Rosenfeld Gallery,
New York
(Plate 71)

83. Stuart Walker
COMPOSITION 65, 1934
Oil on canvas
40 × 30"
Collection of Georgia de Havenon
(Plate 49)

84. Abraham Walkowitz
ABSTRACTION, 1913
Watercolor on paper
12 ⅜ × 8 ¼"
Zabriskie Gallery, New York
(Plate 18)

85. Abraham Walkowitz
ABSTRACTION, n.d.
Crayon, watercolor, and ink on paper
12 ½ × 8"
Zabriskie Gallery, New York
(Plate 17)

Exhibitions of Kandinsky's Work: 1912–1950

1912: Exhibition of Contemporary German Graphic Art, Berlin Photographic Company, New York; traveled to Buffalo, St. Louis, and Pittsburgh in 1913

1913: Armory Show: New York, Chicago, Boston

1920: Société Anonyme, East 47th Street, New York

1921: Société Anonyme at the Heterodoxy Club, New York
Société Anonyme at Worcester Art Museum, Worcester, Massachusetts
Société Anonyme at MacDowell Club, New York

1923: Société Anonyme cooperating with Russian Exhibition, Brooklyn Museum
Société Anonyme (first one-man show in America), East 47th Street, New York
Société Anonyme at Vassar College, Poughkeepsie, New York
Société Anonyme cooperating with State Fair Park, Detroit

1924: Société Anonyme, East 47th Street, New York

1925: Forty-Third Annual Exhibition of the Société Anonyme, Brooklyn Museum
Blue Four, Daniel Gallery, New York
Blue Four, Oakland Museum
Blue Four, Stanford University Gallery, Stanford, California
Blue Four, Mills College Gallery, Oakland

1926: Société Anonyme cooperating with Sesqui-Centennial, Philadelphia
Société Anonyme International Exhibition of Modern Art, Brooklyn Museum
Blue Four, California School of Fine Arts, San Francisco
Blue Four, San Francisco Conservatory of Music
Blue Four, Los Angeles Museum
Blue Four, University of California, Los Angeles
Blue Four, Denny and Watrius Studios, Carmel, California
Blue Four, University of Washington, Seattle

1927: Société Anonyme International Exhibition of Modern Art, Anderson Galleries, New York; Albright Art Gallery, Buffalo; The Grange, Toronto Museum of Art
Société Anonyme at the home of Mrs. Caroline O'Day, Rye, New York
Société Anonyme at the Cosmopolitan Club, New York
Société Anonyme at the Art Center, New York
Blue Four, Spokane Art Association
Blue Four, Fine Arts Building, San Diego
Blue Four, Oakland Museum
Blue Four, Portland Museum, Portland, Oregon

1928: Société Anonyme at Arts Council's Gallery at Barbizon Hotel, New York
Société Anonyme at Worker's Center, New York
Société Anonyme at Women's City Club, New York
Blue Four, Los Angeles Museum
Blue Four, Withorne and Swan Department Store, Oakland

1929:	Société Anonyme at the Daniel Galleries, New York
1930:	Blue Four, Braxton Gallery, Hollywood (one-man exhibition)
	Société Anonyme at Rand School, New York
1931:	Société Anonyme at New School for Social Research, New York
	Société Anonyme at Rand School, New York
	Société Anonyme at Albright Art Gallery, Buffalo; Fine Arts Academy, Buffalo
	Société Anonyme at Women's University Club, New York
	Blue Four, California Palace of the Legion of Honor, San Francisco
1932:	Blue Four, Faulkner Memorial Art Gallery, Santa Barbara, California
	Blue Four, Arts Club of Chicago
	Valentine Galleries, New York (one-man show)
1933:	A Century of Progress, Art Institute of Chicago
	Blue Four, Oakland Museum
	Blue Four, Los Angeles Museum
1935:	Société Anonyme at Black Mountain College, Black Mountain, North Carolina
1936:	"Cubism and Abstract Art," Museum of Modern Art, New York
	Stendahl Art Gallery, Los Angeles
	"New Forms in Art," Société Anonyme–College Art Association (traveling exhibition)
	Société Anonyme at Delphic Studios, New York
	Blue Four, Cornish School, Seattle
	Blue Four, Henri Art Gallery, University of Washington, Seattle
	Solomon R. Guggenheim Collection of Non-Objective Paintings, Gibbes Memorial Art Gallery, Charleston, South Carolina
1937:	Nierendorf Gallery, New York (traveled to Cleveland Museum of Art)
	Blue Four, San Francisco Museum of Art
	Blue Four, Los Angeles Museum
	Blue Four, University of California, Los Angeles
	Solomon R. Guggenheim Collection of Non-Objective Paintings, Philadelphia Art Alliance
1938:	"Masters of the Bauhaus, Kandinsky, Klee, Feininger," Nierendorf Gallery, New York
	Société Anonyme cooperating with Columbia University Art Department, New York
	Solomon R. Guggenheim Collection of Non-Objective Paintings, Gibbes Memorial Art Gallery, Charleston, South Carolina
1939:	Société Anonyme cooperating with Springfield Museum of Fine Arts, Springfield, Massachusetts
	"An Exhibition of Contrasts," Société Anonyme/Nierendorf Gallery, New York
	"The Development of Cubism to Abstract Art," Museum of Modern Art, New York
	Société Anonyme at the George Walter Vincent Smith Art Gallery, Springfield, Massachusetts
	Golden Gate International Exposition, San Francisco

Solomon R. Guggenheim Collection of Non-Objective Paintings, Baltimore Museum of Art

1940:   Société Anonyme at Wadsworth Atheneum, Hartford

1942:   Société Anonyme Opening Exhibition of Collection at Yale University, New Haven, Connecticut

1942/43: Nierendorf Gallery, New York

1944:   "First Exhibition in America," Art of This Century, New York

1945:   "Memorial Exhibition," Museum of Non-Objective Painting, New York (one-man show)

          "Memorial Exhibition," Museum of Non-Objective Painting, The Arts Club, Chicago

1946:   "Memorial Exhibition," Museum of Non-Objective Painting, Carnegie Institute, Pittsburgh

Index

Italic page numbers refer to illustrations.